Local education

Local education

Community, conversation, praxis

Mark K. Smith

Open University Press
Buckingham · Philadelphia

Open University Press
Celtic Court
22 Ballmoor
Buckingham
MK18 1XW

and

1900 Frost Road, Suite 101
Bristol, PA 19007, USA

First Published 1994

A catalogue record of this book is available from the British Library

ISBN 0 335 19274 2 (pbk)   0 335 19275 0 (hbk)

Library of Congress Cataloging-in-Publication Data
Smith, Mark, 1950 June 25–
    Local education : community, conversation, praxis / Mark K. Smith.
        p.   cm.
    Includes bibliographical references and index.
    ISBN 0–335–19275–0 (hb)—ISBN 0–335–19274–2 (pb)
    1. Education—Social aspects—England.   2. Non-formal education—
England.   3. Popular education—England.   4. Community and school—
England.   I. Title.
LC191.8.G72E538   1994
371'.03'0942—dc20   94–14186
                                                                CIP

Typeset by Graphicraft Typesetters Ltd, Hong Kong
Printed in Great Britain by St Edmundsbury Press,
Bury St Edmunds, Suffolk

Contents

Acknowledgements

A large number of people have freely given of their time and their thinking: in individual conversations, workshops and sessions or in written responses to material. In particular, I wish to thank Irene Abel, Jane Caley, Ian Campbell, Carys Charnley, Amardo D'Arbo, Liz Fisher, Yvonne Gilligan, David Hughes, Don Irvine, Vivian Janes, Chris Jones, Colin Jordan, Kamil Khan, Sue Lambert, Richard Larkins, Patsie Little, Lyne Loach, Jo Marchment, Moira McManus, Bob Mardle, Steve Mason, Dervisa Mustafa, John Paxton, Pauline Riley, Gavin Sealy, Hazel Stapleton, Graeme Tiffany and Simon Vincent.

Students and staff at the YMCA National College have also suffered from various attempts to formulate the ideas that follow. In particular, those involved with the Dip. H.E. and degree programmes in Informal and Community Education between 1991 and 1993 made significant contributions both within sessions and in response to the first draft.

Some of the research drawn upon here arose out of work undertaken for the Rank Foundation, which I must thank both for its financial support and the opportunity to take part in the *Youth or Adult?* Initiative. The research and this write-up were supervised by Gwyn Edwards and Vic Kelly of Goldsmiths' College, University of London; their questions and suggestions have been invaluable. Chris Gibbs has commented on all the various research memos and the first draft. Our conversations about the research over the four years have opened up new directions and encouraged me to press on. Some aspects of this research grew out of work undertaken with Tony Jeffs and I have benefited from his research into the development of community schooling. I also need to thank Stephen Brookfield and two

Open University Press referees who provided suggestions for further reading and helpful comments both on the arguments and on the sticky problem of how to cut the thing down to size. Everyone at the Open University Press has been as efficient and supportive as ever.

Previously I have acknowledged my debt to Josephine Macalister Brew. She wrote not only the first 'modern' youth work text, *In the Service of Youth*, but also one of the first substantial studies of informal education, *Informal Education: Adventures and Reflections*. Some twenty years after her death I worked for the organization to which she devoted much of her life (then known as the National Association of Youth Clubs). Without really being aware of it at the time, I took on a great deal of her thinking. It was only later that I realized, with a shock, just how important she was. Now I have to acknowledge my debt to a group of men who have made fundamental contributions to adult education: Eduard Lindeman, Basil Yeaxlee, Robbie Kidd and Malcolm Knowles. This time I was aware of their significance, but there was still surprise. One by one I discovered that, like me, they had worked for the YMCA.

A note on quotations

I have left quotations in their original gendered state, and without any additional comment: it is not always clear whether writers have used 'he' and 'she' as inclusive terms. Almost all emphases in quotations are as in the original. All unattributed quotations are from participants in the study.

Where material has been omitted, this has been shown in the usual way by three dots '. . .'. I have not attempted to transcribe conversations phonetically, but have used normal dictionary spellings. 'Ums' and 'ahs' have also been left out. Any additional material or change is contained within square brackets [ ].

In the few examples where an exchange is reported, workers are shown by [W], the researcher by [M]. Any quotations marked with [F] come from my fieldnotes written up immediately after the event. All other quotations from study participants are transcriptions of tape-recorded material.

Introduction

I want to look at the work of educators who engage with local networks and cultures, and who build ways of working which connect with local understandings. Their main workplace is not the classroom. Shops, launderettes, streets, pubs, cafés, and people's front rooms are the settings for much of their work. Where they do appear in schools and colleges, it is in corridors, eating areas and student common rooms that they are most likely to be found.

Their work is not organized by subject, syllabus or lessons. Education, for them, is about conversation and community, and involved with the whole person. They are not interested in possessing knowledge as one might own objects. Rather, they look to the way people are with themselves and the world. Such education is, as a result, unpredictable, risky and, hopefully, emancipatory. As Lindeman put it in 1951, it is education

> which is not formal, not conventional, not designed merely for the purpose of cultivating skills, but . . . something which relates [people] definitely to their community. It is an educational venture that is localized, has its roots in the local community. It has for one of its purposes the improvement of methods of social action . . . There are methods which everyone can understand. No conspiracy. No manipulation about this. We are people who want change but we want it to be rational, understood.
>
> (Lindeman 1987c: 129–30)

This way of working can be seen among the activities of some community workers, youth workers, community-based adult educators and community

educators – but they are not alone in this. Among those describing themselves as health promoters, probation officers, church and religious workers, teachers and social workers, there are also those who attempt to work
in this way. However, it is with the work of the former that I want to stay
for the most part.

Local education

When seen in a European and North American context, much of what we
look at here could be viewed as an aspect of social work. The concern with
social action has parallels in the tradition of community organization in
the USA, *Sozialpädagogik* in Germany, *animation* in France and socio-
cultural work in Belgium (Cannan *et al.* 1992: 73). It also calls on the
thinking and practice of those who have worked for community-based and
democratic schooling (Moller and Watson 1944; Seay *et al.* 1974; Allen and
Martin 1992). We can also approach it in North America and the UK
through the idea of informal education (Brew 1946; Knowles 1950; Marsick
and Watkins 1990). If we were examining similar work in many southern
countries, then our focus would most likely be non-formal education
(Coombs 1968). It could be seen as close to the Latin American tradition
of popular education (see Hamilton and Cunningham 1989), with its
concern with voice, culture and power, or the French tradition of *la vie
associative*, with its emphasis on association (Toynbee 1985).

I have used the term 'local education' here in the hope that we can look
at this work in a fresh way. I want to explore a form of education which
draws on ideas and ways of working well known to the ancient Greeks, and
to twentieth-century readers of Dewey and Freire. It also attends to the
everyday, to people's sense of themselves in time and place. As Yeaxlee,
the popularizer of the notion of lifelong education, argued, we must
attend to such elementary and informal forms of education.

> Insignificant and troublesome to the expert, these have a charm for
> the common man: he can appreciate them just because they are not
> elaborate and advanced: they meet him where he is, and do not
> demand that he shall make a long journey, or make a violent and
> unnatural effort, to reach them. They are the only recruiting ground
> for higher educational adventures on anything beyond the present
> small scale. But also they are the only ground wherein a very large
> number of people will ever find themselves at home at all.
>
> (Yeaxlee 1929: 155)

This is the realm of local educators and the focus for their labours. They
may seek to 'meet people where they are', and to address the familiar and
the taken-for-granted, as well as work with others to come to terms with
the strange or the new.

One advantage of approaching things in this way is that it allows us to
move beyond the largely spurious case made for the distinctiveness of

community work, adult education and youth work as educational methods and philosophies. I have not looked at questionable notions like andragogy at any length, as this job has been done elsewhere (Jarvis 1985; Brookfield 1986; Tennant 1988; Davenport 1993). As Kidd (1978: 17) has said, what we describe as adult learning is not a different kind or order from child learning: 'man must be seen as a whole in his lifelong development' (see also Houle 1972). When looking at the work of local educators it is what they hold in common that is most striking. Traditions of practice cut across sectors, and for this reason I have freely mixed accounts from separate arenas. Situations and experiences may differ, but the responses made connect directly with long-standing educational traditions.

Community, conversation and praxis

Running through all this is a vision of what makes for human flourishing, and of the social and political struggles involved. I argue that we need to foster those forms of life that nurture community, conversation and praxis. Solidarity and mutuality, engaging with others in a search for under-standing, and acting in ways that embody these are, I believe, central to well-being (for an exploration of this ethical-political position, see Bernstein 1983; 1991). In the United Kingdom such virtues have been particularly under threat in recent years. I say 'particularly', because there is a sense in which working for human well-being is always an uphill task. However, in the 1980s and early 1990s we saw a growing gap between rich and poor, an attack on local and national democracy, philistinism in education, and an emphasis on self-serving and the short run. Unfortunately, the problem is not confined to the UK. As Galbraith (1992) has shown, it will not be easy to break free of the stultifying 'culture of contentment' characteristic of better-off, and politically dominant, groups in northern capitalist countries.

So what is to be done? Part of the answer is that we must learn to understand ourselves as social and connected beings, we need to 'cele-brate the other' (Sampson 1993). In Mills's (1959: 226) memorable words, we have to discover that 'many personal problems cannot be solved merely as troubles, but must be understood in terms of public issues – and in terms of the problems of history making'. Similarly, we must learn that 'the human meaning of public issues must be revealed by relating them to personal troubles – and to the problems of the individual life'. Part of the task is to work for a political community in which democracy has some meaning.

Within local education there is a strong emphasis on promoting associational life and democracy (Hirst 1993); on working with people to identify common interests, to co-operate and to organize. This is clearly seen in the activities of many community workers and their concern for community development, mutual aid and collective action (Thomas 1983). Many adult educators, too, whether it be in the realm of trade union education, the development of work in community groups or through their involvement in the women's movement, have been committed to furthering democracy and self-organisation (Thompson 1980; Lovett 1988). Voluntary youth organizations, with their stress on self-organized activity and involvement, have also played a part. There are, of course, countervailing forces – but possibilities remain (Smith, M. K. 1991). We have the chance to work, as Dewey (1966: 7) put it, so that people may 'share in a common life'.

The research

In what follows I will weave back and forth between the concerns of key writers such as Dewey, Geertz and Gadamer, and accounts of practice. As well as interrogating my own practice, I have worked with over 30 individuals (neighbourhood and detached youth workers, community educators and community workers) to explore theirs. Much of the research was carried out in East London and involved both state and voluntary sector workers. Along with these workers I talked with local educators from other areas. I have also used material from workshops involving a further 60 community educators, social workers, community workers and youth workers. The research took place between January 1990 and June 1993.

I did not set out to prove or dispute particular theories. Instead, I began with an area of work. Through talking to practitioners and reading around the subject, I have tried to develop theory that is grounded (Strauss and Corbin 1990: 23). Just about all that follows has been used in some way with people involved in the study. They in turn have made further comments. In making sense of all this I have drawn on images, ideas and routines from a wide range of sources, but this has been informed by my particular orientation. The references so far to Dewey, Gadamer and Mills situate that quite well. Those wanting a discussion of the methodology can find it in Smith (1993).

Overview of contents

I have organized what follows around certain dimensions. These emerged in my conversations. Some were predictable – like engaging in conversation – but most I did not foresee. The processes identified do not work in a series – the local educators I talk with do not begin by being local and then move on to being educators. Rather, things tend to happen all at once. The work is often erratic and influenced by chance and situation. However, this does not mean that workers sit back, waiting for things to emerge. They are active agents. Their practice – or, better still, praxis – is underlined in the chapter titles. I have used verbs – being, structuring, thinking – to emphasize this.

In Chapter 1 I look at what it means to be a *local* educator. While much has been written about 'community education', little attention has been given to the importance of place and the impact this has on professional identity. I also try to show why local knowledge is an important focus for practice. In thinking about this the work of Cohen, Geertz and Giddens has been especially useful. Based on this discussion, I begin to argue that much can be gained by setting aside 'community education' and instead exploring the idea of 'local education'.

I then move on to look at local educators as *educators* in Chapter 2. The themes and emphases that are highlighted are familiar, and can be located in major educational traditions. These include the significance of choice and voice, the setting for the work, using experiences and situations, conversation and interaction, and educating as a fully human activity. Standing behind much that is said here is the figure of Dewey.

Conversation provides the focus for Chapter 3. More particularly, I look at the various strategies and tactics that local educators may use to initiate or join in conversations, to maintain them, and then to leave them. This is an area that is strangely absent from the professional literature, other than in rather abstract discussions of Freire, or exhortations to engage in dialogue. Here I have used the idea of conversation as it better catches the spirit and nature of the exchanges involved. To help me make sense of what the workers talked about I have turned to writers such as Goffman and Wardhaugh.

In Chapter 4 I explore how local educators can make decisions about the direction their work takes. For much of their time they are not operating within what might be called a 'curriculum mode', so that many common 'explanations' of the educational process do not fit. I try to capture some of the complex interactions in a model which brings in the worker's disposition and repertoire as well as various aspects of the situation. My work here parallels that of Louden (1991) and, more recently, Brown and McIntyre (1993) in respect of classroom-based practice, and develops some earlier work I did with Tony Jeffs (Jeffs and Smith 1990a).

Having established something of the nature of local education, I then turn in Chapter 5 to how workers go about structuring their work. Several modes or ways of being are identified and discussed. The only other writer to approach this area in the UK in recent years is Barr (1991) with regard to community workers. I look at the implications of the requirements for flexibility in the work for the overall planning process.

The process of engaging with local life, of embedding practice, is explored in Chapter 6. A number of key themes are again identified: the role of groups; questions of power relationships; networks; and exploring cultures. These emphases will come as no surprise to those familiar with the area – but, again, there has been little systematic attempt in recent years to explore this area of practice.

In Chapter 7 I examine reflection-in- and -on-action. What do workers say about 'thinking on their feet', and how does this relate to key writers such as Dewey and Schön? I try to build a model that more closely resembles the zigzagging, jumps and hesitations that are revealed in accounts of practice and informed by the 'situatedness' of reflection.

I finish with a chapter that looks at three key ideas: community, conversation and praxis. My focus on these reflects a concern for the 'ethical-political'. While looking to difference and the local, I also want to attend to that which we may share, and may be global. This has led me to a particular mix of writers – but my debt to pragmatism (whether it be in the shape of Dewey, Mead, Schön or Mills), and to hermeneutics (largely through Gadamer, Ricœur and Geertz) is obvious. Other names also crop up like Freire, Gramsci and Habermas. The 'constellation' they form allows us to explore local education while attending to the 'mood' that is 'modernity/post-modernity' (Bernstein 1991: 8–12).

Local education and local educators

I have not set out to demonstrate that local educators think in this way or act in that. I do not claim that this form of work is well developed in large numbers of workers. There is no one person who is the educator described. Individually, those who talked with me differed in various ways, but some come very close in the essentials. Where I do make more general claims about local educators I have tried to provide a source – and this accounts for a higher level of referencing in the text than I would have liked.

My interest here has been to explore with a number of local educators particular aspects of their work. I have linked these conversations with a reading of what I saw to be key writers. I have looked for things shared and points of departure – and there has been a great deal of 'toing and froing' as a result. In the process I have identified some themes and tried to bring them into a creative relationship. This grouping of commitments, ideas and metaphors concerning practice I have called 'local education'. In what follows I generally use the term 'local educator' as a shorthand way of referring to community educators, community workers and youth workers; and 'local education' as a constellation of practices. This latter construction is not normative – I am not saying, for the most part, that this is the way things should be, nor that this is the way they are. My concern has not been to formulate some tidy definition of local education nor to amass quantitative data about its prevalence. Rather I have looked to the language of possibility – I am saying 'this is the way things could be'.

I hope people will discover that there is a set of practices worth exploring and researching here. My conversations with practitioners revealed a range and depth of work that is not seen clearly in books and journals. The quality of that work gives grounds for hope (while the political and economic context in which it takes place is extremely depressing). What follows is offered as a contribution to conversation of practice.

Chapter 1

Being local

> There are those that say you go into the area, you work in the area.
> You don't attach yourself to it in any way. I don't think that is for me.
> It may be valuable in other settings. It may have advantages for
> particular styles of work or worker. It just don't happen to be mine.
> I want to belong in as strong a way as possible.

Being part of a local scene is essential to this worker. He sees the scope
for education within the daily round and would, no doubt, sympathize
with Pestalozzi when he argued nearly 200 years ago that 'within the living
room of every household are united the basic elements of all true human
education in its whole range' (quoted by Sadler 1974: 81). What is more,
not only does the everyday and close-to-hand provide scope for education,
but also coming to terms with the local, having a sense of place, is necessary,
I want to argue, to building robust identities and relationships. The everyday, the taken-for-granted, has to be explored if people, and the communities they form, are to flourish. We may mostly take the 'ordinary' for
granted, 'but it is also a range of experiences we can least afford to suffer
because it is so closely tied to the sensed humanity we share with others'
(Gunn 1992: 110).

Local educators take a further step. This, in the words of one, means
'reaching out to people on their own patch, territory, call it what you
want; and initiating projects where they are at'. For the most part this
entails working with or within local institutions, networks and practices:
enhancing relationships and practices (Smith 1988: 129–30). Thus, local
educators may work with tenants' groups or churches to develop and

extend their activities; they may look to enrich existing networks and relationships so that these become more rewarding. Sometimes they will have a hand in forming new groups with local people, but here again their interest is not usually in importing some prepackaged design but in building something out of local commitments, enthusiasms and expertise (Standing Conference on Community Development 1990). As one worker put it:

> One of the keys to community education [is] having a strong, vibrant community association which isn't run by professionals. It needs to come from the communities themselves. Those that live on estates, that attend classes, who have children at schools.

Some groups may become established fixtures on the local scene. Others may flourish for a short period as a 'spontaneous' response or passion (Kuenstler 1955) and then fade. This can mean that achievements are less visible, dozens of classes or new groups do not suddenly emerge. Those wanting to see local educators' handiwork have to look at the changes in the fabric and routines of daily life.

Most local educators try to work within fairly tight physical boundaries (Barr 1991: 48–61). They base their activities around a few streets, an estate (or two), a neighbourhood, a village or small town. In other words, they look to territorial communities as the site for their work. For the most part, when such workers talk of local work or 'community initiatives' they refer to 'areas smaller than wards, with populations of up to 5,000 or so' (Willmott 1989: 10). However, it would be a mistake to view such activities simply in terms of place. Many also use interest communities to help define what they do. These groupings share some special interest or characteristic, and it is in this sense that we talk of Irish, Muslim, Greek or gay communities. Workers may have a brief that is focused on such groupings – and this could mean operating across a large area. But territory and interest often tend to overlap, centres of population develop. Thus, for example, someone working with Somali community groups in East London could focus on just a few areas (see El-Solh 1991). However, some communities, such as that of deafness, are dispersed and this in itself can be a major problem. It means that opportunities for people to be together are restricted.

In this chapter I want to look at what having a sense of place can mean for local educators and those with whom they work. Locality and local relationships play a powerful part in our lives. The way we live has changed substantially, and with this has come a growing need to handle relationships across time and space and a developing role for educators. While my focus is on educators who work in specific areas, much of what I say relates also to those linked to interest communities. While people may not be in one place, educators still have to attend to networks and the ways of life they express. They also have to deal with issues of distance in time-space.

At one level, of course, there can be no practice without place: interactions have to happen somewhere. Being 'local' involves more than operating in some place; it is also to do with identity and how people approach their work as educators. In this way, when I talk of 'being' local it goes beyond physical location, to the relationship that place has with workers' sense of themselves and of the world. However, we first need to think about how, generally, people experience localness.

Localness

'Localness' is linked to proximity. The local shop is the one at the top of the road, the 'local' is the pub close to home or to work. A local, when applied to a person, is an inhabitant of the area. The most local of locals in this respect are neighbours – those living in the same street, block or building (Bulmer 1986: 18). 'Closeness' increases the likelihood of interaction or of being seen: there is more chance that people may 'bump' into one another and share common concerns like poor garbage collection.

> There is a sense of community in [this] area because people are around more. They know their neighbours better. They may not get on with them. They know the people on the estate who will get things done . . . they talk about a sense of belonging; and perhaps a sense of other people's needs on the estate.

However, 'being around more' does not guarantee people will speak to each other or take an interest in their needs. As studies of neighbourliness have shown, how long people have lived in an area, their age and stage in the life cycle, their culture and class, and their kinship ties are all important factors (Bulmer 1986: 83–99).

Localness is a relational category: for something to be local, something else has to be distant. This process of differentiation allows us to feel that we belong somewhere – we are a part of this place rather than that. To make this judgement we reason or believe that we share certain things with others in the locality.

> Each of the neighbourhoods are villages to themselves. They do not consider themselves as one area. They are individual communities. For example, in one the railway runs one side and on the other side there is the docks – so it is a bit of an island. People see themselves as separate, forgotten by the local authority. There is high unemployment, a lot of young single mums, poor housing, a limited bus service and only a few shops. Once they get to know you the people are quite friendly. It does take a long while unless they know someone that you know and that makes things a bit easier.

This sense of difference may be enhanced by the landscape, as with these dockland neighbourhoods. They are like islands. There are expanses of water between them and the 'mainland', and like some rural island communities which have suffered economic decline, there is a tendency on the part of local people to put down local ways of life (Mewett 1982: 225). We also find the divisions between insiders, outsiders and newcomers that are part of village life – the 'real' or 'old' inhabitants and the 'new' (Strathern 1981: 72–100). In areas where the landscape does not mark off one place from another in the same definite way there will be more argument about boundaries. But people will still seek to make sense of their area's position in the landscape by looking for differences between others and themselves (Cosgrove 1989).

Localness is also about place. Place in this sense not only is an arena for everyday life but also gives meaning to that life. 'To be attached to a place is seen as a fundamental human need and, particularly as home, as the foundation of our selves and our identities' (Eyles 1989: 109). Our knowledge of the 'local bond of social life' (König 1968: 9) is sketchy, but many attach significance to where they live, or were brought up. At the same time places can provide not only a sense of well-being, 'but also one of entrapment and drudgery' (Eyles 1989: 109). We can feel confined and want to escape.

> This is a close, small community with not a lot going on in it. It does feel to be a very unmotivated town although it is improving now. Growing up in it seems like struggling out of a bog sometimes. The money is to be made in the tourist industry. There is nothing exciting happening, they don't have opportunities, the cultural thing. There is no excitement of another culture here. So it is a very bigoted place.

Thus, to talk of place is to refer to understandings and feelings – it is not simply a matter of the area within lines drawn on a map. Physical areas or spaces provide settings for interactions; we draw upon them to live our lives (Gregory 1989a: 90). In so doing, we construct meanings, certain spaces can be seen as places, and this is also helped by people thinking about them in relation to the wider landscape.

Locality also connects with culture: within areas distinctive ways of life evolve. Shared conditions can lead people into making sense of things in ways that are different from other places. It is in dealing with everyday events that people come to know their way of doing things. These will be carried with them when they migrate. We can see this, for example, in the contrasting ways in which Hindu temples have developed in London (Vertovec 1992). There are basic differences which have grown out of contrasting regional backgrounds, religious orientations and histories of migration and settlement. Such factors also affect the way people learn to use language. People have different ways of communicating, 'because their communities have different social legacies and ways of behaving in face-to-face interactions' (Heath 1983: 11).

Exploring localness involves looking at how people express and experience their difference from others, and what they share with people. How does a sense of difference become part of, and inform, the nature of social organization and process? 'This sense of difference ... lies at the heart of people's awareness of their culture' (Cohen 1982: 2). Where there are a number of cultures in contact with each other, the valuing of differences is part of survival (Cohen 1982). As one worker put it:

> It certainly isn't a melting pot. The groups are very distinct. There are lots of suspicions about each other. The question is how you get people working together without making them feel that they are losing something of their culture.

What we also need to focus on here is the interrelatedness of local ways of living and space. We are dealing not with simple linear or one-way processes, but with a complex array of relationships. Aspects of space will influence local ways of living; and those very ways of living will affect how place is experienced. Place and even 'space' is socially constituted. It is created out of 'the vast intricacies, the incredible complexities, of the interlocking and the non-interlocking, and the networks of relations at every scale from the local to the global' (Massey 1993: 80).

Localities change – they are in a state of permanent flux. They are 'constantly being formed and reformed, constructed and disintegrated' (Massey 1984: 105). East London, where much of the research for this study took place, is an example of this. As each new group has become established, its members tended to move north or east. One group followed another: Protestant Huguenots from France in the seventeenth century, Irish labourers fleeing the potato blight, Jews escaping Russian pogroms, Indians, Pakistanis, Bangladeshis (Palmer 1989). Like all local economies, East London's has grown and declined unevenly. Differences in forms of work and production led to major inequalities both between and within regions and localities (Harvey 1982).

Yet it is not only localities that change – people's sense of them also differs over time, and from person to person. We may know this from our own lives. When returning to childhood haunts or to our first school, things are often not as we remember them. Our appreciation of size and distance differs with age. This is both as a result of physical changes in ourselves – we see things from a different vantage point – and in the way we interpret the world. Our sense of place and landscape is bound up with our experience of culture, and the forces within which this is formed (Cosgrove 1989: 122–6).

To sum up, localities can give a sense of identity to parts of the landscape. They can help people to build a feeling of belonging and security – people know where they are. They are places where you 'belong', and where 'spontaneous and organised social contact can take place' (Walmsley 1988: 121). But they are forever changing. People move; cultures evolve; housing alters; and work comes and goes. More than that, we refashion our understandings and responses.

Modernity

How are we to come to terms with these changes? What of the impact of new technologies and evolving patterns of working and living? In northern countries, for example, jobs, shops and leisure facilities are now less likely to be close to where people live. Friends and families may be more distant than in the past. At first sight it might appear that there are now fewer chances for people to create local attachments and associations.

In 'pre-modern' societies, space and place largely coincide. Social life is, for most people, and in most respects, dominated by 'presence' – by local activities (Giddens 1984; 1990). In 'modern' societies space is increasingly torn away from place; relations are often between 'absent' others. Local areas are 'thoroughly penetrated by, and shaped in terms of, social influences quite distant from them' (Giddens 1990: 19). For Giddens, routines and distance are central to thinking about modernity. Hence, even in rural regions in northern societies, people will share a common range of goods with those in urban areas. People watch the same television programmes, and read almost identical newspapers. Many activities that used to need face-to-face contact can now be done at a distance. When we look back at older studies of communities such as Middletown (Lynd and Lynd 1929; 1937) or Ashton (Dennis *et al.* 1969) there seems now to be less mutual aid and trust; less co-operation. With greater affluence, changes in private and state welfare, and shifts in work and leisure patterns (thanks in large part to technology), traditional patterns seem to be breaking down.

The danger here is that we are not comparing like with like. There have always been great differences between communities (Bell and Newby 1971), even those of apparently the same 'type' (Wright 1992). And for all this talk of distancing, so much of life still depends on routine face-to-face contact. That is to say, interactions between people who are co-present in time and space. In emergencies we need to turn to people who can respond then and there (Bracey 1964: 76–9). Raising children, or caring for adults with health problems, requires presence. And while the private and individualized world of the home may have become the key site for our leisure, team games and group activities continue to thrive (Rojek 1985: 176). Our sense of identity and being remains wrapped up in face-to-face contact. The sound of a person's voice on the telephone or the sight of that person's words on paper is not the same as *being with* that person. Thus, academics flock to conferences to meet and listen to papers, and to 'be' academics; and families have get-togethers. In the same way, friends meet in pubs or do things together. We are routinely with others in everyday life.

We also need to be aware of large differences of access to, and use of, technologies and space. For example, in Britain, while 98 per cent of homes where the 'head' is a 'professional' have a telephone, 71 per cent of those where the person is 'unskilled manual' do so (Central Statistical

Office 1993: 83). Changes in retailing, for example, have hit many low-income households. With the decline of the 'high street' and growth of out-of-town stores, they have to travel further to shop cheaply. Also they lack the means to take full advantage of the changes (Cahill 1992; Worpole 1992). On top of this are powerful forces shaping the use of time and space by age, gender, physical ability and by ethnicity. For example, women generally carry the burden of childcare, and do most of the shopping, cleaning and cooking (Pahl 1984). They are less likely to have access to a car. They are more likely to be living in poverty (Oppenheim 1990: 93–105) and to be economically dependent on others (Joshi 1989: 157–76). There are areas of public space where it is either dangerous or difficult for them to go (Woodward and Green 1988; Worpole 1992: 50–65). Taken together, these have a profound effect. Women are thrown back on local networks and facilities; they have, for example, been central to the activities of community groups (Gallagher 1977; Dominelli 1990). Children, too, will be particularly thrown back on the resources and opportunities in their local areas (Heath 1983: 344–50). Parallel arguments can be made for other groups such as those without work and those with differing abilities – and these are cut across by class. For example, Callaghan (1992) found that 'localism' appeared to be a working-class strategy for coping with structural change. People are able to stay in place because 'local networks of friends and kin operate to support them against the worst aspects of unemployment or sub employment' (1992: 31). Thus, far from making local ways of life marginal, modernity still involves many people in making significant links with the local. As a result, we need to focus on the complex relations between local involvements and interaction across distance (Giddens 1990: 64).

Locality, modernity and local education

Everyday routines and locales are the sites for local education. Workers have to be able to align themselves with these but not be consumed by them. However, paying attention to routines is not simply born of the concern to be around when potential clients are about. It is also linked to an interest in problematizing the everyday. Also, it may be difficulties with 'interaction across distance' that push people to make use of what local workers can offer. Dealings with complex systems such as those linked to the law, housing and income maintenance often occur at points where routines have been disrupted. Some of these crises are predictable as they arise as a part of a life cycle – for example, adapting to the birth of a child. Others are more unexpected, or spring from wider forces, and can threaten whole communities – such as the closure of a major employer or the growth of racist attacks. The problems that arise are often only partially concerned with a lack of knowledge about the system. Typically they also tie into the way people feel about themselves and others. There are often questions around literacy, power, and the use of different forms of social interaction (Levine 1986: 156–64).

In this way the work of these educators is tied into the rise of modernity. This is hardly surprising. Professions 'permeate, and, some more than others, dominate modern societies' (Perkin 1989: 25), a process that stems from the division and reintegration of labour. In this we can see a paradox. While local educators may be working to cultivate some feeling of community, it is possible to talk of the liberatory impact of the breakdown of homogeneous communities.

> The modern city can turn people outward, not inward; rather than wholeness, the city can give them an experience of otherness. The power of the city to reorient people in this way lies in its diversity; in the presence of difference people have at least the possibility to step outside themselves.
>
> (Sennett 1991: 123)

This is a theme also taken up by Wilson (1991) with regard to women's experience of the city. In such settings it is possible to escape the supposedly patriarchal social controls of smaller communities. However, at the same time, women have often been represented as dangerous and as a threat to order and have thus been subject to control – informal and otherwise (Wilson 1991: 157).

For all the talk of change, locality and localness remain powerful elements in people's experiences. At the same time, the diverse cultures and traditions that can often be found in local neighbourhoods, or close by, open up possibilities, some of which are experienced as threatening, some as promising. Patterns of living have altered, but people still have to come to terms with local routines and with handling the relationship between that which is close at hand and that which is 'distant' and often 'strange'.

Local knowledge

Education is a craft of place – it 'works by the light of local knowledge' (Geertz 1983: 168). Thus, one of the valued things that local educators bring, and what those new to an area have to gain, is such knowledge.

> I spent a long time walking about the neighbourhood; getting to know the names of the streets and the different types of facilities on offer to young people. I tried to cover the patch at all different times of the day and night, so that I could soak up the flavour, and see if particular patterns emerged about where young people went at certain times or on certain days. This meant that, on many occasions, I did not meet anyone to talk to, and it was in these moments I wondered about what I was doing and if there was a purpose to my wanderings.
>
> (Wild 1982: 23)

Knowing the 'patch' or the 'ground' – where things are and what is going on – is essential to locally based practice (Twelvetrees 1982: 20–38). As Yinger argues, learning place means learning how practitioners fit into surrounding life.

> It involves learning in detail about the participants in practice, their lives, their histories, and their relations to one another. It includes learning the characteristics that define a place: family, neighbour-hood, community, culture. It also includes learning aspects of the physical world defining a place.
>
> (Yinger 1990: 90–1)

Workers can find out much, as Wild (1982) indicates, by systematically observing the area and what is happening. However, observation can only take them so far. It is through continuing conversations with people that workers can both enhance their local knowledge and engage in the central elements of their task. They are there not simply to learn about the area but to intervene. To do that effectively over a period of time entails know-ing more about the area than where streets lead and what facilities there are. It involves gaining an active appreciation of local networks and rela-tionships; of how things work; of the norms and values of different groups within the area; of power relationships and 'important' people; and so on. Sometimes the scale of the knowledge we perceive as being required is such that we either become immobilized or we resort to long and detailed research programmes (see, for example, Henderson and Thomas 1987: 54–91). In reality, much of the local knowledge workers need can be learnt 'on the hoof' as they work with individuals and groups. At other times, and often related to a specific problem or question, they are able to draw on the expertise of particular local people or workers who 'know' the area. As they find out more about an area things can begin to fall into place:

> More and more I am learning about the history of the place and the whole thing is starting to fit into a complex pattern. The stuff the kids are doing now, they are not going to stop, not after hundreds of years of racism, sexism, and the whole lifestyle being the hidden economy sort of thing. You can't change that overnight. It takes time for all this to sink in.

This worker had been an 'outsider' who had had to work at being ac-cepted into the neighbourhood and to spend time picking up local knowledge. 'Insiders' may come with some local knowledge and perhaps even with more realistic expectations, but they still have the task of gain-ing acceptance as workers rather than as neighbours, as family or as friends.

> I was brought up just down the road and that was a good starting point. Like I didn't come in with any great high-falutin ideas – like

I was just going to walk in and change it . . . When I was 15 I wished
I had something, somebody who you could talk to, who could show
that you had more to your life than being told what to do and fitted
into a little compartment. That is like a really personal thing, and
that is the one thing that has kept me going. I really do believe in
what I am doing. I really do believe that young women should have
more choices than what they have got.

For all the apparent differences, these workers share something fundamental. They are both considering the local in relation to other situations
and possibilities. The worker who was the outsider is linking what he is
learning with larger concepts such as racism and sexism. The worker who
was a local is similarly placing her understanding and experience within
the language of possibility. She has broken through the taken-for-granted,
seen that there are alternatives for herself and for other women, and
sought to work to change things.

When we consider the local in relation to the general, or to other locals,
we can see that both the 'inside' and the 'outside' worker are faced with
a similar task. Both workers have to adopt the same mode of thinking,
namely 'a continuous dialectical tacking between the most local of local
detail and the most global of global structure in such a way as to bring
them into simultaneous view' (Geertz 1983: 69). We begin to see the local
in terms of the global and the global in terms of the local:

> Hopping back and forth between the whole conceived through the
> parts that actualize it and the parts conceived through the whole that
> motivates them, we seek to turn them, by a sort of intellectual per-
> petual motion, into explications of one another.
>
> (Geertz 1983: 69)

What both these workers bring in their own ways is the ability to stand
both inside and outside the situation. They can see the *part* (for example,
a young woman's deference to her boyfriend's opinion) as an aspect of a
whole (the subordination of women within a class society). At the same
time, the second, woman, worker knows that subordination as a living
thing, not as some slogan or abstraction. She allows one to inform the
other. In many respects this tacking between the local and the global is
not only what workers have to do. It is also what they need to be cultivating in those with whom they work.

To see ourselves among others, to place the part by other parts to make
a whole, we have to approach experience not just as something we have,
but also as something we *know* (Dewey 1929: 1a–39). In thinking about
how we may do this as educators, the distinction Geertz uses between
experience-near and experience-distant concepts can help.

> An experience-near concept is, roughly, one that someone – a pa-
> tient, a subject, in our case an informant – might himself naturally

and effortlessly use to define what he or his fellows see, feel, think, imagine, and so on, and which he would readily understand when similarly applied by others. An experience-distant concept is one that specialists of one sort or another – an analyst, an experimenter, an ethnographer, even a priest or an ideologist – employ to forward their scientific, philosophical, or practical aims.

(Geertz 1983: 57)

Keeping a balance between the immediacy of experience-near concepts and the abstractions of experience-distant concepts, and allowing one to inform the other is difficult. Yet it is an essential part of workers' jobs. There are, for example, great dangers in the 'I have been there myself' approach. We can either become drowned in immediacy or have our perceptions over-affected by our own feelings, rather than informed by what the other person is saying. Perhaps the important word to hold on to here is 'concepts'. What these workers are seeking to do is encourage and help people to *think* about their situation so that they may *act*. They are 'absorbed in the artisan task of seeing broad principles in parochial facts' (Geertz 1983: 167).

This leads on to a further, fundamental question: to what extent is all knowledge 'local'? Ideas and images are not things that we simply retrieve from our memories, but have to be created at the time of use.

Understanding is not reconstruction but mediation. We are conveyors of the past into the present. Even in the most careful attempts to grasp the past 'in itself', understanding remains essentially a mediation or translation of past meaning into the present situation.

(Linge 1976: xvi)

The form of our understanding will depend on our emotions and disposition at the time; and on the context which engendered thought. In this sense learning is situated; meaning is created in relation to the specific contexts in which we act. Understanding, as Gadamer (1979) has so eloquently argued, is never complete, it is built in specific circumstances, is always open and looks forward. In this sense, all effective criticism 'must be local and specific and dependent on local contexts' (Bernstein 1991: 318). In this way we can guard against the 'inhibiting effects of global, totalitarian theories' (Foucault 1980: 80). There is no set of standardized procedures for 'cranking out the truth' (Young 1992: 16). While educators may be engaged in the task of looking for broad principles in parochial facts we may also recognize that such principles are only of use if they can be related to the situation. This is the significance of Geertz's (1973: 53) call for us to attend to the particular and the general and their interrelationships; and Mills's (1959: 226) concern for 'both troubles and issues and both biography and history, and the range of their intricate relations'.

Localness and professional identity

Describing people as 'local' educators, therefore, is not simply to do with the fact that they operate in a certain area; it is also to say that they belong in some further way. They are part of the fabric of daily life, like the local priest or local policewoman. They are part of a whole network of relationships, they are greeted on the street, they are associated with the area. They are in and out of local shops, homes and organizations. More than that, learning place implies commitment. 'The specialist practitioner too often is passing through on a "career path". The conversation of practice is rooted, grounded, and locally committed' (Yinger 1990: 91). It involves placing the local in a dynamic relation with both the global and other areas of local knowledge.

All this impacts upon the professional identity of workers. Being local involves adopting a particular frame of reference or 'locus of identity' (Wallman 1984: 214). That is to say that workers' professional self-definitions are sustained in vital ways by forms and symbols they associate with the area (Smith 1988: 119). These forms and symbols may be provided by association with local organizations such as temples and tenants' associations, neighbourly networks and a variety of other everyday situations. Workers can use various markers as symbols of attachment to 'their' areas: their office in the church hall; membership of a local club; and their way of greeting others. When workers fail to take on or acknowledge these symbols or rituals they may be seen as aloof, as not committed and as outsiders. In other words, local workers need to be seen as one of 'us' rather than one of 'them'. Or perhaps more accurately, as both one of us and one of them, for they are in a position which sets them apart. They are paid to be in an area; and they are usually there to further in some way the interests or wishes of people and institutions outside the locality.

The question of professional identity is significant for another reason. These workers are not able to draw on an especially stable public understanding of their role, especially in contrast to, for example, teachers. Their presence *as workers* in settings where people are generally participants, does mean that they have to pay careful attention to the way in which they are seen by others, and the way they see themselves. For some an important way of dealing with the situation is the adoption and declaration of a statement describing who and what they are.

> I have learnt that the best thing to do is to say straight out that I am a community educator; that I work where people are; and that my job is to help people to learn to do things for themselves.

Such statements carry important messages about where workers place themselves in relation to other forms of educational intervention. 'Working where people are' is not simply a statement about physical location. It is also about working with people's current understandings and interests, about engaging as educators with 'the ways' of those worked with. To this extent, the identities of local educators are woven in with the forms and networks they encounter in their day-to-day work.

There is a further sense in which many workers are local. Most of the workers quoted here work in, or close to, the area where they have been brought up or have lived in for a considerable time. Not only do they share some of the experiences common to the area, but also both their personal and professional identities are to some extent wrapped up with the locality and/or the cultures with which they are engaging. This can come out as a particular type of commitment.

> I am glad, and it sounds corny . . . , because I have been able to give something back. So I feel in a privileged position really. Because I have been given that little bit of power, that go-ahead, to do what I believe in and a lot of people don't have that, do they? They just have it all inside . . . That's what's good for me. It's something I wanted to do, [and my employers said] 'right, there you are, go and do it'.

There are important considerations concerning identity here – for example, to what extent workers adopt models of 'professionalism' that take them away from their roots. As well as dealing with the effects of possible changes in class location and identity, there can be further questions and dilemmas relating to ethnic and religious identity, for example. What is at issue here for all these workers is that they could lose touch with who and what they are themselves.

> I look at the people I work with and I ask 'is that how I want to be?' I go to the pub with people I grew up with and start talking about 'interactions' or 'groupwork' and they look at you a bit strange. So you have to spend a lot of time thinking about identity. [F]

Unfortunately, there is no reliable, recent research concerning the backgrounds of local workers in the UK that can be used to approach this area.

In summary, it can be said that being 'local' requires that educators develop an identity which connects to, and belongs with, the institutions, networks and ways of living found in that area. Workers must gain an understanding of life within the area and how such local knowledge relates to the world beyond. In a very real sense they have to become 'part of the local community': to participate in local ways of life; to engage in a living relationship with people and place.

Local educators, community educators or educators in the community?

Given the focus here on neighbourhood it is worth concluding this chapter by looking at the notion of 'community education' in relation to the practice examined here. Were I, and all those quoted, working in Scotland there is a chance that I would not have focused on 'local education'. We would, for the most part, have shared the traditions that have developed around community education since the Alexander Report (Scottish Education Department 1975). It is possible in this context to talk of work with young people and adults being informed by a reasonably common set of educational understandings and which attends to community development (Principal Community Education Officers 1989; 1990; 1992). For example, Community Education Validation and Endorsement (Scotland) defines community education as

> a process designed to enrich the lives of individuals and groups by engaging with people living within a geographical area, or sharing a common interest, to develop voluntarily a range of learning, action and reflection opportunities determined by their personal, social, economic and political needs.
>
> (CEVE 1990: 1)

There are of course, questions about just how this translates itself into actual work, but at least there is some sort of framework to appeal to.

Against this, the English, headteacher-dominated, tradition of community education is perhaps better described as a community school movement. It has 'captured buildings rather than minds' (Jeffs 1992: 26). In this setting 'community education' is used by both policy-makers and commentators with a looseness that makes it problematic. For some it can simply be a way of cloaking administrative changes – for example, where schools or authorities have encouraged outside-hours usage to spread costs. Putting 'community' in front of 'school' does soften the image. Others have used the label to describe compensatory forms of education such as those associated with the Educational Priority Areas (Halsey 1972; Midwinter 1972). These tend to stress pre-school provision, home–school liaison, and the development of a 'community curriculum' as ways of improving the performance of some students in schools. At the same time, community education has had a progressive tinge. It has been used as shorthand for the need to 'renegotiate and reconstruct the ways in which the education system relates to its constituent communities of interest and residence' (Allen et al. 1987: 1). However, even in this sense it remains stubbornly focused on the school and college – both in England (Cowburn 1986) and in North America (Seay et al. 1974). It represents a 'bureaucratic, institution-based and "handed down" model' (Poster 1990: 27). Such a focus is of little use here. In many respects, as we will see in the next chapter, the school is a model against which these educators define their work.

'Community education' has also been used in the context of what might be called radical adult education to refer to work more fully grounded in local communities (Lovett 1988). To some extent this is a possible option. Writers such as Lovett use community-work concepts such as community development, community organization, community action and social action to order their different pedagogic approaches (Lovett 1975; Lovett et al. 1983: 36–40). For some of the workers quoted here this would be a comfortable route, especially those who define themselves as community workers. However, there are problems for us in this approach. First, these ways of viewing practice do not do full justice to the range of work they undertake – they go beyond a concern with community. Second, we are still left with the confused usage to which the term 'community education' is put.

A rather more attractive option is that of 'educators in the community'. Much of the work described and analysed by Brookfield (1983) in his discussion of learning in the community would fit this title. It is a world of informal education (Brew 1946; Knowles 1950; Jeffs and Smith 1990a); learning projects and self-planned learning (Tough 1993); learning networks and non-formal education (Fordham *et al.* 1979); and 'organizing around enthusiasms' (Bishop and Hoggett 1986). This is the right territory; however, as a title it is simply too clumsy for workers. In use it quickly becomes reversed to the more comfortable 'community educator'.

An added concern here surrounds 'community'. The growing popularity of the word to describe social and commercial initiatives has not made its meaning any clearer (Willmott 1989: 2). Some influential sociologists such as Stacey (1969) gave up on the word as a 'non-concept' and instead studied local social systems. Others, such as Cohen (1985), have explored community as a symbolic construction. He looks at how people define themselves: the boundaries they draw around 'their' community and the symbols they use to mark that boundary. I do not want to dismiss community as an idea – it does hold special significance for educators (see Chapter 8) – but I do think there are certain advantages in following Stacey's example and using 'local'.

Calling this area 'local education' helps concentrate attention on the interaction of individuals and institutions in specific localities (Bell and Newby 1971: 49); puts a proper emphasis on place; and brings out the significance of local knowledge. This is of special importance if, as Westwood (1992: 243) and others have argued, the 'new politics' is marked by local narratives. 'Homogenous conceptions of the working class, women, black people and community require deconstruction if they are to be in any way effective starting points for a politicized adult education' (1992: 243). The concern with the local links with the idea that learning is situated. Such understandings as we have are not 'things', they are not bundles of set images which can be simply taken from a shelf, dusted off and used; rather we build them in specific instances. So it is that I will talk of local educators and local education.

Chapter 2

Being an educator

> I wouldn't want people to associate the education we do with school, not because it is a bad thing, but because I wouldn't want people to get mixed up between the academic and the informal, or formal and informal education . . . People only know about one form of education. If someone said to me 'what do you think of education?' I would think of schools and colleges . . . So many people have negative feelings about education.

This local educator is not alone in defining her work against schooling – but what exactly is her 'form' of education? Locality and local knowledge bring a special dimension, but is there anything else distinctive about the shape of such workers' practice? Here I want to report on some of the themes that have emerged in my conversations with local educators around these questions. These include having a regard for:

- choice;
- voice;
- convivial settings for learning;
- reflection on experience;
- conversation and interaction;
- education as a fully human activity.

I cannot claim that all or many workers share these interests exactly in this way, but I can argue that these concerns provide a useful starting point for exploration. By engaging with these we can better name and shape our practice. Taken together, they do hint at a distinctive form – one that is centred around being and interaction – but it is not unique to local education. What I also hope to show is that we need to move beyond simple oppositions, and to reflect on what we mean by 'selfhood' and 'learning'.

Choice

Words like 'chance', 'choice', 'opportunity' and 'possibility' recur time and again in the conversations and writings of local educators (see, for example, Flynn *et al.* 1986; Jeffs and Smith 1987; and Poster and Krüger 1990). As one worker put it, 'there are choices but these people are never really shown those choices. They are just sucked into things or they are not given space to think.' This concern connects with an attention to relationships between people. It entails a simple premise: that if people are to learn that they have, and can make, choices, it is important that they are in conversations by choice. As Gibbs (1989: 54) has argued in respect of youth work, the main plank is consent: 'Young people choose whether or not they will engage in a relationship with a worker, which worker, and at what speed the relationship will develop.' In adult education, too, voluntary participation is promoted as a basic principle (Cross 1992). People should engage in learning as a result of their own volition. 'It may be that the circumstances prompting this learning are external to the learner (job loss, bereavement), but the decision to learn is the learner's. Hence excluded are those settings in which adults are coerced, bullied or intimidated into learning' (Brookfield 1986: 9–10).

It is easy to fall into crude contrasts between schooling where attendance is compulsory and other settings where people 'choose' to be. To move on we have to attend to the experiences and perceptions of those involved. For example, as Blackburn and Blackburn (1990) have shown with regard to residential social work, because people have to be in certain settings this does not mean that there can be no space for choice in learning. The requirement to be in a place does not necessarily imply a demand to do certain activities or learn particular things. Furthermore, the 'voluntary principle', applied in a crude way, can lead to elitism. For example, it can be argued that the result of relying on learners to articulate their demands has been that education in many southern countries has reached only a small and socially discrete sector of the population (Rogers 1992: 42). We should examine the quality of the relationships and how questions of content and outcome are resolved before dismissing those programmes which attempt to compel attendance.

One key device used by workers to handle questions of choice is the making of implicit or explicit contracts. We can see how these are formed in this account of a worker who was funded to work with offenders.

> I explained a little bit about the group, told the young people where
> I got the money from and arranged to meet on the Tuesday . . . The

first session would be going off to McDonald's and having a chat and that's where our very informal contract was drawn up. I didn't use the word 'contract', I can't remember the terminology I used, it was something like 'let's sort things out, how we are going to run this group'. And the issues which came up first were drugs and were the contents of the programme: 'what's in it for us, what are we going to get out of it?'

The group developed its own programme, and negotiated the 'rules' with the worker. As the worker put it:

They are actually setting the boundaries and saying you don't overstep this and we won't overstep that. I think that it is important to let people know what you are about and let them tell you what they are about and take the relationship or take the group from there.

However, these people were in a situation where, although they could choose not to attend, there were various external pressures (from the social work agency and the courts) for them to do so. By making a 'contract', questions around this were approached and space for choices carved out.

Voice

Closely linked to the idea of choice is that of voice.

When you watch television, read the papers and listen to what politicians say, you only get part of the story, you only get the views of a small group of people. Look at the books they are recommending for the National Curriculum – they are mostly by men and just about all the writers are white. There is a whole world of experience out there that doesn't get a look in and the result is that people do not get a proper chance to explore who they are and what they may be. [F]

People do not come to conversations on an equal footing. They bring histories and identities which have been deeply inscribed by social forces. The experience of being members of particular classes, cultures or races; and the pressures and expectations which people feel because of their body, gender and sexuality, interact and are at work in such exchanges. Educators must, therefore, look to questions of identity and power.

Over the years I have tried to replace the external definitions of my life forwarded by dominant groups with my own self-defined standpoint . . . I now know that my experiences are far from unique. Like African-American women, many others who occupy societally denigrated categories have been similarly silenced. So the voice I

now seek is both individual and collective, personal and political,
one reflecting the unique biography with the larger meaning of my
historical times.

(Collins 1990: xi–xii)

Working with people to name themselves in this way, to 'gain a voice',
forms a fundamental strand of local education practice. There is a long
history of work which is grounded in the experiences of excluded groups
and movements (Lovett 1988).

When we turn to these developments it is clear that 'voice' is not only
a matter of speech, but also has to do with how people are seen and
heard. Excluded groups tend to become a powerful motif in the minds of
the dominators. They are viewed both as a threat to order – politically,
socially and sexually – and as existing for the benefit of the powerful.
Examples abound: the Victorian bourgeoisie's concern with the emerging
working class (see Pearson 1975); the development of slavery in the British Empire (Fryer 1988); and the domestication of women (Oakley 1982).
All involve simultaneously defining a group as a 'problem' and casting
them as 'objects rather than subjects, beings that feel yet have the ability
to think, and remain incapable of considered behaviour in an active mode'
(Gilroy 1987: 11). This process involves a simple either/or distinction –
something is not just different, it is opposed. As Collins (1990: 69) put it,
whites and blacks, males and females, thought and feeling, are not
complementary counterparts but opposites. In this the opposing group is
seen not as people but as the 'Other' – a dangerous phenomenon to be
controlled.

As soon as we move beyond the language of either/or we have to live
with uncertainty. We can begin to attend to the experiences of those who
are excluded and those seeking to exclude; the relationships between
them; the context in which these are formed; and our place in all this. To
engage with the politics of difference and the forces that feed simplistic
oppositions is not to act in the belief that we are 'all the same under the
skin'. Rather it is to recognize and celebrate diversity, while at the same
time looking for what we hold in common. The danger with an emphasis
on difference is that we focus on particular groups and cultures, we begin
to see them as self-contained, and so ignore the 'blurred zones' between
them (Rosaldo 1993: 209). Yet these blurred zones or borderlands are
central to our lives and hold within them considerable possibility (Giroux
1992). As Anzaldua has argued with regard to the experience of Chicanos,
'the new *mestiza*' (person of mixed ancestry) copes by developing a tolerance for contradictions, for ambiguity.

She learns to be Indian in Mexican culture, to be Mexican from an
Anglo point of view. She learns to juggle cultures. She has a plural
personality, she operates in pluralistic mode – nothing is thrust out,
the good the bad the ugly, nothing rejected, nothing abandoned.

Not only does she sustain contradictions, she turns the ambivalence
into something else.

(Anzaldua 1987: 79, quoted in Rosaldo 1993: 216)

'Turning ambivalence into something else' is a powerful phrase, especially
when reading it as an educator. The 'something else' involves both having
voice and engaging with other voices.

This is not always a pleasant experience. Working in the borderlands
involves listening to, and meeting head on, much that we may despise.

One group I am working with is very racist – but I feel it is important
that I keep talking with them, that I hear what they are saying when
they are being racist; that I allow them to say those things. It is
perhaps easier because I am a white worker. I feel I have a responsibility to work with that racism, not simply reject it. I still go
and see the group . . . you try to work against these prejudices and
the self-destructive things.

This is where it becomes difficult. To work in this way involves entertain-
ing the possibility that there may be some truth in what, in this case, the
members of the tenants' group are saying. But the 'truth' lies behind, or
is enmeshed in, a tissue of feelings, prejudices and 'common-sense' explanations. We ask what is it about people's situations and experiences that
leads them to their particular understanding. The politics of voice and
difference entails something fundamental. To have something to say,
people must address their experiences and identity and understand themselves as 'active authors of their own words' (Giroux 1989: 199). It also
means cultivating tolerance – respecting 'the other as what it is: other'
(Derrida 1978: 138) – but that can only be gained if we work for justice
and democracy at the same time.

Settings

The plan is to create an environment before, during and afterwards,
where you can work with these kids. You can engage them in the
kind of things they are thinking about and even in the things they
are not thinking about. You try to set the environment.

The settings in which local educators work do not, for the most part,
resemble classrooms, but are often 'social' in character or arise out of
direct encounters with the physical environment. Workers have to be sensitive to the feelings and responses that such settings evoke (Tiffany 1993).
To a great extent, 'the setting dictates a large amount of the aims and
objectives of the group and both directly and indirectly constrains the
manner in which those aims can be achieved' (Douglas 1991: 118).

As educators we cannot change people's minds for them – nor should
we wish to. 'We never educate directly, but indirectly by means of the
environment. Whether we permit chance environments to do the work, or

whether we design environments for the purpose makes a great difference' (Dewey 1966: 19). One problem for local educators is that for much
of the time they have to foster such environments within settings over
which they have limited control.

> If they were coming to the centre then I would do things to create
> an environment here that is friendly, welcoming and all those sorts
> of things. If I am going and doing things in their space then I am
> not going to necessarily alter that.

On the street, in people's homes or in the supermarket, workers' main
points of intervention are likely to concern the social setting or context
and the subject for conversation. There is little they can do about the
physical setting. In contrast, when working in space which they manage,
they can make use of the usual array of tools. There is no shortage of
guidance for workers in this area. In youth work, for example, setting out
rooms, the use of equipment and the design of settings have long formed
part of the standard textbooks (see, for example, Russell and Rigby 1908:
40–52). As Brew put it:

> A club is a community engaged in the task of educating itself. It
> therefore follows that a youth organization can meet anywhere. There
> are only three necessities – light, preferably the sort that cannot be
> turned off or blown out by the practical joker – warmth, and if you
> cater for boys this means a 'fug' – and comradeship.
>
> (Brew 1943: 67)

Youth houses, clubs and projects usually reflect this with comfortable
seating, different lighting textures, various leaflets, magazines, books and
board games scattered around and so on. Care is also taken about the
possible impact of both the structural and socio-cultural context. By 'structure' I mean the established roles and relationships, 'including operating
procedures, shared beliefs, and norms' (Cornbleth 1990: 6). The sort of
questions that can arise for workers here include how various activities are
administered; how order is kept and by whom. I am taking the socio-
cultural context as something wider and as including social, political and
economic conditions, traditions and ideologies and events that actually or
potentially influence interactions.

However, a concern for setting can go beyond facilitating interaction; it
may move into stimulating the senses. Within local education there is a
strong tradition of encouraging people to enter new situations and settings. This may range from visits to theatres and art galleries, through trips
to cities and other countries, to use of the outdoor environment. The
latter has been a key aspect of most youth movements, whether out of a
concern for health, both physical and mental – for example, in the girls'
clubs of the late nineteenth century (see Stanley 1890) – or to further
manliness, independence and self-reliance (Baden-Powell 1909: 56). It has

also been a feature of work with adults and of mutual organization in the United Kingdom – for example, the cycling touring clubs associated with churches and Sunday schools in the 1870s; and the Co-operative Holidays Associations in the 1890s (Kelly 1970: 195–215).

For adult educators detailed advice was a later innovation. Discussions have been an aspect of provision in the United Kingdom since the days of the mutual improvement societies and the start of university extension in the mid-nineteenth century (Kelly 1970: 221). However, it is only with a growing appreciation of the way groups function that setting has been properly attended to. Thinking about group work as a method really began to take off in the United States in the 1930s, and owed much to the work of Coyle (1930) and others (see Lieberman 1939). It was enhanced in the 1940s by work on the functioning of small groups (see, for example, Lewin 1947; 1948; Homans 1951). Insights from these studies found their way into adult education texts. Notions such as 'realness', acceptance and empathy were also creeping in via counselling and especially the work of Rogers (1942; 1965). Knowles (1950: 33), for example, looked to the creation of favourable physical conditions and friendly and informal climates as basic principles of adult teaching. By the 1970s, substantial sections are devoted to such topics as seating arrangements and atmosphere (Rogers 1977: 101–5).

In all this it is helpful for educators to have a certain humility. Their work on the physical environment, the impact they may have through work on the structural and socio-cultural context, and their participation in situations can be significant. However, much of the strength of local education lies in the ability of educators to be participants, to involve themselves in the action without becoming an overwhelming point of reference. The value lies in the total experience, in the interactions and activities – and in the feelings and understandings that people have. Educators and learners, alike, are active agents in the situation.

What is fascinating about all this is the extent to which the links and parallels with schooling are now largely unacknowledged in the literature (and the conversations I have with local educators). Yet behind much of this writing lies the hand of Dewey. Coyle drew extensively on his work (Reid 1981: 113); Rogers was deeply influenced by his follower, Kilpatrick (Thorne 1992: 104); and Lindeman was both his friend and his disciple (Stewart 1987: 136–49). While Dewey may have stood outside or beyond the main protagonists in the struggle for the American curriculum (Kliebard 1987) and had limited overt influence on debates in British schooling, there can be no doubting his impact on adult education theorists (Elias and Merriam 1980: 68). Similarly, to understand outdoor work, we have to look to the influence of Rousseau and the Romantics; the New School Movement; and the pioneering work of Pestalozzi, Froebel and Montessori (Putnam 1990: 23). Many of the elements at work in organizing a primary school classroom can be directly transferred to working with youth or adult groups. We might look to the physical design and layout (see, for example, Stewart 1986: 29–62); the impact of context on relationships (Kutnick 1988); or how group work might be initiated and sustained (Galton and Williamson 1992). Running through all this is a shared concern: how do educators intervene in settings so that a better environment for learning is created? By failing to explore practice that lies beyond traditional occupational boundaries much can be lost.

Experiences and situations

> I start worrying about my own children growing up here when you come in contact a lot with the drugs and the thieving that supports the drugs. Or you are talking to young people that have been in trouble or whatever, and there is no learning . . . But usually that's balanced by others who have suddenly grabbed hold of something or suddenly had an opportunity . . . It is experiences rather than activities. A new experience can usually draw things out.

I have been struck just how my conversations with local educators are littered with references to experience – mine, theirs and others'. In many respects these are *the* starting point for workers' efforts. As Lindeman argued in respect of adult education, their approach is via situations rather than subjects. 'Every adult person finds himself in specific situations with respect to his work, his recreation, his family-life, his community-life, et cetera – situations which call for adjustments. Adult education begins at this point' (Lindeman 1989: 6). Here we can see echoes of the Progressives' epithet that 'we teach children, not subjects' (Brookfield 1987a: 6). However, there are important differences – for while local educators may begin with situations, their response may not be to build a curriculum. There are moments when they set up special projects that are, in effect, curriculum-based or when they take on a more didactic role but, for much of the time, the concern of the workers I talk with is to move with the questions and interests of the learners.

Local education involves learning 'that occurs as a direct participation in the events of life' (Houle 1980: 22). As such it is a refinement of the processes that we all go through. We all have to think about, and learn from, our experiences of daily living (Jarvis 1992: 3–16). Local educators can try to enlarge these experiences by encouraging people to take up new activities and by working with people to come to a deeper understanding. To do this they often set up specific opportunities, such as camping trips, residentials and so on. The various decisions and interactions involved in such projects can provide rich pickings:

> The activity and skills learning is just one small part. Living together, making decisions, dealing with the elements, dealing with disputes that happen when people get on top of each other. Making decisions about what we are going to eat . . . There is so much to talk about.

Figure 2.1: Experiential learning (after Kolb 1984: 21)

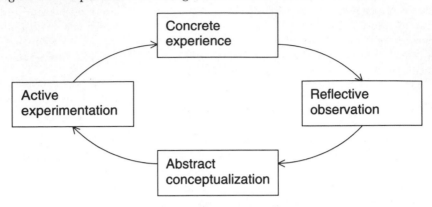

It may also involve workers in encouraging people to undertake self-directed learning projects such as visiting museums, reading specialist magazines or following a series of television documentaries. These can be seen as deliberate and focused efforts to gain and retain definite knowledge and skill that involve some commitment of time (Tough 1993: 58–60). Research such as that of Sargant (1991) reveals that a significant number of people are engaged in such self-education efforts.

In recent years, there has been a growing awareness of what educators outside schools must do if they are to engage with experience. Much of this has arisen under the guise of 'experiential learning' and particularly through the influence of writers and trainers who have taken up the work of Kolb (1976; 1984). The model most usually associated with him was drawn from the work of Lewin (1951). In this, people begin by carrying out an action. They then observe the effects of this action in a given situation and attempt to understand them. The third step involves generalizing and understanding the principle under which the situation falls. This may not involve putting the understanding fully into words. When the general principle is understood, the last step is its application through action in a new circumstance within the range of generalization. In some accounts these steps (or ones like them) are shown as a circular movement. In others, to show learning has taken place, the process is shown as a spiral – because the action takes place in new circumstances and the learner is better able to anticipate the possible effects of action. We can see the simple circle in Figure 2.1.

Two aspects were seen as especially noteworthy: the use of concrete, 'here-and-now' experience to test ideas; and feedback to change practices and theories (Kolb 1984: 21–2). Kolb joins these with Dewey's emphasis on the developmental nature of the exercise, and with Piaget's appreciation of cognitive development. There are various criticisms that can be made of such models (see Jarvis 1987), but there can be no denying their practical use and influence (Tennant 1988: 105; Thorpe *et al.* 1993: 7).

The emphasis on experience does leave some questions about the role of what might be called 'information assimilation' (Coleman 1976) where material is transmitted from teacher to learner for use in future situations. Workers may need to brief groups on new housing legislation; take them through safety procedures for an outdoor activity; or provide information about different study opportunities. This links with a problem Freire recognized when talking with community educators in Scotland. A number defined themselves as facilitators. He argued with them:

> I am an educator. I am *not* a facilitator. The act of teaching is not included in the concept of facilitation. As a teacher, I know I have things to teach. I don't need to feel ashamed. If a teacher says he is equal, he is incompetent, or trying to get some favour from the students. But being different from the students does not mean being authoritarian. It means being *competent* in order to get the respect and support of the students.
>
> (Quoted by Kirkwood 1991: 43)

The problem here is that local educators may well develop an appreciation of their role in the context of 'counselling' and 'group work' and in so doing define themselves primarily as facilitators – seeing teaching as 'instruction'. For them, as for Rogers (1983: 228), 'teaching is a relatively unimportant and vastly overvalued activity'.

Conversation and interaction

> Why come to see me? All I do is talk with young people.

Such has been the emphasis on activity and organizing things in community education, youth work and community work, that 'simply' sitting and talking with people is sometimes not seen as real work (Davies and Gibson 1967: 99–120). Linked with this is the idea that having conversations is something that anybody can do well – it is part of living. Yet conversation lies at the centre of local education. We can see its place in the following example.

> We do an activity, people feel good about it, they want to do it again. Now when the women I work with go home and say to their husband 'I went out today and it was really, really good' now he has got to cope with that because he has never let her have that before. The women come back and say 'My man wasn't very happy and he is not going to let us go again.' So it is saying to them there are choices here, but it is not making the choice for them. It's about saying let's look at what you could move on to and what would happen if you did that, and then letting them do it.

This worker was using various outdoor activities to stimulate thinking. In conversation she picks up on people's experiences and helps to create an environment in which they can think about them. She does not list the choices for the women she works with. Rather she encourages them to sketch out options and possibilities. She then works with them to build opportunities to test out their choice. To do this she has constantly to be thinking about what she has heard and what she is doing. It is not possible for her to follow some preset plan. She has to reflect-in- and -on-action (Schön 1983). Without her questions, suggestions and engagement – her conversation – I suspect much would have been lost.

Listening to local educators evaluating sessions I have heard phrases such as 'there was a real buzz' or 'people have really been talking'. On closer inspection what this boils down to is a recognition that people have been:

- talking about something 'important', such as the way they relate to each other or the way they experience racism;
- listening to each other;
- thinking about what they have heard and said, and how this relates to what they believe;
- expressing respect for, and interest in, other people in their actions and words.

Talking, listening, thinking, respecting: listed in this way it is clear that conversation is fundamental activity. It is also easy to see why it can be a problem: we do not always listen, engage with what is being said, and treat each other with respect. Moreover, much of what we talk about is seemingly unimportant.

There is a trap here. A focus on overt significance of the subject matter – whether we label it as trivial or important – can lead to an undervaluing of conversation. It does not seem to be scripted and organized around the delivery of 'knowledge' in the same way as lessons may be. For much of the time, as local educators, we are talking in an everyday way about children, television, school, the lack of things to do. It all seems quite pale when compared with the process Freire (1972) describes as dialogue. Through dialogue people are supposed to create new understandings which are 'explicitly critical and aimed at action, wherein those who were formally illiterate now begin to reject their role as mere "objects" in nature and social history and undertake to become "subjects" of their own destiny' (Goulet 1974: viii). Yet we overlook two aspects here at our peril. First, the very fact that much of the subject matter is the stuff of everyday life means there always is the possibility of unmasking the taken-for-granted. We can ask why things are as they are in relationships; or why is it that there is so little provision in a neighbourhood. Second, and crucially, conversation like dialogue is, at heart, 'a kind of social relation that engages its participants' (Burbules 1993: 19). The act of engaging with another – whatever the subject matter – is significant in itself. The process entails virtues and emotions such as concern, trust, respect, appreciation, affection and hope (1993: 36–46).

I want to look at these matters at some length in later chapters but before leaving things here it is important to comment on my focus on conversation. In seeking to make sense of local education I initially turned, like others (for example, Rosseter 1987), to the idea of dialogue and the work of Freire. However, several factors have led me away from this. First, the workers I talked with did not, for the most part, describe their inter-actions in terms of dialogue. Instead, they used words like talk, chat and conversation. At this basic level I wanted to stay as close to their vocabulary as possible. Second, when I analysed the types of activity that they were involved in, the word 'conversation' seemed appropriate and to allow the necessary fluidity. Describing an exchange about the state of the kitchen or the price of children's clothes as dialogue sounded rather pretentious. It was more comfortable to talk about different forms of conversation: some were 'passing', some were 'playful', some were 'serious'. One tended to flow into another – they were, in effect, changing conversations. Third, I did not want to privilege 'serious conversation' too strongly. Yes, local educators engage in activities directed towards discovery and new understanding – what Burbules (1993: 8) describes as 'dialogue' – but they are also concerned with being and belonging. Here, as I will argue in Chapter 3, seemingly trivial exchanges are of central importance and, if neglected, lead to major problems. Dialogue in the sense that Freire uses the term is only one element of the work local educators do.

Education as a fully human activity

It is about not labelling them. Not saying you are an A-level student or a dunce or this, that or the other, but taking them as a person and starting from there. Yes it is dealing with feelings, but it is more than that. It is saying you have got capabilities more than people have given you credit for . . . Rather than stating that you can do this or that, it is about people trying for themselves and setting their own limits. It is about a roundness.

Ideas about choice and voice shade into an overarching concern, expressed by some workers, for the 'whole person'. This has several dimensions including valuing yourself; being in touch with your capacities; working to integrate different parts of yourself. It also focuses on the relationship of individuals to others and to the world (the whole and the parts); and that between values, thinking and action (praxis). For them, no doubt, as for Kidd (1978: 125), '*being* and *becoming* are not only what living is about, but also the chief object of learning'. As Jarvis (1992: 101) notes, such words are relatively rare in the educational vocabulary.

A key aspect of this orientation involves encouraging people to see and treat themselves, and others, as acting, thinking, feeling people (subjects) rather than as things (objects). As a result, feelings are paid considerable attention.

> I think that if some people don't experience their feelings and don't question why they are feeling that way they will not move on. It is enabling that to happen. So that when they do move on they can think 'Right, that person is there.'

The focus on emotional matters is not simply to do with things that are happening 'out there', but also with the feelings involved with learning. This means exploring the various anxieties people have as their understanding of themselves alters. There are the possible impacts that these changes might have on people's relationships and lives. It also involves getting and staying in touch with the emotional nature of the relationship between educators and those with whom they work – looking at questions of dependence, expectation, transference and so on. It is a recognition that affective and cognitive aspects of learning are closely linked and interdependent (see Salzberger-Wittenberg *et al.* 1983).

The attention paid to feelings and the changing nature of relationships brings workers back to the self.

> You have to be honest with yourself, and accept yourself with regard to your own hopes and fears, feelings, thoughts and capabilities. When you can do this, you can then enable other people to value themselves, and to explore and express their own feelings, anxieties, hopes, fears and ambitions, and enable them to believe in themselves.

Workers may also feel they have to show some of their frailties and limitations.

> I make mistakes, I am human. I have no wish for them to think I am just this perfect person whose life is . . . like they'll say I just want to be like you. You have got out of it, ain't you. I say it ain't that easy. It hasn't been smooth. I don't mind letting them see my weaknesses. It's important, because that is part of being a whole person.

Here we can see how the emotions of workers may come into play. They make a commitment; have a vision of how relationships can be and what might make for human flourishing; and some feeling and liking for those they work with. Indeed, it is difficult to see how they can function as educators without these things. They have to be experienced as thinking, feeling people if they are to work in this way – and with this go certain costs and risks. Things will cause pain and hurt, at times the work will be an emotional roller-coaster, there will be times of loneliness, embarrassment and fright (Collins and Hoggarth 1977: 16–18). For example, one worker described how she became stuck up a tree on an assault course when working with a group of women. It had taken the women 30 minutes to talk her down.

> It was then that the women realized that on the assault course everybody could do something, but not everybody could do everything. And then they put it into other situations. Yes, there are certain

things that we can do and feel OK about. And there are certain
things that you have got to let go.

This highlights a further dimension: the relationship of oneself to others
and the world. All the local educators quoted here worked with both
individuals and groups. Relationships in groups were a key focus and a
source of emotion.

One of the most important things is relationships between the group.
That's been the big key thing for me, how they treat one another,
how they behave, all those sorts of things. That's the depressing one
for me.

Beyond the concern with immediate relationships with friends, families,
teachers and bosses, these educators may also look to the way in which
people place themselves with respect to wider collectivities. What sense do
people make of their living in a particular neighbourhood; of being
members of a particular class or culture; of being male or female; of being
white, African, Panjabi or Irish; and so on. What is their attitude and
behaviour towards people they see as different to themselves?

In some respects this concern with the 'whole person' and with promoting human flourishing links with that tradition known as 'person-centred'
practice. Notions of wholeness overlap with what Rogers describes as
congruence or 'realness'; and the attitude embodied and conveyed by
educators may be accepting and valuing of the other (Rogers 1965).

When the facilitator is a real person, being what she is, entering into
a relationship with the learner without presenting a front or façade,
she is much more likely to be effective. This means that the feelings
that she is experiencing are available to her, available to her awareness, that she is able to live these feelings, be them, and able to
communicate them if appropriate. It means that she comes to a
direct personal encounter with the learner, meeting her on a person-
to-person basis. It means that she is *being* herself, not denying
herself.

(Rogers 1983: 121–2)

The concern with congruence (genuineness) and acceptance may well
come close to two of what are sometimes described as Rogers's (1974:
61–3) 'core conditions' for counselling relationships. However, his third
condition, 'empathetic understanding', marks a point of divergence.

Rogers emphasizes achieving as full an understanding of the other
person as is possible. This involves a willingness and ability to enter
'the private perceptual world of the client without fear and to become
thoroughly conversant with it' (Thorne 1992: 31).

When the teacher has the ability to understand the student's reactions from the inside, has a sensitive awareness of the way the

process of education and learning seems *to the student* then again the likelihood of significant learning is increased.

(Rogers 1983: 125)

Many local educators may be happy to work in this way (see, for example, Fisher 1993). However, as we explore the notion of conversation, it becomes clearer that the task is not so much to enter and understand the other person, as to work for understanding and commitment. This is not achieved simply by putting oneself into the shoes of another. Conversation involves working to bring together the insights and questions of the different parties; it entails the fusion of a number of perspectives, not the entering into of one (Gadamer 1979: 271–3). As Freire (1972: 63) put it, at the point of encounter, 'there are neither ignoramuses nor perfect sages; there are only men who are attempting, together, to learn more than they now know'. In this respect the approach I am arguing for here is not person-centred, but conversational or dialogical. And this is subverted when the educator 'concentrates on the other person as such rather than on the subject matter – when he looks *at* the other person, as it were, rather than *with* him at what the other attempts to communicate' (Linge 1976: xx).

Looking to the self and learning

People are social beings. We are created out of social interactions. We need other people to be fully human.

We can get locked into looking exclusively for outcomes in individuals. Working in a way that attends to the politics of difference, and to the nature of conversation, entails a major shift of focus. Instead of aiming for particular changes in individuals, we look to the nature of the interactions we foster – we move from a focus on product to a concern with process and praxis (Grundy 1987). Associated with this is the idea that people's lives

are characterized by the ongoing conversations and dialogues they carry out in the course of their everyday activities, and therefore that *the most important thing about people is not what is contained within them, but what transpires between them.*

(Sampson 1993: 20)

Here we return to Mead's argument that our selves are formed in inter-action with others and to Vygotsky's (1962) linking of inter- and intrapsychological processes. We 'read' others' gestures (behaviour), and so become conscious of ourselves. The essence of the self 'lies in the internalized conversation of gestures which constitutes thinking; or in terms of which thought or reflection proceeds. And hence the origin and foundations of the self, like those of thinking, are social' (Mead 1934: 173). But while the self emerges in society this does not mean it is completely determined by others. To be a self is to be in two more perspectives at once:

> This enables the individual to understand his own behaviour as a participant in the social act in relation to the behaviour of other participants . . . In order to be a self, then, one must also enter into the perspectives of others, but entering into their perspectives does not obliterate one's own. The seller must take the attitude of the buyer without being the buyer.
>
> (Miller 1973: 166)

In this way our identities are constituted through living relations with others – there can be no separate self apart from others (Gadamer 1979: 271).

Many in the West are caught up in a particular view of the self, and find it difficult to come to terms with ideas such as these. Their thinking has become infected by system and machine-like images. Routinely, brains are likened to computers, thinking processes to software, and experiences and memories to data. The body is seen as a machine. The individual is understood as discrete, the cornerstone for activities. As Sampson (1993: 59) put it, people start to think of the self as a bounded container, separate from other bounded containers, with the body housing the individual. This is linked to a tendency in some ways of thinking where wholes are habitually reduced to parts. The parts then become *the* path to an understanding of the whole. In contrast, Dewey (see, for example, 1929: 1a–39) argued that we would be better rewarded if we attended to the inclusive and connected, and looked to a process of differentiation within wholes.

> Our knowledge of the 'external world' is not something put together out of self-contained independent particulars. It is something that begins as a whole, large in terms of what it includes (which is everything) but small in terms of the differences, detail, complexity and relations of significance which it incorporates.
>
> (Tiles 1988: 22)

A further, crucial, assumption is of possessive individualism: 'every man is naturally the sole proprietor of his own person and capacities (the absolute proprietor in that he owes nothing to society for them)' (Macpherson 1962: 270). This view has become so pervasive that it can be difficult to argue for alternatives. Yet, as Macpherson has shown, ideas about personhood change over time; they also vary cross-culturally (Marsella *et al.* 1985). Indeed, the ideas around the self that many western educators hold as 'obvious' are rather peculiar within the context of the world's cultures (Geertz 1983: 59).

> To members of sociocentric organic cultures the concept of the autonomous individual, free to choose and mind his own business, must feel alien, a bizarre idea cutting the self off from the interdependent whole, dooming it to a life of isolation and loneliness. Linked to each other in an interdependent system, members of organic cultures take an active interest in one another's affairs, and

feel at ease regulating and being regulated. Indeed, others are the means to one's functioning and vice versa.

(Schweder and Bourne 1984: 194)

Selves in interaction are complex and connected beings. Feelings, hopes, beliefs, ideas, and experiences mix and are shared.

I know how difficult it is to move from a focus on individuals to one on interaction. It is something I come across time and again as people begin to see what is involved in working with groups. One step involves focusing on 'the space in-between' rather than the individual. Another entails exploring the extent to which our focus is conditioned by carrying definite ideas about learning outcomes into exchanges instead of 'going with the flow'. If we are to take conversation seriously then we have to learn not to cut off possibility. This is a frame of mind that we also need to consider in our one-to-one work. We can approach learning as situated – as lying not so much in the individual mind as in interactions between people in communities.

> Activities, tasks, functions and understandings do not exist in isolation; they are part of broader systems of relations in which they have meaning. These systems of relations arise out of and are reproduced and developed within social communities, which are in part systems of relations among persons. The person is defined by as well as defines these relations. Learning thus implies becoming a different person with respect to the possibilities enabled by these systems of relations.
>
> (Lave and Wenger 1991: 53)

This is not to imply that all learning has to happen in groups, or face to face. What it does mean is that as we reflect on something we inevitably draw upon language, resources, ideas, images, that we share with others. We also, in our thinking, routinely make reference to what others might say, how they may view us.

In conclusion

Earlier I said that this was an area rife with crass polarizations. In some ways it is easy to see why – occupational groups tend to use stereotypical images of others to mark out boundaries and buttress their professional identity (Hugman 1991: 101–4). Adult educators want to establish their specialism; youth workers want to differentiate themselves from teachers; community workers from social workers; and so on. But there is something more here. Influential writers such as Freire are prone, for other reasons, to posing one form against another as if they were opposites. A central example of this is the contrasting of banking and dialogical approaches to education (Freire 1972). Other examples include Knowles (1970) and his setting of andragogy against pedagogy; and Rogers's (1983) dismissal of teaching. However, we should be deeply suspicious of this strategy. As Dewey has argued, an either/or approach to such matters in education is misguided. 'The fundamental issue is not of new versus old education nor of progressive against traditional education but a question of what anything whatever must be to be worthy of the name *education*' (Dewey 1963: 90).

The constellation of qualities that I have been describing as local education holds a great deal in common with other educational endeavours. The emphasis on localness is significant but this should not set it apart from other educational traditions that value being and interaction. In many respects, such educators seek to foster what Habermas (1984) calls 'communicative action'. This is action that enlightens and connects; that is orientated to mutual understanding. In interaction we can explore our thoughts, beliefs and feelings, our relationships, and the world we inhabit (Habermas 1984: 308). As educators our aim may be to foster an environment in which we can come to an engaged understanding with another person about some aspect of these.

> It is basically listening to what the groups have to say, joining in with what they are doing. It comes from seeing oneself as an 'outsider'. It allows you to take a phenomenological approach if that is not too distant. The thing that I have been able to do is to go into meetings with the Muslim group and listen to what they have to say about religion and to discuss religion with them. I think that approach is appreciated. It is not me sitting back and being the secular facilitator. It's being a participant, perhaps from another perspective, but one who respects the fundamentals of religion. It has basically been the same with the Gujarati/Hindu group although they are overtly religious in what they do.

Just how workers begin to approach this task is the subject of the next chapter.

Chapter 3

Engaging in conversation

> I have become very conscious of the language that is used. When you
> look at it a lot of it is terrible. That is why I refuse to use the word
> 'counselling' ... Often a chat with a young person is built up into
> something else: 'I really had a heavy counselling session.' I absolutely
> hate that because I feel it is incredibly patronizing.

Usually, chapters in education books with the words 'talk', 'conversation'
or 'dialogue' in the title mean readers will be treated to either a discussion
of Freire or an examination of classroom interaction. In contrast, the
focus here is everyday talk and the way it is thought about by local educators. I want to argue that their work is grounded in conversation and
that with this comes a problem. In many respects their practice is 'unseen'
– it centres around something we all do, and take for granted. Local
educators thus have to think carefully about communicating and responding
to other people. As well as being in touch with their own thoughts and
feelings, and how they act, they also have to engage as educators with
those of others – with what happens between people.

It is easy to overlook the meaning of 'everyday' talk, and undervalue
what local educators do. Things are not helped by the sway held by idealized
or normative accounts of dialogue, largely after Freire (a theme I develop
further in Chapter 8). Sometimes the conversations of local educators
could be called dialogue: they are 'directed toward discovery and new
understanding, which stands to improve the knowledge, insight, or sensitivity of its participants' (Burbules 1993: 9). However, much of the time
they appear more prosaic. The behaviour of neighbours, partners and

children; the previous night's television; stories about media personalities; requests to borrow money; offering cigarettes – this is the stuff of everyday talk. At least these are the types of things we label as commonplace – but as soon as we list them the debates begin. What is everyday to one person is not to another. Further, and crucially for local educators, the ordinary can become the extraordinary as we explore it. One particular writer, Goffman, provides us with a range of images and metaphors in this respect. As Manning (1992: 3) has commented, with the exception of Simmel's, his general descriptions of face-to-face interaction are unmatched. Sometimes though, his actors seem terribly calculating, and his account both arguable and uneven (see Giddens 1987: 109–40). However, his insistence on the significance of the 'trivia' of encounters, and his focus on what is happening *between* people (Burns 1992: 25), are crucial insights for our purposes here.

Conversation

Conversation may be thought of as two or more people talking either face to face or at a distance via technologies such as the telephone. We may routinely learn that conversation involves a good deal more than speech. For those who have sight, conversation is enriched by visual signals: raised eyebrows, wagging fingers, smiles, the direction of looks and so on. Points may also be underlined or communicated by touching.

> So much of what I do involves touching, particularly when I am working with people who have difficulties communicating. One young woman in the group at the moment is not able to put much into words, but she says a lot by the way she touches me.

In this way, it is possible to have a conversation without a sound. We might use signing, or write things down, or type them into a text telephone. For this to happen there has to be a shared language and the opportunity for immediate response. Writing things down, for example, slows up the rate at which we can exchange information. With text telephones it is just a case of waiting for one person to finish typing. However, with letter writing the time elapsing between each exchange significantly alters the process. The lack of immediacy and the thought involved in committing things to paper gives such exchanges a formal air.

From this we can see that conversation is usually a social activity, involving interaction with other people (talking with an 'abstract other' or conversing with the self are special cases). Three things are quickly apparent. First, for it to work those involved must co-operate. Second, for this to happen, those concerned must have some appreciation of what the others are experiencing. Third, they must give each other room to talk. It is, in other words, a reciprocal process. Conversation cannot be properly entered into if one person is seeking to act on the other, as a potter might shape a vase. These aspects are significant for local educators. Much of their work can be concerned with encouraging people to think of others, and themselves; and with fostering co-operation and mutual respect (Davies and Gibson 1967).

To engage in conversations certain 'rules' and procedures have to be followed. These vary from group to group, relationship to relationship – see Wardhaugh's (1985) excellent discussion of conversation for an exploration of this and other aspects raised in this chapter. We also have to take a great deal on trust. In conversation each party has to assume that there is some truth in what the other is saying. Apparently simple matters such as promising to be in a particular place at a particular time are a good example of this. If we did not broadly trust others to keep to such promises then there would be chaos. With individuals we may be cautious or questioning, but if we cannot routinely believe in some way what others are saying then co-operation is difficult.

Conversations also leave their mark. We change the world in some small way every time we speak with another. People think and act in response to what we say; the experience becomes a 'memory'. This we may not fully recognize, but it is there. Language allows communication, social interaction, thought and control. It is a means of relaying ideas and perceptions of experiences between individuals. It also provides a medium through which people can categorize, order and direct their experiences and understandings and relations with other people. However, putting things in words for other people is something more than exchanging information. It contains the possibility of experiencing, of making things real and so bringing one's world alive:

> An event or experience can, by being put into words, crystallise itself into a certain insight or emotion. A thought or feeling, if articulated for the first time, or expressed in a new way, might become tangible and thus find its place in the configuration of one's thinking or emotional life. Our experience can thus become embodied in speech and, once clothed in words, it can take on form and substance.
>
> (Spurling 1988: 164)

Having taken on form and substance, the words are an aspect of new actions in the world.

As a result conversation can be a risky business. A striking experience for local educators in this respect can flow from their having to start conversations with strangers, and with people they hardly know. This is all right where there is a clear task and clearly understood ways of doing things, such as when giving out leaflets. However, in other situations where there may be no apparent agenda and procedure, the situation is more fraught.

> It's not just that young person being vulnerable to you, it is you being vulnerable to that young person because you are around there. Nobody knows who you are, nobody likes being told to fuck off. You

have that fear when you walk up to people that you are going to make the biggest mistake in your life.

While there are risks around conversations – dangers, as here, of being rejected, or of making a gaffe – they can also be a source of great pleasure. They can be infuriating, informing, hurtful, loving. In short, conversation is an emotional as well as an 'intellectual' activity. We may want to communicate our feelings or concern for another – and this is often far more important than the overt words we use. We want to show we are 'with' the other person. Given a concern with the affective domain, this aspect of conversation comes to the fore. Workers then have to be sensitive, 'moment to moment, to the changing felt meanings which flow in this other person, to the fear or rage or tenderness or confusion or whatever, that s/he is experiencing' (Rogers 1980: 142).

Conversation is also a deeply political activity. The labels we give to things, the ideas evoked by a particular word or phrase, are a double-edged sword. They allow the possibility of knowing more, and of being controlled or misled. As Habermas (see, for example, 1984: 332) has consistently pointed out, our communication can be systematically distorted. Such words as we have may not fully describe or capture an experience, situation or idea. The context in which they are heard or read may be flavoured by a wish for submissive silence.

> The repression used to return the masses to their silence is preceded and accompanied by a myth-making effort to identify as diabolical all thought-language which uses such words as *alienation, domination, oppression, liberation, humanization* and *autonomy*. To counter this effort . . . de-mystifying work is necessary to show what the words really stand for: the expression of objective, socio-historical and political categories whose dramatic character in the Third World allows no one to be neutral.
>
> (Coutinho 1972: 16–17)

When approaching conversation it is crucial that we do not fall into the trap of seeing the participants as operating on a level field. The language we use is inevitably flawed. Moreover, people have widely different opportunities to develop their vocabulary. The material and social conditions in which they live foster contrasting ideas of what is important and what is not, and of what is possible. Seeing conversation as a social practice infused with a complex, interacting and often conflicting range of forces, allows us to get a grip on the nature of people's relationships. While we may seek to be open to the truth in what is said, and hope to engage with each other as 'equally knowing subjects' (Freire 1985: 51), this does not mean that we have had the same access to knowledge or the same opportunities to develop our understandings. In conversations there are considerable differences between the actors and this can be obscured by the apparent informality or the overt nature of the encounter – see, for example, Goffman's (1961) discussion of games.

We can also turn to the ways in which relations of power become expressed in conversation – how one group assumes dominance and another is muted. Here we can call on Spender's (1980) work on the participation of women and girls in mixed groups. She found that males often consider female talk as trivial; that women are frequently interrupted by men and tend to defer to them; and that women's contributions tend to be both more co-operative and tentative. Here we need to avoid crude essentialism, a belief, for example, that men are inherently more disposed to 'having' and women to 'being'. We do need to consider how language is 'man-made' – in what ways women have been 'excluded from the production of cultural forms' (Spender 1980: 52); and the ways in which the voice of the dominated has generally been excluded (Parkin 1979).

Making contact

Where can local educators start? While they may do some of their work over the phone, most of their conversations involve their being with people. Their first step then, is to work their way into being within conversing distance of the people to whom they want to talk. They have to make themselves part of the 'scene'. The second, and tricky, step is to move from being part of the scene to being present in a direct way as a person. It means moving from unfocused to focused interaction. The former consists of those signals that have to be made because individuals are co-present in a situation – signs of mutual awareness. The latter involves people paying direct attention to what others are doing or saying (Goffman 1961: 58). Moving from silence to speech, or from being part of the scene to a focus of attention is made more difficult by all the various rules or norms concerning 'talking to strangers'.

Workers seeking to make 'openings' can employ one of four basic moves or tactics:

■ Greeting or speaking to a member of a group or gathering to whom they are already known or can legitimately speak. They can then use that as an introduction to the other people present. Classic variations on this theme include making a fuss of a pet, pulling a 'funny' face at a small child, and then greeting the accompanying person.
■ Becoming recognized as someone who is routinely around, who is a feature of the scene. This involves spending a lot of time 'being around'. Contact can then be made by building on greetings or routine episodes such as asking the time; or by using the situations that occur.
■ Going up to people, saying who they are and what they are doing and then asking questions or offering information. This tactic can range

from giving out leaflets, through simple questions ('I am new to this area, what is there to do round here?'), to introductions ('I am the local community worker . . .').

- Doing some activity that attracts attention or interest. In building-based settings this can be simply sitting at a table doing some craft work. People come up to see what you are doing. Outside, workers may use devices like stalls and displays, mobile coffee stands and so on.

A lot of thought can go into selecting the appropriate tactic or move. Workers need to be able to handle their anxieties (Rogers 1981: 18–21), and these sorts of situation are fraught with problems, as Goffman (1969; 1972) has shown. Initial moves are often accompanied by an apology: 'I'm sorry, but could you tell me . . .'. Workers may routinely ask questions like 'What are these people likely to think of me?' in order to ease the choice of move or, indeed, whether to make an approach at all. Having made the move and got an opening, workers can use this to ease interactions at other times. They have established what could be described as a 'relationship wedge' (Goffman 1963).

Establishing the basis for conversation/beginning routines

We have seen some of the ploys local educators use in trying to make the move from being part of the scene to being an object of focused attention. In making this move, they have to:

- ensure that the situation is one where conversation is generally appropriate or acceptable;
- judge that it is appropriate for them to be approaching the particular individual/group in this situation;
- present themselves in an appropriate way, put on the right 'face', express the correct level of involvement;
- judge the content and level of the conversation.

They may come up against the feeling that workers should not 'invade' other people's time and space. Their presence has to be acceptable to those involved; initial contacts should be brief unless there is some confirmation that it is OK for them to be there.

> You can often pick up when they want to talk to you . . . You can use your body language and say 'Look I am going off now, I'll be around.' Then you go round the corner and they will catch up with you. So it is about that approach.

With groups and individuals we do not know, as we start engaging at these early moments, we are often acutely aware of their response. How are they responding, what signals are they giving, how are they thinking and so on? Workers have to read situations carefully.

You are constantly looking for their response. Are they looking away, are they looking bored? Should you change the subject? The aim is to get them to talk, not for you to keep talking at them.

What usually happens at the start of conversations is a set of routine exchanges – inquiries about family, friends, general introductory questions such as how the person is getting on; references to outside events such as the weather, TV and so on (Wardhaugh 1985: 116–38). Those conversations where we get straight down to business are either fairly trivial, or formal and involve various known rules. An example of the former is stopping someone and asking for the time (because you want to know the time!). A visit to the doctor is an example of the latter. The doctor asks what is the matter with you; or you go in with your speech worked out, explaining what your symptoms are.

There are some parallels in what local educators do. They might go straight up to someone and ask, for example, if they want to go on a trip or take part in some activity. At other times workers may be in a more formal 'counselling' setting, where others expect to walk in, much as we enter the doctor's surgery. However, mostly we have to go through the preliminaries. These establish the fact that we are having a conversation; that our lives are somehow connected one to another (however loosely).

Probably if I don't know them I would talk about things that are pretty common with people in that age group. Done anything nice lately? Been anywhere, done anything? Have you left school yet, got a job? What you doing? Nothing too nosy. Just like chattering on. Bits and pieces. I might tell them a bit about what I do, to give them an in into me. That's probably how I'd deal with someone I didn't know. But then if I did know them, I always seem to talk about them, so that they can talk about themselves. They always take up on that. They like talking, like I do now. To chatter on about yourself a bit, because you don't get the opportunity. Nine times out of ten that seems to be the key. People like telling you, because you appear interested in them, which you are, and they warm to that.

We can see here a process of feeling out, of establishing oneself as an educator, and who the other person is. Names might be exchanged; care taken about the topic: 'nothing too nosy', or too risky for that matter. Somewhere in these opening moments it is also necessary to establish a framework for the situation so that it becomes intelligible to participants. Things can get put in boxes like 'chance meeting', 'sales', 'asking direction', and so on. These labels provide a frame 'around a spate of immediate events, determining the type of "sense" that will be accorded everything within the frame' (Goffman 1961: 20). This is a process that occurs throughout encounters – if participants did not constantly 'frame' encounters (see Chapter 7) they would find themselves 'listening in on a meaningless jumble of words and with every word [they] injected, increasing the babble' (Goffman 1986: 546).

Where workers have to make a 'cold contact' the initial approach can parallel a sales talk. This, however, is less about selling than about enabling both the worker and the other person to be comfortable.

> You check somebody out and if they look like they are homeless we will go straight up to them. We have a card. The usual one is 'Hello, my name is blah blah blah, I am from [agency name]. We work with people who find themselves homeless' and we hand them the card. The trick is keep talking when you hand them the card and not let them say anything. You find that most people you come up to coldly, they are in such a shock first of all that someone they don't know is speaking to them, that they don't have time to say 'Go away, leave me alone.' They go 'What?' and take the card and they look at it and they see 'homeless' and if it relates to them they pick it up themselves.

This educator establishes the nature of the contact: he is a worker for an agency working with homeless people, not from the police or a con artist or someone looking for a pick-up. The emphasis on the word 'homeless' also establishes the topic of the conversation. It sets out a key part of the agenda for discussion. In these opening stages it is important to give the right signals about possible content. Sometimes these are overt, as in the example above, often they lie rather more in the sort of person people see you to be – how you are with them, what they have done with you in the past and so on.

> I just think they view me as someone they can talk to. Someone that listens and says 'Right if I can't do it, I'll put you in contact with someone who can.' Just someone who has a positive input in their life. Probably!

Such responses have to be finely balanced. One of the most intractable dilemmas facing educators, as Brookfield (1990: 207–8) comments, is balancing support and challenge.

Taking turns, matching performances, keeping face, being sincere

Having made contact, established the basis for conversation and gone through the opening routines, local educators then have to make decisions about how they manage their contributions. Some of these are likely to be directed at enabling the process of conversation; some will be concerned with the topic under discussion.

There are a number of rules or maxims guiding productive conversation. Participants have to work out what is intended, they 'must reconcile what they hear with what they understand the immediate purpose of the activity to be' (Gumperz 1982: 94). Grice's (1975) influential 'co-operative principle' comes in here. 'Make your contribution such as is required at the stage at which it occurs by the accepted purpose or direction of the talk exchange in which you are engaged' (Grice 1975: 67). This involves certain maxims concerning:

- *quantity.* You have to include as much information as is necessary for the task. There should be neither too much nor too little.
- *quality.* You have to be truthful, avoid lies and statements for which you have no evidence.
- *relevance.* The comments made must relate to the topic.
- *manner.* You must avoid ambiguity and obscurity and make sure that what you say is in some order.

There has been some empirical support for these maxims (see Argyle 1992: 12). However, there are times when such rules may not be appropriate – we may break them in the interest of politeness, for example. Strict application would also make for 'very boring, formal kinds of conversation – no jokes, metaphors, amusing exaggerations or irrelevancies' (1992: 13). Indeed, it could be said that these maxims relate more to telling – they have no dialogical structure (Burbules 1993: 73). Not only that, viewing encounters solely through such maxims fails to contextualize properly what occurs – as events riven through by relationships of power, for example.

Conversation is a complex affair. We need to know what we can and cannot say; how we may be experienced by others. We have to be able to call upon a range of behaviours appropriate to particular situations: when to stand or sit; what gestures to use (or to avoid); whether to look someone in the face; how close to get and so on. Above all, we have to appear sincere. As Goffman put it:

> When an individual plays a part he implicitly requests his observers to take seriously the impression that is fostered before them. They are asked to believe that the character they see actually possesses the attributes he appears to possess, that the task he performs will have the consequences that are implicitly claimed for it, and that, in general, matters are what they appear to be.
>
> (Goffman 1969: 28)

We do not necessarily expect to hear everything – the 'full truth'. However, we do expect not to be deliberately lied to. We also know that we should not take everything literally – we have much experience in 'using language to express what we mean indirectly and obliquely rather than directly and unambiguously' (Wardhaugh 1985: 36).

This disposition comes through in those workers seeking to be 'non-judgemental' and accepting of other people.

> I think it is about accepting and working from where they are and their point of view. Not putting your own priorities or whatever,

accepting the ducking and diving, not accepting the racism, but hearing what they are saying. Working from there. You would very quickly get shut off if you went in there with your structure of what you are going to do for them.

While we may begin as potential believers, experience of particular individuals and situations may lead us to put this disposition to one side. Alternatively, we may strongly 'bracket' what other people are saying. We might judge that they believe what they are saying, but that other things we know lead us to a different interpretation of the 'facts'. In this, there is a concern to display respect for the other person, while seeking to question.

The judgement I make is based on what people say to me. I need to check that out and by questioning in an appropriate manner and not by challenging . . . in terms of the person or the personality. It is about what is actually being done, not about the individual who is doing it.

To block out the possibility that what another person is saying is true is to make conversation impossible. It also, as a result, means that work cannot be done with that person.

Making judgements about appropriate responses is often difficult within a particular social or cultural group. They often require a great deal of 'local' knowledge. However, communication across cultures can be particularly fraught in this respect (Gumperz 1982: 172–86). This is not simply a matter of an inability to match understandings, it is also an expression of the role of language in affirming identity and in resisting attempts at external definition and political domination. An example of this is the use of Creole within the British black community 'as a language of power and solidarity' (Wong 1986: 109). It is hardly surprising that many, if not all of us, experience substantial problems in conversations from time to time. We can also see that engaging in conversation is not simply a means to an end for local educators. It also forms a significant focus for intervention. We engage in conversations as relationships so others may value the process and develop their abilities as conversationalists.

Process, face and respect

Given that the fostering of conversation is a key aspect of the work of local educators we would expect them to make interventions around process. The way in which encounters unfold, the moves, jumps and hesitations of conversation, do not often become a sustained focus for reflection by participants. The process is simply something that happens, it is taken for granted. Local educators can move beyond this. They can ask what has been going on. They may create or foster environments in which people can reflect on the way in which they speak to each other.

Of course, at one level, all people, as they engage in conversation, have to monitor what they are doing and to redefine or develop their perform-ance in relation to the feedback they are getting. This tacit phenomenon, what F. Smith (1992) calls 'commonplace thinking', when it breaks down in some way, can become the focus for intervention by educators. For example, they may work with people whose anxieties lead them to focus on themselves and to overlook the impact they are having on others. It might involve encouraging groups to adopt certain ways of behaving.

> I have this real important rule when I am working with groups. One person speaks at a time. It's about respect, but it's also practical. How can people be heard if everyone is speaking at once?

One approach is to flip between attention to what is being said and to the mode of expression, the 'here-and-now'. Workers may draw parallels between the way things are said and the subject matter. Much talk consists of 'replayings', of telling stories – 'often what talkers undertake to do is not to provide information to a recipient but to present dramas to an audience' (Goffman 1986: 508). In this sense, talkers are re-creating something, rather than simply describing it, and in so doing are revealing more of themselves. They do not simply emit messages, but animate them (1986: 518); they literally breathe life into words. As such, two things are of immediate importance for educators. First, the sought-for response is at the level less of a cognitive engagement than of what Goffman (1986: 541) calls 'murmuring': 'the clucks and tsks and aspirated breaths, the goshes and gollies and wows – which testify that the listener has been stirred, stirred by what is being replayed for him'. Second, the act of animation involves the expression of feelings and the re-creation of events. Here educators have a window into both the interaction and the processes of the person – the switch into the experience of the 'here-and-now', draw-ing attention to the nature of the performance, can thus be a source of rich material for reflection.

Another tactic or move may be to refer back to previous discussions and perhaps suggest that there is a certain pattern to what is happening:

> 'it seems to me that each time we talk about this you get very aggress-ive. Is it something about the subject, or is it about us as a group?' [F].

There are problems around this as it involves a shift from the abstract world of the object of the discussion, to the risky terrain of the interper-sonal. Within interactions people have a certain amount of 'face' to keep, appearances have to be maintained. Participants usually have an interest in enabling others to 'save face'. This is to do with both self-respect, and because one person's loss of face may actually threaten the success or satisfactions that the encounter provides to others. The combined effect is that individuals tend to conduct themselves during encounters so as to maintain both their own face and the face of other participants (Goffman 1972: 11).

> I had to do something – I wasn't going to bawl him out then and there, but his behaviour was unacceptable. I didn't want to make it into a joke, I didn't want to be sarcastic. But I was angry. I hate bullying. I had to signal something both to him and the group. So I said that it really pisses me off when people do not treat each other with respect and asked what had happened to create the situation. [F]

This worker tried to demonstrate both her feelings (anger) and her values (respect) in the manner of her response. She asserts a general principle and then asks the group to look back. Sometimes exploration happens, sometimes it does not – at least not at that moment. Some workers view the latter as a failure, many view it more philosophically – hoping that consistent response will get through eventually.

Topic/finding a focus

Many 'conversations' appear to be nothing of the sort. They resemble two or more monologues being performed by people who happen to be in the same place. All of us will have listened in to, or taken part in, 'conversations' where people take it in turns to talk about completely separate things. Sometimes people stick tenaciously to their particular track throughout. At other times, the monologues meet, perhaps as one person realizes what is happening and feels he/she ought to do something about it.

The fact that the overt topic is not shared should not lead us to think this performance is without meaning or value. What we might be witnessing are simply the preliminaries before the 'real' business begins. It may be a way of signalling topic; a setting out of potential areas for conversation before participants 'tune in' to the others' ways of speaking (Gumperz 1982: 167). There does need to be a certain amount of shared background information – often conversations begin by someone telling another person about something – so that the substantive discussion can then begin. Alternatively, this might be the 'real' business – a moment where in our speaking to one another we affirm our place with other people. There has to be some shared focus or common ground – but this might not be immediately apparent from the words that are said.

The question of topic can loom large in local educators' actions.

> When something happens on the spur of the moment, that time of instantaneous dialogue, I really don't know how you can set out objectives for that. It may be that you could do something during the conversation, if you get a pause or interruption. You either have to be there like a dummy and not return the conversation, or you have got to lead in.

'Leading in' involves trying to find some common ground. This does not mean that the subject is completely shared. Participants look at the topic from different angles. Conversation depends upon achieving some overlap in our frames of interpretation. The participants' horizons of understanding may barely touch. However, through the encounter they will hopefully grasp each other's standpoint, without necessarily having to agree with it, or to 'get inside each other'. As Ricoeur puts it in relation to texts: 'To understand is not to project oneself into the text but to expose oneself to it; it is to receive a self enlarged by the appropriation of the proposed worlds which interpretation unfolds' (Ricoeur 1981: 94). This provides an important insight, a counterbalance to the emphasis given to empathy by some. The danger is that a concern for the experiences of another is transformed into 'temporarily living in his/her life, moving about in it delicately without making judgments, sensing meaning of which he/she is scarcely aware' (Rogers 1980: 39). Rather than trying to live another's life, our concern lies in appreciating what is being 'said' both cognitively and affectively.

Some of these elements are at work in an example given by a worker who had just begun to work in a new neighbourhood when the Gulf War began in early 1991.

> During the Gulf War did we have some conversations. They were brilliant conversations. They were incorrect, ignorant conversations. They were based around all sorts of imperialist notions. But they were marvellous conversations because out came whole histories that these young people didn't even know they had. About their families, where they lived, the kinds of work that were and had been around in the docks. I have got some nice recordings on them. I was fervently anti-war and I wore lapel badges to say so. Standing up and being counted for the nonsense that war was. I know that some of those conversations had stuck with some of the young people. They had been thinking. That was the one thing that tipped the scales, it was such an issue, it was the one thing that we could all talk about. It happened as I started work there. It helped me get in and settled reasonably quickly. It was a kind of catalyst. It enabled me to do some real face-to-face work much quicker than I expected.

Here we see a worker jumping in with both feet on an issue that was very much on people's minds. It was approached in what at first sight might appear to be a highly partisan way. It is a stance which displays commitment. The worker does not pretend to be neutral but engages with the young people as someone who has sincerely-held views. There is no initial sense that this is someone acting, playing a role, saying something simply to stimulate debate. It is an encounter with someone's beliefs. Yet, for all this, the worker is playing a role. Sometimes we are acutely aware of this – we sense a gap between our words and feelings. The thing about such

'acting' is that it has to be seen as 'natural'. It cannot be seen as acting
– that would introduce an element of falseness, or insincerity, a 'put-on'.
There is a sort of double-take here. We all know it is acting, but it cannot
be seen as acting. Or, more accurately, it has to be seen as a form of acting
that is an expression of what we feel or are.

The real test in this example concerns not the 'balance' of the worker,
but whether the conversations were entered with an openness to the
possible truth of what others might be saying; whether the educator's
performance is experienced as sincere or 'natural'; and whether the
educator is orientated to the learning of the others involved. The worker
clearly had a sense of what was happening as an educational process and
was using recordings to reflect on things. What is also significant is that
these conversations led on to other matters concerning family and local
history.

Matching performances, using routines, improvising, reacting

In conversation, local educators have to match their performance with
that of the others involved. The way they speak and the language they use
have to connect. The topic has to be shared. Workers have to think on
their feet.

> The conversation was flowing quite easily, but it is quite easy to put
> in one sentence. You think, right, this is my time now to intervene
> and this is where you just put in the one sentence, that's it. The
> debate starts again. It's very easy. I know what I want to do in my
> mind, and I know what point it is to put in a sentence. 'Have you
> thought about this . . .' or 'Have you thought about it in this way?' It
> is planned in my mind . . . Maybe I have noticed that everybody has
> said their piece, and that they think they have sorted it out and they
> have decided what they think, then just to change the direction of
> the conversation. So I suppose it is in my head, 'Well, OK, you have
> all had a little bit of air space, now I'm going to put in my tenpenny
> worth and see what you think.'

What this worker describes as 'very easy' is a rather sophisticated ability.
She is 'going with the flow' and then putting in a point or question when
she judges the moment is right.

Good conversationalists are able to use routines and to improvise.
The person who simply uses routines will either sound like one of those
incredibly boring people who appear in sketches in *Monty Python*; or will
end up sounding like a tired salesperson, going through a form of words
without having any real connection with what is issuing from his/her
mouth. He/she will not appear sincere. In a similar fashion the person
who does not use routines will be viewed as distinctly odd – lacking social
graces. Certain things have to be gone through before most conversations

can occur. We have to achieve another balance between improvisation and routine.

> You need a basic routine which can be modified at your discretion. If you get stuck in your situation then you fall back on your routine and that gets you out of that situation. If you are working well with someone you can modify the routine. Open it up as wide as you dare let it go. The routine is there to help you. It means you can take it in different directions but bring your safety nets with you.

The ability to combine routines and to improvise lies at the heart of professional practice. As Louden has argued in relation to teaching from the practitioner's perspective, it is 'a struggle to discover and maintain a settled practice, a set of routines and patterns of action which resolve the problems posed by particular subjects and groups of children' (Louden 1991: xi). Local educators also need these patterns, but the rhythm of their practice may be less settled than that of teachers. For much of the time they are engaged in apparently casual conversation. They will then move into conversation formats that are more formal and uniform as 'difficult' or 'delicate' matters arise, or as someone asks a question or makes a statement which demands a 'teaching' response. These more formal patterns or formats use the same tools as are applied in ordinary conversation (Peräkylä and Silverman 1991: 647). Workers have to put on a different 'face', draw on a particular element of their role. They organize talk in a different way. Rather than chatting, they may ask short questions: 'How did you feel?' or 'What did you think?' They may make statements which further encourage the other person to reflect on his/ her situation. In other words, particular routines tend to be associated with different conversation formats.

A further aspect is that local educators can feel guilty about the apparently reactive nature of their work. There is some sense in which they may feel they ought to be more proactive. To some extent this may be a feed-through from the more overt goal orientation of formal approaches. What local workers have as informal educators is a particular orientation and frame of reference which they then employ (see Chapter 4). While it is important that they think about what they are doing, not all that they have to say has to be carefully measured. Someone might show us a picture or article in a magazine and we respond 'Yuk' or 'That's horrible!' We haven't thought long and hard about what we have said. Indeed, there may have been little conscious thought at all. This worries some workers, who feel that each word ought to be chosen. When some apparently unconsidered thing they have said encourages a deep debate or seems to enable other people to talk about something quite difficult (as is sometimes the case) they can become even more worried. Much here has to do with whether what they do is interpreted by the others involved as a readiness to engage with the subject; to value conversation with them – and this is *the* significant factor (Howe 1993: 15–41). The 'instinctive' response can stimulate.

Thinking about context, thinking about meaning

When we speak we do not necessarily put things in the order that makes them most understandable by others. Also, not all the necessary information for another to gain a substantial understanding can be communicated instantaneously. It is delivered in various chunks, often with important details or elements missing.

> You sit there thinking 'When is this all going to make sense?' The other person is going on about this, that and the other. What is it that they are *saying*?

In conversation we consider what speakers are trying to say; what is it that they intend? The 'chunks' of talk need not follow any obvious order. We can see here why beginning as 'believers' is so important. If we began as disbelievers, we would soon find material to support our orientation. (Perhaps, more accurately, it is the absence of material that might confirm our position.)

As listeners, from the outset, we fill in holes in the account. Often we have to make sizeable assumptions to make sense, and hold on to all sorts of ambiguities. Much that is said would make no sense at all if it were taken out of context.

> People everywhere say things whose full meanings you can appreciate only if you are sensitive to the circumstances in which they are used: the total physical, social, and psychological setting. In other words the total meaning of an utterance derives from its context as well as from the actual grammatical form it takes.
>
> (Wardhaugh 1985: 89)

We also have to remember that the meaning is not necessarily in the particular content – but in the act of engaging. Many conversations are banal, but they can be an act of commitment or affirmation. Also everyday language is 'open' in an important sense. 'Most of the words and phrases used in everyday talk do not have precise lexical definitions . . . Ordinary language is not thereby necessarily vague or indefinite. What gives ordinary language its precision is its use in context' (Giddens 1987: 104). The interpretations we are continually making are judgements not so much about individual words – although these do matter – as in relation to context: who is saying something, what has gone before, what a particular word means in our organization and so on. As Goffman argued, the meaning of our actions is linked to the context in which they arose – there has to be 'situational propriety' (Manning 1992: 10–11).

Leavings and endings

The last element to consider is the delicate matter of ending. Most practice texts tend to focus on beginnings and the process of working. Little attention is generally given to endings, except in the context of facilitating the ending of formal groups (see, for example, Whitaker 1985: 361–71). Even here the focus is on 'finishing a group' rather than drawing a session or encounter to a close. The same applies to many of the standard guides to classroom teaching (see Kyriacou 1986; Cohen and Manion 1989), although some mention is made of closure in terms of helping students to focus on the learning that has taken place. When working in formal settings with clear time boundaries 'endings' are to some extent managed by the clock (or the bell). It is usually obvious that the session is coming to a close. Those operating in informal settings have to handle endings and transitions often without such clear external stimuli. Where they do occur – as when a bus appears at a stop, or a guest at the door – we can simply make reference to the event and move on.

If the ending is too abrupt it will be interpreted as rudeness. To take us through these problems we resort to various routines and rituals. We have to give off various signals as endings have to be shared. Certain things have to be said or done to signal the end and to ensure that people do not lose face. In other words, endings have to be negotiated. Often there is an apology involved, linked usually with some sort of explanation: 'Sorry, I have got to rush – I have to pick my son up from school.' Sometimes there will be thanks: 'Thank you, I have found what you have been saying very helpful.' To end the conversation we have to exchange signals; then enter the routine.

Local educators can use a number of basic approaches to handling endings. These include:

- Signalling the timespan of the conversation from the outset: 'I was just on my way to the shops, so I thought I'd drop in for a few minutes to see how you are.'
- Introducing external constraints, so that the occurrence of that factor terminates the exchange: 'Hi, are you wanting to see the welfare rights adviser as well?' Often this can be easily 'read' by the participants from the context – the queue in the post office; the start of the film at the cinema.
- Identifying the business, so that, once concluded, the encounter can be closed: 'I wanted to talk to you about next week's committee meeting . . .'. As one worker put it:

  Sometimes conversations end quite naturally. You have said every-thing you need to say. What you need to think about the conver-sation is that it can only go so far.

- Focusing on the timespan of the other: 'I can see you are in a rush but could I just ask you about . . . ?'

Farewells share a number of characteristics with greetings except that, of course, the movement is from focused attention to inattention. A key element is to signal that you are not rejecting the person but simply taking leave:

> You know when a conversation is coming to an end so you end. That person knows as well – so there is no point in prolonging it. You end it in a way that comes back on you. 'Catch you later, you know where we are.'

There are other differences between farewells and greetings, as Goffman (1971: 108–20) indicates. Among them are concerns with the impact of raising expectations.

> Since a greeting marks the initiation of a period of easier social contact, the participants may be concerned to constrain their enthusiasm so that a misleading indication of what is to be expected will not occur. Closing salutations figure differently. Since participants can assume that they soon will be less available to each other, at least for a time, the way is opened for supportive accesses which otherwise might create burdensome anticipations.
>
> (Goffman 1971: 115–16)

Yet preparing for farewells is still a sticky manoeuvre. One party may be less inclined to get on with the process, 'thereby obliging the other party to instigate the process in advance by cues that are effective but not blatant' (Goffman 1971: 120). These typically include diminished eye contact, checking the time, signalling some external dimension. As Wardhaugh (1985: 159) says, it is difficult to close a conversation if the other party is unwilling or unable to do so. They may refuse to acknowledge signals, or bring up new topics. In these circumstances we may make some excuse or act in some blunt way to show the encounter is over. However, there is in this plenty of material for educators – the very difficulties that may be involved here can, through the shift from overt subject to process, become in itself a matter for exploration.

> On occasions I have just had to say 'Do you find saying goodbye to people difficult?' or something like that. One person thought I was incredibly rude, but on the whole you do seem to get somewhere. [F]

Local educators and conversations

Local educators have to engage in encounters such as these with a consciousness and intention often very different to those around them. To conclude, I want to draw out two crucial, linked, themes arising from this: first, that we should guard against our consciousness privileging particular forms of conversation; second, that we must take care to move with the various forms that conversation takes.

Everyday conversation and educational conversation

Given the concern with subject and activity in much of formal education, it is not surprising that local educators can worry about the amount of time they spend listening to talk about the daily round.

I do worry sometimes about what I am doing. I mean you just sort of sit there talking about boyfriends, or children, or television, or friends – whatever. You ask, 'What is it that I am doing here that is educational?' It's not like standing in front of a class.

This question is also central to Burbules's (1993) exploration of dialogue in teaching. He argues that only some forms of conversation are dialogical, the basic dividing line being whether the relationship is directed towards discovery and new understanding. He sees dialogue as a 'pedagogical communicative relation' (1993: 8).

At one level, the concern to distinguish between 'educational' (dialogical) and 'everyday' conversation is pointless. All conversations, however we label them, involve the possibility of change and learning. At another level, the worry is real enough: that possibility may not be realized. Educators, presumably, should be working to make conversations 'edifying'; fostering the search for 'new, better, more interesting, more fruitful ways of speaking' (Rorty 1980: 360). The danger is that our desire for edification can lead us to sabotage conversation or look to the parts rather than the whole. First, the wish for understanding can encourage a focus on overt content as against the significance of relationships and process. We can easily remain stuck in the cognitive domain. Simply being with another person, talking with him/her, can be both important in itself, and a prelude to more difficult or 'serious' conversations. Enabling people to be comfortable in conversation, to feel they have something to offer, are important aims. Spending time with people, valuing their presence and words, are similarly significant. If we are orientated to 'doing things', striving to 'create change', the meaning of being with people can be easily overlooked.

Second, the desire to promote change can lead us to undermine conversation. This can happen in a number of ways. Most obviously, we can fall into the trap of not listening to what others are saying because we label it as trivial. We may dismiss, for example, the endless talk about who has fallen out with whom, or the recounting of incidents that is the staple fare of drop-ins and clubs. We may get frustrated at our inability to engage with people about local housing conditions, their attitude to education or whatever. Rather than trying to explore why the former topics are important, to go with the flow, we can end up seeking to impose our own agenda. Seeking to alter the subject in a conversation is not a problem in itself; it is how it is done, the values it expresses, and the extent to which it sweeps other matters under the carpet that are a concern.

We have to learn to trust in the relationships forged in conversation. Conversations take place between people; they are public rather than personal and private; they involve one person addressing another in a specific situation; and they encompass a range of communicative forms (Sampson 1993: 97). Given the meshing together of these elements, if we engage with what people are saying – at both the cognitive and affective levels – then there is always possibility. As Howe (1993) has shown through his examination of counselling from the client's point of view, relationships in which people feel welcomed, accepted and understood are powerful. In such relationships, for those wanting to give new meaning to experience, there is the chance to talk. The question Howe (1993: 4) poses is whether it is the act of talking in itself that is potentially helpful 'rather than talk acting as a vehicle for carrying the actions and content of a particular therapeutic technique or counselling style'.

Changing conversations

Trusting in the relationships forged in conversation is not a recipe for inaction. As participants we have a responsibility to work with others to make encounters as fulfilling as they can be. We may act to alter the nature of the exchange – to move from description or story-telling, for example, to exploration and analysis. We may seek to give information. For example, a worker wanting to encourage young women to think about sex and sexuality might pick up on a comment and launch into a 'spiel' concerning contraception. One concern that arises regularly when local educators explore practice concerns the impact of such interventions: have they, for example, undermined conversations by slipping into a 'telling' mode?

    We need to recognize that conversations change. As Gumperz (1982) has noted, the picture of everyday talk that emerges from studies is of an interactive and dynamic process. It is characterized by moves from one mode of speaking to another:

> shifts from informal chat to serious discussion, from argument to humor, or narrative to rapid repartee, etc. In other words, speech routines, which when seen in speech act terms constitute independent wholes, here serve as discourse strategies integrated into and interpreted as part of the broader task of conversational management.
>
> (Gumperz 1982: 159)

Once we see the ebb and flow of conversation, then our own worries about making interventions can be better handled. Workers who reflect on their work can soon recognize the patterns.

> You start trivial talking and get on to all sorts of things – what they want to do, where they want to go. It is surprising how quickly you can move from the trivial stuff, to talking about leaving school and so on.

One way of looking at this process is as a movement between different conversation formats (Peräkylä and Silverman 1991). Changing ideas about what the topic of conversation is, or might become, leads to shifts in the 'face' or role of the participants. Where workers believe that others are about to raise a difficult or delicate matter they may well adopt a more serious persona. Some workers describe this process as a sort of 'clicking into place' of different elements of their role – the counsellor, the teacher and so on. Associated with these are different ways of labelling the exchange. We might call it therapeutic, instructional, enquiry-based and so on (see Burbules 1993: 110–30). As this business comes to an end, there is often another transition. We might move into a conversation format which allows us to say goodbye.

Looking out for the changing character of conversations, and the shifts in role and perception involved is central to the work of local educators. As participants they also play their part in altering the tempo and focus of encounters. Because people recognize them as educators there may also be some expectation that they will introduce matters and ask questions about which others may not feel so comfortable.

In conclusion

> We say we 'conduct' a conversation, but the more fundamental a conversation is, the less its conduct lies within the will of either partner . . . The way in which one word follows another, with the conversation taking its own turnings and reaching its own conclusion, may well be conducted in some way, but the people conversing are far less the leaders of it than the led. No one knows what will 'come out' in a conversation.
>
> (Gadamer 1979: 345)

Dominant models of education tend to be didactic, planned and task-centred. Conversation can thus be difficult for educators. However, things do not stop with its unpredictability: part of the problem is that conversation is often seen as a method rather than a social relationship. We need to think about it less as something that we do or use, and more as part of our engagement with others (Burbules 1993: 19–49). We have to look to the processes that occur between people – we are conversational beings. Fromm (1979) talks about two fundamental modes of existence, of orientation to the self and to the world. These he describes as *having*, which is concerned with possessing and owning; and *being*. These entail contrasting views of conversation.

> While the having persons rely on what they *have*, the being persons rely on the fact that they *are*, that they are alive and that something new will be born if only they have the courage to let go and respond. They become fully alive in the conversation because they do not stifle themselves by anxious concern with what they have. Their own aliveness is infectious and often helps the other person to transcend his or her egocentricity. Thus the conversation ceases to be an exchange of commodities (information, knowledge, status) and becomes a dialogue in which it does not matter any more who is right.
>
> (Fromm 1979: 42)

While I may want to dispute the extent of such a polarization, it is a useful sensitizing device. In a 'being' mode, conversation is not about trying to win an argument, but about engaging with another, and furthering understanding and our ability to act in the world.

In this way, educators engage in conversation as both learners and contributors. They pay attention to both what they are learning and what other participants are experiencing. Through being with an enquirer, and, furthermore, an enquirer who is interested in the thoughts of others, people are given the chance to learn. In this there is a degree of vulnerability for educators. If they are open to the possible truth of what is being said, it means that they may change as a result of the encounter. They may have their own beliefs and thinking challenged. At one level, this allows for the possibility of enrichment; on the other hand, it may be a very uncomfortable experience. As Collins (1991: 48) put it, 'in remembering always to *let* the learner learn, the teacher has to be open to being taught'.

Chapter 4

Thinking about direction

In many of the work situations that have cropped up, you forget the building, and forget all those sorts of things, because it has been about a process; it's been about talking to young people . . . and I have needed to respond to things there and then.

In conversation we can never be sure of the way things will turn out. People appear with something on their mind that they 'just have to talk about'; events occur which alter the subject. Above all, as we engage with ideas and situations our understandings and feelings change. If we are to begin with situations rather than subjects (Lindeman 1989: 6), what guides our thinking and acting? How do we make decisions about the direction that encounters are taking?

Thinking things through

The local educators I talk with, like schoolteachers, do not appear to think things through in the- linear way proposed by 'scientific curriculum-makers' such as Tyler (1949) and the 'problem-solvers' such as Priestley *et al.* (1978).

The rational 'formulate objectives, identify appropriate learning activities and evaluate the achievement of objectives' is a favourite . . . approach in teachers' initial training; but there is little evidence that it reflects the thinking of practising teachers.

(Brown and McIntyre 1993: 18)

Workers have to 'improvise, contemplate and prepare' (Yinger 1990: 85). In this, 'purpose and intention may not . . . always be marked by closely specified goals' (Brookfield 1983: 15). However, while much learning may at first seem to be incidental it is not necessarily accidental: actions are taken with some purpose. The specific goal may not be clear at any one time, either to educators or learners, yet the process is deliberate. Educators in these situations can seek to foster an environment in which conversation can take place.

This process of thinking things through, of practical reasoning, still needs clear reference points. The talk of local educators can be littered with links to these. Words like 'aim', 'role', 'values' and 'tactics' are used to describe why workers did this or took that decision.

> My style of work involves reaching out to young people who normally don't have contact with the service . . . which is why I go out to them rather than them coming to me . . . It's about creating new opportunities for them, giving them new experiences and having a chance to participate – I know the word is thrown about rather a lot – in different activities. And then once they are doing those things, I think my agenda is certainly a lot about looking at their lives; looking at the influences in their lives; looking at all the different issues that affect them; and creating time and space to talk to them about some of those things . . . looking at all the processes that happen there.

In these few sentences this worker uses a number of organizing ideas: the impact of her style of work; the concern with participation; the desire to create space so that people may reflect on their lives; the focus on process; the wish to enable people to be themselves. These are common concerns and the pivotal place they occupy indicates the beginnings of a framework for thinking about direction.

Creative participation

The starting point for this worker, and many others I talk with, is a picture of the relationships and activities that they want to see in a situation. While this varies according to situation and worker, for most it boils down to an emphasis on participation in 'meaningful' activities (see, for example, Department of Education and Science (DES) 1982). Central to this, as the worker suggests, is space to talk about experiences. As another put it, 'you look to create environments where something can happen'. Much like the teachers in Brown and McIntyre's (1993: 54–61) study, this worker seeks to establish and maintain a 'normal desirable state of activity'. For local educators I suggest this state is 'creative participation'.

Given the significance of choice, setting, experience and conversation to local educators, the emphasis on creative participation is hardly surprising.

> I know when I'm with a group like the [Pensioners'] Group, what I
> tend to do is look to see if everyone is involved: that they have got
> something to do, someone to talk to. I don't try to force things,
> move people about or really jolly things along . . . What I do is to sit
> down and talk, make suggestions about activities, connect people up
> with similar interests and so on. A lot of the time I don't have to do
> much – just pick up on the 'strays' – people by themselves or the
> ones who appear to be in a mood or upset . . . You can hear when
> things are going well, the noise level goes up.

When people are not involved and things do not appear to be 'happening' this triggers various interventions to move things on or to address a
particular worry or question. Where people are involved, workers have the
chance to 'get alongside them', to join in activities and conversations, and
to encourage creative participation.

This way of describing the state of relationships and activities in a situation brings out a number of motifs in workers' thinking. First, it highlights involvement – and for youth workers, community workers and
community educators this is one of the most enduring of concerns (see,
for example, Thomas 1983: 66). Second, 'creative' carries the notion of
possibility; people's engagement allows for the chance of becoming something more (Rosseter 1987: 52). Third, the label expresses a desire for
agency – that people should be encouraged to be creators rather than
consumers of situations (Smith 1980). Last, the idea of participation
carries a social dimension.

> As an aspect of social practice, learning involves the whole person;
> it implies not only a relation to specific activities, but a relation to
> social communities – it implies becoming a full participant, a mem-
> ber, a kind of person. In this view, learning only partly – and often
> incidentally – implies becoming able to be involved in new activities,
> to perform new tasks and functions, to master new understandings.
> (Lave and Wenger 1991: 53)

Agency, involvement, the sense of being part of a group, and the chance
to be something more – before going much further it is worth looking at
these and rehearsing the other themes concerning purpose that can emerge
from the way that workers may talk about their work.

Aim or purpose

Once we recognize that the nature of people's participation may be the
first port of call for local educators, it is then possible to approach the
'larger' purposes in their labours. Here I want to highlight seven themes
that have emerged from my conversations with local educators.

Crap detecting

Much of the practice I have heard described has been directed at identifying and challenging assumptions; developing an understanding of the context in which people act and how this has helped to shape their thinking; imagining and exploring alternatives; and developing what Brookfield (1987b: 9) – after McPeck (1981) – describes as a 'reflective scepticism'. In short, it has been concerned with developing the ability to think critically; with the cultivation of wisdom or what Postman and Weingartner (1971) called 'crap detecting'. Some seem to approach this as a skill, but, more accurately, it is a disposition or frame of mind. It also depends on having the necessary knowledge. 'There is no formula for distinguishing fact from opinion, no litmus test of veracity, even for our own ideas, let alone those of others. Everything depends on our knowledge . . .' (F. Smith 1992: 98). One key aspect of this process is then the provision of information, for example, through the publication of a regular neighbourhood newsletter giving details of local developments, housing news and local campaigns.

Opening up new experiences and new opportunities

Overlapping with the desire to foster critical thinking can be a wish to give people a chance to experience new sensations; to do things that they would not normally do. This concern is often linked to a desire to get away from the neighbourhood. This can be eagerly taken up by workers in the forms of residentials, trips and events. The hope is that getting people away from their immediate neighbourhood and doing different things might help them to develop a more critical perspective on their situation and to have some sense of alternative possibilities in their lives.

Promoting mutual respect and fairness

A third key theme concerns the promotion of mutual respect and fairness. Some workers use organized, structured programmes in this area, some look mostly to matters arising out of everyday interactions – someone mouthing off about 'blacks' in the drop-in; young women being pushed off the pool table in the pub by young men; people jumping the queue at the bingo hall; a member of the community association committee getting free drinks in the bar; and so on. One form of intervention made is in the shape of a question: 'Is that fair?'

Wholeness

Some workers have a concern with wholeness, a desire to work for the development of the whole person. This has several dimensions, including such things as valuing yourself; being in touch with your capacities; working to integrate different parts of yourself (see Chapter 2).

Thinking about others

A fifth theme concerns thinking about others – what they might be experiencing, what their needs are. Clearly this overlaps with the wish to cultivate mutual respect, but it was also doing something more. Underlying this may be a concern that people should not always put their needs first, that they should think of others.

Developing a sense of community

There is also some talk of the importance of creating an environment in which people feel they belong, and of people being part of something greater than the immediate groups to which they belong. This feeling or sense may be given many labels – for example, neighbourliness, solidarity, sisterhood, brotherhood and comradeship.

Collective action and mutual aid

The last key theme is that of working with people so that they may work and act together both to organize activities and groups for their own satisfactions, and to understand and act on the institutions and processes that significantly affect the lives of people in particular neighbourhoods or communities. The orientation is to community development and organization: an emphasis on 'self-help, mutual support, the building up of neighbourhood integration, the development of neighbourhood capacities for problem-solving and self representation, and the promotion of collective action to bring a community's preferences to the attention of political decision-makers' (Thomas 1983: 109). As Barr's (1991: 65–72) study of community work shows, 'community development' is the preferred and dominant model informing practice.

Different workers have different emphases – for example, youth workers may stress the first themes; community workers the last two themes in particular. This 'difference' is not something that should be pushed too far. It is not very clear-cut and, anyway, all these statements of overall aim involve coming to some understanding of what makes for human well-being or human flourishing. They have within them an implicit or explicit view of the good, or what makes for the good life. This is then reflected in the picture workers have of the relationships and processes that they feel characterize a good session or desired state of activity.

Role

If we return to the local educator cited at the beginning of this chapter, we can see that she put a lot of work into exploring people's expectations of her as a worker – how she would act in different situations (for example, when people were discussing illegal activities); what legal powers she had; what sort of things she would be organizing; whether she could help with particular problems; and so on.

> He knows I am a youth worker now, not a social worker. What he would probably say, what some of the young people would say, 'Oh you can talk to X and she can help you sort out your problems . . .'. The other part is the label attached to me: 'If you want to go away X will take you away on trips.'

Over the next few pages I want to focus on what she said, as it was in conversation with her that the framework set out in this chapter emerged.

Attention to role is particularly important in the case of local educators. They are not able to draw on a strong public understanding of their work. People are less sure about what behaviour to expect. A common view of youth workers, for example, is as ineffectual leftovers from 1960s hippydom such as Rick Lemmon in Townsend's (1984) *The Growing Pains of Adrian Mole*. Another sees them as social workers. Indeed, in one study of adolescents' views of social work it was found that there were fewer differences between the perception of social workers and youth workers than between social workers and other occupations (Jones 1987: 198–9).

This inability to draw on a coherent set of public expectations concerning local educators' behaviour is not simply to do with the public's lack of knowledge. People's identities as workers are bound up with local networks and practices. Local educators operate within fluid settings. Within these social interaction generally follows less explicit rules and conventions than, say, in a classroom. These have to be learnt, and different behaviours negotiated that are specific to the situation. As Banton has commented:

> A loosely textured social structure in which roles are less clearly defined offers less resistance to change but can also give less protection to the people that have to play roles in it.
>
> (Banton 1968: 198)

The relative openness to change and the lack of protection contributes to a considerable amount of uncertainty concerning role and purpose within the various professional groupings examined here (Smith 1988: 75–84). It is not only that the public are not clear about what local educators do (or should do). Practitioners may lack a fully worked-through understanding of their role and purpose.

Being in a position where less can be taken for granted, practitioners have to pay special attention to role-making; to explore how expectations about their behaviour are reworked in the interactions they have with people. This tentative process (Turner 1962) involves changes both in the practitioner and the person worked with. Roles have to be made and accepted by the various parties. Practitioners cannot simply say 'I am a community worker' and expect those with whom they work to accept it. The role of local educator requires the existence of another role: that of local learner. Thus, people have to accept workers as workers, and understand themselves as in need of being 'worked with' before a full working relationship can be established.

Much of the interaction that follows is then concerned with the testing of roles; with participants looking at the other's behaviour and as a result maintaining or modifying their own actions in role. When engaged in conversation, one of the key aspects of our performance concerns staying in touch with our capacities and our understanding of our role in the situation.

> When an individual plays a part he implicitly requests his observers to take seriously the impression that is fostered before them. They are asked to believe that the character they see actually possesses the attributes he appears to possess, that the task he performs will have the consequences that are implicitly claimed for it, and that, in general, matters are what they appear to be.
>
> (Goffman 1969: 28)

When it comes to the practice of education within local networks and everyday settings, matters are rarely what they appear to be. For example, the casual conversation of workers is not primarily about socializing and spending a pleasant half hour (although it may involve these things). It is work. It has further purpose. The danger in this situation, as Goffman (1969: 28) has pointed out, is that we can be fully taken in by our own act and so lose touch with the reality of our performance; or that we may have no belief in our 'act' and no ultimate concern with the beliefs of our 'audience'. In other words, we become so distanced from our behaviour that it becomes false, or involves the cynical manipulation of those with whom we are working.

There is much more to pull local educators off course. The 'testing', the impact of changing circumstances, and the difficulty of operating for long periods of time can all act to fog their sense of themselves in the situation. There is also the continuing likelihood of roles being defined differently by people in the situation. While we may understand ourselves as 'educators', those we are attempting to work with might stubbornly define us as 'friends'. This may be a try-on, the result of misreading the situation, or a statement of fact, but until roles are defined and accepted there is likely to be conflict and drift. We may, for example, seek to retrieve the ethical notion of local education as 'friends educating each other' (Collins 1991: 48–9).

It is also misleading to talk of 'role' in the singular in these circumstances. While there may be an overarching concept of the role of the educator, there are associated with it a number of sub-roles or behaviours which are specific to situations. For example, in order to undertake their educational function, many local educators have to be able to organize play schemes, drive minibuses, mend inflatables and so on. It is often when these different behaviours do not fit with one another, when they are not experienced as coherent, that workers begin to pay deep attention to their role and purpose.

Agenda and tactics

In what our worker had to say about her aims another concept appears important: agenda. This notion is a part of the vocabulary of a large number of workers I talk with. It is used in much the way it would be in a meeting: as a list of items to be attended to. Statements like 'My agenda at that moment was to . . .' are common. Indeed, the very commonness of the word was (I suspect), a key factor in 'agenda' not being seen as an organizing idea by the workers I talked with:

> W. That's funny, because that is not a word I associate with myself. Yeh.
> M. How would you would talk about aim?
> W. That's what I am trying to sort out. I use the word 'agenda'. Is the way I use it different to the aim? . . . The aim is something much bigger; the agenda might be something that varies from hour to hour or day to day. It's something that is determined by what is going on at that moment in time to some extent.

On the whole, 'agenda' seems to be used in relation to particular situations, although it does sometimes find its way into broader statements of aim, such as in the original statement by the worker. It is something that moves with the situation. Items are dealt with, forgotten or deemed not to be appropriate. In contrast, some local educators, perhaps working within a narrow brief, will have fairly fixed agendas. For example, those specifically promoting 'drugs awareness' may seek to confine their interventions to these areas, but this can be a source of tension as conversations are not that neat and tidy (see Fisher 1993).

There is no way of knowing how 'agenda' has come into common usage by practitioners, but the way workers conduct their meetings and their group sessions does appear to have been influential. Sessions often begin with a period of agenda-setting and some negotiation about order and emphasis. People are seen as bringing their own agendas and as having some rights in how sessions are conducted and what business is done. More than that, in encounters there may be a common wish to bring these out into the open; a hope that hidden agendas could be eliminated or at least minimized. This is not to say that there is not some 'smuggling' of items going on – but as Lindeman (1987c: 130) said, the methods are ones that everyone can understand: 'No conspiracy. No manipulation about this.' In conversation there has to be some agreement as to subject. However, as Taylor (1993: 77) has shown in relation to Freirian approaches to literacy, even where there is an explicit commitment to dialogue, the hidden or personal agendas of educators can easily have a controlling influence over key aspects of the encounter.

Figure 4.1: The beginning framework

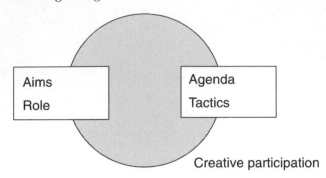

Another idea was commonly associated with agenda by more than one worker: a concern for employing the right tactics.

> One of the interesting things for me about having conversations and discussions is trying to change your tactics in terms of how you bring up conversations . . . Yes, you have got to get your tactics sorted out. It can be quite interesting being in a difficult situation with a group, when you feel the atmosphere building up, thinking to yourself, 'Right I have got to bring them down a little bit, how am I going to do it?' You might make allegiances with certain people and it's all thought out. And you have to work out what the different roles people are playing and if you spend a bit of time with so and so then maybe they could influence so and so and all those sorts of things.

'Tactics' as used here appears to refer to the moves workers make in order to address items on their agenda or to connect what is happening with their overall aims. There is attention to detail and to the particular. In this last comment by the worker we can also see 'role' appearing again, but here in connection with the behaviour of others in the situation. It is a key element in the decisions she makes about which tactics to employ.

Framing direction

These four ideas, when linked to a concern for creative participation, provided the beginnings of a framework for thinking about direction in dialogue (Figure 4.1). What seems to be of importance here is the way practitioners frame situations. This framing allows workers to make sense of their practice and the experiences and situations they encounter. At any one time we may apply several frameworks or schemes of interpretation (Goffman 1986: 25). What separates the two boxes in Figure 4.1 is the extent to which their contents changed with the situation. In other words, practitioners appeared to have an overarching understanding of their aims and roles as workers. While these altered over time, they were nowhere near as fluid as the content of their agendas or the tactics they employed. Thus, when working, the local educator on whom we have been focusing takes stock of the situation, and reasons her way through to what is the best course of action. In this she is guided by her understanding of what makes for well-being, and what is the proper way of working. The notion of 'creative participation' provides a picture of the interactions involved and connects with all elements. It is a touchstone. As another worker put it:

> You don't have to worry anymore about being in control or knowing everything. You can get involved and work things out as you go. It's liberating when you realize that the group has a responsibility. You are only there to help them take that responsibility – not keep it for yourself.

This is how the original worker responded to the diagram in relation to some work she was undertaking around pregnancy:

> 'Role' would fit into it first. That would be above 'aim' because my role is seen as a sort of friend, whatever. I am known for being able to give so-called 'advice' for people who need it. That is the first thing that comes into people's minds. So I am approached, then the aim comes next, and the aim is about looking at first of all is that young person pregnant and dealing with that. Secondly, what has tended to happen is it's raised massive issues about the lack of sex education. Those would be the general aims and an aim that has now come out of that for me is that I need to go to school and say 'What is going on?' But then the agenda and the tactics are quite important because my agenda is interlinked with the general aims. But then, day to day, the agenda changes according to what experience that young woman has with her boyfriend.

This response highlighted a growing uneasiness I had about the notion of 'aim'. The original worker was not alone in using the idea at both a general overarching level and in thinking about particular interventions. Workers can oscillate between the general and the particular in relation to aim. For this reason, it is important to free up the concept: to leave 'aim' as a way of thinking about intentionality at all levels and to find another way of describing what might be called 'general aims'. Here, 'purpose' seemed a suitable replacement. Thus purpose, the reason for which the work exists and is done, found its way into the first of the two boxes.

Repertoire

I then overlaid a further element: repertoire (see Figure 4.2). The idea of repertoire came from Schön (1983). He argued that practitioners build up a catalogue of examples, images, understandings and actions. This

Figure 4.2: Repertoire

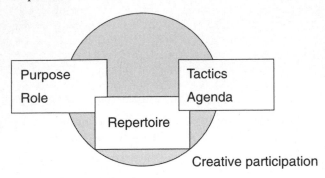

repertoire includes the whole of their experience in so far as it is accessible to them for understanding and action (1983: 138). It is by drawing on some aspect of repertoire that workers are able to make sense of the situations they encounter:

> When a practitioner makes sense of a situation he perceives to be unique, he *sees* it *as* something already present in his repertoire. To see *this* site as *that* one is not to subsume the first under a familiar category or rule. It is, rather, to see the unfamiliar, unique situation as both similar to and different from the familiar one, without at first being able to say similar or different with respect to what. The familiar situation functions as a precedent, or a metaphor . . . for the unfamiliar one.
>
> (Schön 1983: 138)

In working with individuals and groups, things occur, an expression, a word, that evoke previous experiences or bring an image to mind. We might then use that image or experience to develop an understanding of the new situation. We can draw on other responses or ideas so that we may act on our new understanding, testing it, seeing if it works. In so doing we have to try to ensure that our sense of what is happening now is not overpowered by the past or by the image or metaphor that has been evoked.

The idea that practitioners carry with them a catalogue of ideas, images, understandings and actions, and that they draw upon this constantly in action is a powerful one. As Calderhead (1989; 1990) has shown with regard to teachers, mental pictures – images of the way classroom activities should and could be – are central to the way that both experienced and new teachers think about situations. Thus, in Figure 4.2 thinking is structured by reference to creative participation and our understanding of role, purpose, tactics and agenda. We are then able to draw upon our repertoire in making sense of both the particular (tactics, agenda, the situation) and the general (role and purpose).

Issues

When thinking about this framework it was clear that there was something missing. For example, a number of practitioners use the notion of 'issues' when discussing the direction of their work. The worker we are focusing on here was no exception.

> For me [pregnancy] is really such a crucial issue ... The lack of discussion about contraception is absolutely shocking ... But there are then much wider issues about relationships, contraception, that sort of thing, which nobody is dealing with at the moment. There is this massive myth that the school is doing such wonderful work really.

At one level the introduction of issues was obvious, there being a desire to promote 'issue-based' approaches within some quarters. Such approaches take a specific dimension such as sexism, racism, unemployment or drug abuse and then use the phenomenon as the basic rationale for prioritizing and directing interventions and resources (Jeffs and Smith 1990c: 16). However, the way 'issues' is used by many of the workers I talk with does not fall in line with what might be expected from an issue-based model. Issues are things to look out for rather than the basis for allocating resources or the major reason for intervention – although there is some prioritization on the basis of people's experiences. For example, several workers have talked of looking for, and working with, 'burning issues', those concerns which were felt to be especially important or critical by participants.

The final clue as to where to place issues came around where 'pregnancy' fitted into our worker's scheme of things when working with young people. How did it relate to aim (purpose) and agenda? She described it as a crucial issue. What became clear was that something called 'issues' existed in her framework somewhere between aim and agenda. Issues are more flexible than aims, but do not change as much as the content of her agendas. In working with young people she could predict what 'issues' were likely to come up in conversation:

> If I was to look at all the residentials I do then I could name all the issues that I know will crop up over that weekend ... The first ones ... are sexism and racism. Drugs crop up quite a lot, but one of the most important things is relationships between the group. That's been the big, key thing for me, how they treat one another, how they behave all those sorts of things. That's the depressing one for me ... We always seem to have a discussion about gay people. Now I know these are all the classic 'isms'. And we quite often say that school will be a big issue. There is probably another one – growing up, talking about pressures. Families. I know that in the course of spending time with young people we are going to touch on all of those.

Figure 4.3: Introducing strategy and issues

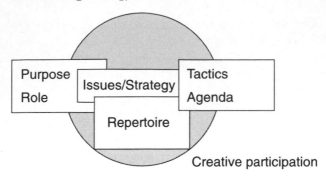

She linked these issues into her overall aim (purpose), which was getting young people to question and to look at why they respond to situations in the way they do. She also translated them into specific agenda items when working with particular groups or individuals. For her a number of issues would always be around when working with young people, but they had to be made sense of within her overall aim. (Her list closely matches the concerns which subsequently emerged in the major study of 16–19-year-olds by Banks *et al.* (1992).) The community workers I talk with are usually similarly able to reel off a list of potential issues: for example, housing, community relations, transportation, schooling, shopping, and local social facilities. What we have here is not 'issue-based' work, but work organized around creative participation in conversation, and through which certain issues are identified and perhaps worked on. We are therefore able to introduce a fourth box overlapping and bridging those containing purpose/role and agenda/tactics (see Figure 4.3).

Strategy

A further dimension has also entered the fourth box: strategy. With the original two boxes we had, on the one hand, an overarching understanding of role and purpose, and on the other, the working out of tactics and agenda items for the specific situation. Missing from this was the middle-range activity of planning:

■ *Target groups.* Which are the main groups that local educators should seek to make contact with and develop work with? Local educators may have a brief to work with specific groups (for example, young women), or may have identified people sharing certain learning needs that accord with the main concerns of their work (for example, officers of tenants' associations needing briefing about new housing legislation).
■ *Primary places for work.* In which neighbourhoods and institutions should the work be concentrated? Once the basic neighbourhood or area is

identified, decisions about specific places of work, such as how much time should be spent in schools, on the streets or in people's homes, will be largely dependent on the other elements discussed here.

■ *Main times for work.* This is really just a case of making bets as to when people will be around and wanting to be involved in the work; and then matching this up with what is reasonable, and what is possible from the educator's point of view.

■ *Basic approaches.* What are the central methods; what is the broad balance between the approaches?

This is an unexceptional list. Most of the projects I come across have some statement concerning target groups, methods and so on. Just about all the workers I talked with for this research had a work plan for the next three months or more. It is this middle-range planning that I am calling 'strategy'.

The idea of 'strategy' has come into progressive use in the field. It dovetails with the use of tactics by the workers studied here (tactics being elements of strategies). Three immediate influences have been at work in this respect. First, there has been the import of business management thinking and practice into the organization of fieldwork. Within that sphere, with increasing scale and the need for forward planning, strategic thinking has developed (Knight and Morgan 1990). Second, and in relation to community work in particular, there has been a long-standing concern with influencing political processes and an explicit interest in building strategies of influence (see, for example, Francis and Henderson 1992: 36–52). Last, and a little speculatively, within youth work I suspect that the notion of 'strategy' has also been promoted by the popularity of sports and games as means of working. Underpinning all this, and somewhat worrying in its implications, is the military origin of strategic thinking (Shaw 1990).

Strategy, in its military sense, is concerned with the planning and conduct of war. It is about making a series of moves or using tricks in order to triumph over the enemy. It is this sense that comes through in some of the ways in which the concept of 'strategy' has been used in relation to schooling. In particular, Woods (1983: 122) has talked about teacher strategies and pupil strategies, the latter being categorized as supportive, oppositional or detached. Usage such as this 'reflects an increasing self-perception of individuals, and basic social groups such as families, as embattled agents, in a competitive social environment' (Shaw 1990: 467). Now it may well be that the use of terms like 'strategy' and 'tactics' by local educators is an expression of their feeling of being engaged in a battle in a fairly hostile environment. A shift into more neutral language, talking perhaps about 'plans' and 'moves', would no doubt sweeten the image, but it would obscure the nature of the feelings and experiences that produced the original terms. I have therefore stayed with them. This is also given some support by the study by Galton *et al.* (1980) of primary school classrooms which links strategy to tactics, aims and student behaviour in much the same way as has been suggested here.

Before leaving the question of strategy it is necessary to make a couple more points. One of the things that has arisen out of the debates about the growing usage of strategic thinking by sociologists is the loose and varied ways in which it is employed. Some writers have talked of 'unconscious strategies', whereas others have insisted that strategies involve conscious and rational decisions involving a long-term perspective (Crow 1989: 19). Similarly, there is always the danger of being wise after the event. We attempt to put a gloss on what were seemingly unconnected responses to situations, or actions with unintended consequences by later calling them a strategy. This is a criticism that Hammersley (1990) makes of notions such as 'pupil' and 'teacher strategies'. Here, for the sake of clarity, I am using 'strategy' to refer to conscious and explicit plans for practice. What others might describe as 'unconscious strategies' are here seen as habits or rituals (Morgan 1989: 29).

Disposition

The framework is still incomplete. In my earlier work on informal education (Smith 1988; Jeffs and Smith 1990a) it became clear that practitioners were going beyond elements such as have been assembled here. When reflecting-in-action they were appealing to wider values and appreciations.

> As a worker you have to hold on to values. At times like that it is your anchor. It keeps you going. It gives me a direction. If I am talking to a particular person, it is not a question of trying to lead someone to my values, but often to try and express some different values. I find that is quite important because each peer group has its norms and they drift along.

Like teachers, local educators 'think on their feet'. Here, I am suggesting that they are broadly guided in this by their understanding of what makes for the 'good'; of what makes for human well-being (Jeffs and Smith 1990a: 17–18). This mode of thinking comes very close to what Aristotle describes as 'prudence' or 'practical wisdom' (*phronēsis*):

> It is thought to be the mark of a prudent man to be able to deliberate rightly about what is good and advantageous for himself; not in particular respects, e.g. what is good for health or physical strength, but what is conducive to the good life generally.
>
> (Aristotle 1976: 209)

Phronēsis involves the disposition to act truly and justly (Carr and Kemmis 1986: 33). It entails an orientation to 'good' or 'right' rather than 'correct' action. This frame of mind allows people to break a rule or convention if they judge that to follow it would not promote 'the good', either generally, or of those involved in specific situations (Grundy 1987: 62). The

Figure 4.4: Disposition and interaction

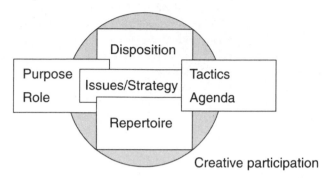

implications of this are drawn out by Gadamer. Phronēsis, unlike more technical forms of reasoning, involves an understanding of other human beings:

> The person who is experienced in the world, the man who knows all the tricks and dodges and is experienced in everything there is, does not have the right understanding that the person who is acting needs; he has it only if he satisfies one requirement, namely that he too is seeking what is right, i.e. that he is united with the other person in this mutual interest.
>
> (Gadamer 1979: 288)

He continues:

> Once again we discover that the person with understanding does not know and judge as one who stands apart and unaffected; but rather, as one united by a specific bond with the other, he thinks with the other and undergoes the situation with him.

In other words, we have a disposition of a peculiarly human kind. Where educators are committed to working out the meaning of the universal in situations, and to exploring how actions may further that which is just and good, this can only happen in interaction with those with whom they are working. The action we seek to take is informed and committed. All of the elements interact, are open to change and are constructed and reconstructed in particular situations and contexts (see Chapter 7). So it is that a fifth box enters our diagram (see Figure 4.4). In some respects, I could have included 'disposition' in with 'repertoire' – but its orientating role indicated that it may be of a different order for workers.

It should be noted that disposition is not simply temperament or personality. It is about a particular orientation. Obviously the intimate and dialogical nature of what we are examining here focuses attention on the person of the educator (Foreman 1990). However, the defining features of the orientation involved in informed, committed action matter, too.

Direction, curriculum and context

Emerging here from the activity of local conversations, walking around neighbourhoods, visiting council offices and working with groups is a particular way of conceptualizing direction in education. It is some distance from curriculum models. Those models which focus on the use of behavioural objectives (curriculum as product) can be immediately ruled out as can those that centre on a body of knowledge-content and/or subjects, 'which are then "transmitted" or "delivered" to pupils by the most effective means' (Blenkin *et al.* 1992: 23). This leaves us with process/praxis approaches to curriculum-making to consider (Stenhouse 1975; Grundy 1987).

Process/praxis approaches are driven by general principles and emphasize judgement and meaning-making. The main difference between them is that the process approach does not make explicit statements about the interests it serves; the praxis model brings these to the centre of the process and makes an explicit commitment to emancipation (Grundy 1987). At its centre is praxis: informed, committed action. We can show this diagrammatically (Figure 4.5).

If we were to substitute 'strategy' and 'issues' (as we have discussed them) for the 'proposal for action' – that is, a curriculum proposal after Stenhouse (1975) – and widen the situations worked in, we would be very close to the conversational practice we have been looking at. But the removal of these elements is highly significant – the character of the enterprise has changed. Basically, we have moved from informal to formal education (Jeffs and Smith 1990a: 14–17). At one level, not too much should be made of this as these form a continuum. Educators will use a mix of the informal and the formal. They will work between points X and Y in Figure 4.6. However, the overall balance of their activity will influence the way they categorize and understand themselves as educators. Local educators will tend to define themselves as informal educators, given that the balance of their work lies in that domain.

The main points of departure between the informal and the formal centre around the nature of the setting utilized and the extent to which the 'proposal for action' is codified and sequenced, that is, formed into a curriculum proposal (Jeffs and Smith 1990a: 14–17). In the case of the former, it is not so much the physical environment that matters as the signals given, the symbols invoked and the props used by the educator. Informal work can happen in classrooms, formal work in the middle of fields (see Tiffany 1993). As for curriculum, as Cornbleth (1990) has demonstrated, it is inextricably linked to milieu. It is not a concept that stands on its own. It developed in relation to ideas like 'subject', 'class', 'lesson', and 'examination', and within particular organizational relationships and expectations. It is simply one 'way of organizing a set of human educational practices' (Grundy 1987: 5). To apply it to all 'human educational practices' is a fundamental mistake, for this entails the 'pedagogization' or 'schooling' of everyday life.

Figure 4.5: Curriculum as praxis

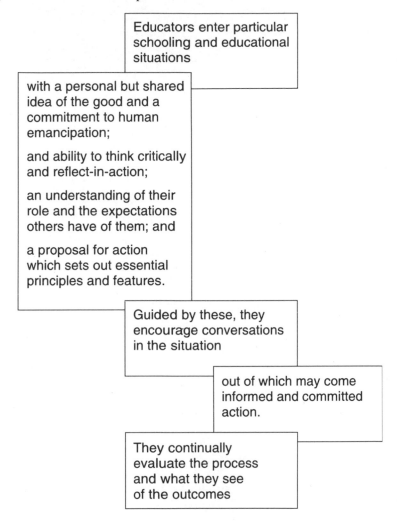

Educators enter particular schooling and educational situations

with a personal but shared idea of the good and a commitment to human emancipation;

and ability to think critically and reflect-in-action;

an understanding of their role and the expectations others have of them; and

a proposal for action which sets out essential principles and features.

Guided by these, they encourage conversations in the situation

out of which may come informed and committed action.

They continually evaluate the process and what they see of the outcomes

Source: adapted from Jeffs and Smith (1990a: 19)

When we participate in the language of an institution, whether as speakers, listeners, writers, or readers, we become positioned by that language; in that moment of assent, myriad relationships of power, authority, status are implied and reaffirmed. At the heart of this language in contemporary society, there is a relentless commitment to instruction.

(Street and Street 1991: 163)

Our language use and definition of space can subordinate groups (Jarvis 1992: 126–9).

Figure 4.6: Informal and formal education

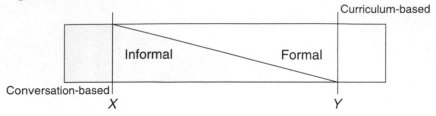

Source: adapted from Ellis (1990: 97)

Any viable curriculum model seeks to set out in some detail the range and nature of the educational encounter beforehand (Barrow 1984: 11), while a 'conversational' approach responds more strongly to the moment. This is exactly the tension that Alexander recognized with regard to primary schooling. 'Genuine open dialogue is unpredictable and can lead anywhere; it is not consistent with the pursuit of a detailed prearranged programme of work, yet it is widely accepted as an appropriate medium for teaching' (Alexander 1992: 78). Stenhouse's (1975: 5) 'proposal for action' includes details of intention or aim; planning principles (for example, around the selection and sequencing of content); and principles concerning the study and evaluation of the process. Local educators, when running residentials, short courses, activity programmes and special or training sessions, do plan in such a way. These are formal interludes and here a 'curriculum' – set or negotiated – is involved. In these circumstances we can reinterpret our model. By specifying more tightly the nature of the issues to be raised and the strategy to be followed in the particular setting, and by planning our tactics and agenda beforehand, we have, in effect, a curriculum proposal. In this way local educators may still be working with notions of 'issues', 'strategies', 'tactics' and 'agendas'. However, for much of the time, I would suggest, local educators are not working like this – they are involved in spontaneous conversations and encounters and all the unpredictability that entails. To make judgements they still need aims and procedural principles, but the nature of the physical and social context, and the character of the interactions necessitate a less prescriptive (in terms of content and activity) form of planning.

Outcomes

The unpredictability of much of the work does not mean that local educators can put thought of outcomes to one side. In some ways, uncertainty leads workers into looking harder. Lacking familiar forms of feedback like test scores, assignments and the like, they have to make use of other means. In addition, they cannot, for the most part, call upon the comfort of subject specialism. This means both that the range of things they may be called to account for is wider; and that what they are doing is less 'obvious'. This worker used recording to reflect on this:

> Within each area there is so much. It is a difficult sifting process. I wrote down my feelings about some of the behaviours I was witnessing. They did not seem in line with group norms. So I was actually questioning in my writing . . . One of the possibilities is that it was a kind of reaching for something; being fearful about it, anxious, confused and, therefore, that's interrupted their behaviour pattern.

Such uncertainty is part of the work. Yet outcome (the impact on society and the individual) and output (the goods and services produced) have become more significant in policy discussions (see Carter *et al.* 1992: 5–24). How do services, for example, justify their existence in an environment where 'value for money' is stressed? The tendency is to look for concrete changes in individuals and to measure in terms of cost any benefits to society as a whole. What happens to individuals in an encounter is important. However, the significance of interactions goes beyond the sum of their outcomes. We need to consider the consequences of interactions that lie beyond manifested outcomes. In interactions there may be three:

- People achieve certain conscious 'understandings'.
- Experiences, images, routines, ideas and emotions become memory traces which can be redeveloped to help make sense of new situations. These are often non-conscious or unconscious.
- Debris is left behind – posters on walls, changed seating arrangements, words on boards, grades, minutes of meetings, new club rules and so on – which others find or are given, and use.

However, as I suggested in Chapter 2, learning is both situated and shared. When individuals seek to make sense of something they draw on images, words and routines which are born of interaction and, as such, are held in common in some way with others. 'Learning, thinking and knowing are relations among people in activity in, with, and arising from the socially and culturally structured world' (Lave and Wenger 1991: 51). In this way learning is not so much what individuals 'do' in their heads as what happens when people participate in certain forms of interaction.

The non-conscious and unconscious

When stressing concrete outcomes we can quickly overlook the deeply private, unknown and in a sense unknowable (for that moment) imprint that encounters make on people and situations. Local educators often cite work which was seen as highly significant some time (often years) after the event, but which initially was unremarkable, and unremarked upon. It may be that at a non-conscious level learning has occurred – that is to say, there has been a process which has led to some tacit understanding (see Jarvis 1987). Much of what we do in our day-to-day lives is informed by action at this level, as those concerned with experiential learning have been at pains to point out (Coleman 1976). Such 'practical consciousness could not be "held in mind" during the course of social activities, since their tacit or taken for granted qualities form the essential condition which allows actors to concentrate on tasks at hand' (Giddens 1991: 36). Thus, we may not be aware of the learning that has taken place. The lesson is clear: we cannot say with any degree of specificity what is gained from encounters. Yet, there is something more here.

Ideas, experiences and images are encoded in memory. Some of these will have been appreciated and placed in relation to other 'understandings'. We may or may not be conscious of this learning. However, some will simply remain as memory traces. They have not been worked into something we can label as knowledge; they remain outside organized sets of ideas. At times we may be conscious of some element of these; for the most part they are submerged. Later they may be evoked and reworked by another experience or through reflection. We see them in a new light; they become significant. At that distance things also tend to overlap. We have a sense of something, but it is often not easy to tie it to a specific event. Instead we may link our feelings or insights to our experience of one person – a special teacher, for example. Or we may associate them with a series of events, such as the time we spent in a youth group.

Those tightly focused on outcomes may well push people too quickly into bringing these experiences to the surface, naming them, tidying them up, and putting them into order. In so doing they may obstruct under-standing. Such feelings and ideas have to be lived with, entertained and experienced before they can be explained. We need to avoid the impulse to explain in advance of experience, to collapse time (Sennett 1973: 27). Those focusing on product tend to be in what Fromm (1979) describes as the 'having' mode of existence (see Chapter 3). Or as one local educator put it:

> A lot of what we do is concerned with process, its about being rather than doing. Doing and being would be the contrasts. You create a state of being. You create an environment.

The difference is between knowing more deeply and having more know-ledge. The value placed on wholeness and 'learning to be', and the training that many have in counselling and working with individuals does mean that there is some awareness among local educators of the dangers of pushing people to name outcomes before they entertained and connected with the feelings and ideas involved (DES 1987; 1990).

Interaction and shared or communal outcomes

An added, and crucial, problem with reducing interaction to outcomes in individuals is that it ignores the communal aspect. As Scott (1908) wrote with regard to group membership: 'The idea of such a group as a whole is not necessarily contained in the brain of any single member, and as the idea develops by social interpenetration, it becomes, in all its many-sidedness, too large for any member to contain.' Conversation allows for common knowledge and memory. It is concerned with the fusion of horizons (Gadamer 1979). The primary purpose, in this view, is not to change the other person, but to advance understanding, and the possibility of action. In it, individuals are led beyond 'private' understanding into a 'more *consensual* world of meaning that is ever *more public* and, in short, more readily communicable among an *ever-widening circle of interpreters'* (Pusey 1987: 62). What I say to one person may well affect how she or he treats another. Crucially, there is a move from a focus on *my* to *our* thought. This includes reflection on my, and on your, processes and thought: what I and you think, what we share, and what we do not share.

There is a further communal dimension. Such encounters leave not only memories but also physical items such as written notes, diagrams, lists, changes in rooms and so on. Participants may return to these later. They are, at one level, concrete products of an encounter. However, what is important here is their social nature. The act of writing something down may be to 'capture' it for me, but it can also provide material for others. The physical debris arising out of conversations also has an impact. There can be a change in the physical setting or in the props available to those that follow.

Evaluation

Within local education there is only a limited amount that can be said about evaluation as a separate phenomenon. It is part and parcel of the work. To work in this way is routinely to make judgements, to judge the worth of what is being done.

> I obviously evaluate as I go along. I don't write a big report at the end of it which sometimes would be a good idea. I am constantly questioning what is going on, and why they behave the way they do, and what are the factors? How they can get more out of the ex-perience, where do we go from here?

Feedback features strongly in models of experiential learning and the value placed on reflection-in- and -on-action (see Chapter 7).

The fact that people can point to a lack of attention to monitoring and evaluation in youth work, for example (Larkins 1991), is partly to do with a failure to understand fully the work as informal education (Smith 1988) and to be clear on matters of accountability and organization (Jeffs and Smith 1988). It is also associated with the extent to which the 'meanings and intentions of evaluation have somehow become twisted and distorted, and making it inappropriate for doing other than supporting the status quo' (Gitlin and Smyth 1989: 9). It can be experienced as something 'external', something that local educators are required to do to prove the worth of their work to managers and to funders. As Gitlin and Smyth (1989) again comment, from its Latin origin meaning 'to strengthen' or to empower, the term 'evaluation' has taken a numerical turn – it is now largely about the measurement of things – and in the process can easily slip into becoming an end rather than a means.

In conversation two aspects of evaluation seemed to be valued. First, some workers see the need for periodic evaluations of different pieces of work with individuals and groups to take stock and think about the future. Examples here include the fairly formal evaluation sessions or 'moments' that local educators may routinely include in the projects, courses, residentials and activities they help to organize. The aim is to encourage people (learners and educators alike) to reflect on their experiences: what it meant for them as individuals; what it meant for the group. There is no shortage of advice for workers in this area: most standard texts on groupwork, for example, have substantial sections on evaluation (see, for example, Douglas 1976: 106–16; Whitaker 1985: 147–70; Preston-Shoot 1987: 140–58). The one dimension that is of particular note here is the extent to which the process is collaborative. As we have already seen, local educators may be concerned to move beyond 'private' understandings into a more *consensual* world of meaning.

Second, some recognize the place of evaluation within the arena of accountability. Leaving aside, for the moment, the complex question of to whom local educators are accountable – funders, managers, learners, local communities – there is some appreciation that the worth of the work has to be demonstrated and communicated to others. Again this may not be a one-way process, but a matter of conversation. Judgements can be made by all parties about the impact of the work. In some agencies and authorities this process has been reduced to rather crude performance indicators: the numbers worked with; the decrease in crime on an estate and so on. This takes us to the all-important question: what criteria are to be used?

As might be expected from what has gone before, questions of method and criteria are highly problematic. The 'truth' of the matter is not arrived at through the uniform application of certain procedures; and such criteria as we have can only be indicative, providing material for debate and reflection. If we have to focus on the interactions, the quality of the discourse, the way people act, then there is so much that we cannot possibly know.

> The interesting thing is to bring it down to what youth work is all about. You can't do anything unless you look at the relationship you have got with that young person. That has got to be your starting point. Which is why when you evaluate it in terms of outcomes and things – how can you judge what will happen in the long term?

In the end we have to make judgements about the extent to which the work furthers human well-being. For example, in what way has it promoted community, conversation, and informed, committed action? In making these judgements we must both recognize the limited base of the possible evidence, and look to the quality of the interactions and what is revealed in them.

If education is a moral and a political craft then we have to ask questions about the 'rightness' of actions. This introduces elements that are not easily contained within dominant, managerial approaches to evaluation (see Gitlin and Smyth 1989). I do not dismiss the use of numbers – concerning, for example, hours of contact time, who has been worked with, the subjects covered. Indeed, many local educators have increasingly sought to keep such data. However, figures are only a starting point, just one reference point in debates about work. And here it is the debate that is important.

Chapter 5

Structuring the work

> It's about being structured in an unstructured job. The problem is
> that once you start trying to structure your week that inevitably
> changes things. If I went out today, saying 50 per cent of my time is
> going to be face-to-face and the other is going to be admin, and I am
> going to be pretty firm about that, then I wouldn't be able to deal
> with any of the crisis intervention work, for want of a better term. So
> I have got to go out in the morning with a plan in my head . . . But
> I must have that flexibility in my mind, 'well the admin can wait', or
> 'this or that can wait'. But you can't always do that . . . I can't just say
> I can't deal with you, I endeavour to go out with flexibility.

'Going out with flexibility' brings out nicely the emphasis in local education on responsiveness, on being able to do something here and now.
While there are occasions when workers have particular aims and use
planned activities, many of those I talk to put regular open 'slots' in their
diaries. These might be for 'being around' or for responding to things
that emerge. Local educators cannot, for the most part, call upon the
daily routines and structures open to most other educators. They organize
time around sessions (for administration, activities, being out and about
and so on) rather than lessons, and around work plans rather than time-
tables. Finally, the setting for their activities is usually space that is used
and designed for activities other than education, and over which they
have little control. This does not mean that they are without structure or
that they have to start afresh in every encounter. There are fixed points
in diaries, there are various routines and rhythms. However, with less

apparently 'given', practitioners have to pay special attention to their work in time-space (Collins and Hoggarth 1977: 16).

In this chapter I want to look at the ways in which local educators can structure their work. By this I mean how they may conceptualize the different forms of work, link them together and plan and manage their practice. To do this I need to look at some questions concerning time-space that arise out of their local involvements. I will then look at the way in which certain distinctive modes of working and being can be used to make sense of practice. Out of this, three particular questions arise concerning: the way local educators move between different modes and how these relate to their sense of themselves as a whole; planning the work; and managing the work across time-space.

Encounters

Local educators seek situations of co-presence; they have to co-ordinate their activities with the rhythms and contours of the neighbourhood. Workers can feel anxious when this is not happening, as, for example, does this detached worker new to an area.

> Sometimes you have to stick around for a bit. That's why it's horrible starting out in detached work, because it is horrible all the time and it is the most horrible feeling. I used to have to force myself to talk to kids at first. 'Just think this is a stupid job.' You can only stick around for so long. It is just not wise to be in that situation.

They use a range of strategies to overcome these feelings. A common approach is to do some work in settings where their role is more clearly communicated by the physical and organizational setting. Workers may make contact with people in a youth club or community association, or do some work in or around a school. They may use various props or things like leaflets or an opinion survey so that they can go up to people or knock on doors. Worries may never fully disappear – the concern to enable co-presence has a number of continuing implications for the work, and for the way local educators engage with time and space.

Catching the moment

The wish to work in ways that connect strongly with participants' everyday lives involves local educators in settings that are not tied to them in the same way that classrooms are linked to teachers. It also means that they do not work to institutional, 'clock', time in the same way. There will be fixed points like appointments but, in general, local educators think in larger and fuzzier blocks of time-space. For example, the contracts of youth and community workers have traditionally been framed in sessions to be worked rather than hours (a session comprising a morning, an afternoon or an evening). Arrangements may be made for people to drop in and see workers in their office on a morning rather than specifying an hour. Similarly, people may know they can catch community workers or detached youth workers 'on their rounds'. Like ice-cream vans, many have their regular stops and times.

> Sometimes it can be the most boring thing in the world. If it is a horrible day why do you want to spend an hour being around? You have got to look at the continuity. It is quite important. If you are in a building or structured setting you get the continuity through clubs and groups. If you are not and people don't want to take part in even semi-structured things, then how do you maintain contact with them? That is when the being around is important.

For some this may link into rather romantic hippy-like ideas on the workers' part about being 'natural'. For others it is simply a logical outcome of this mode of working.

'Starting with situations' involves a particular form of organization.

> Some of my job is focused around small projects. Some of it about having a certain amount of floating time that I can decide how I am going to use it week by week. That's great . . . a crucial bit of the way you organize yourself is to leave yourself with times when you have nothing planned to do.

Workers have to co-ordinate practice with features of the locale and setting. For example, this outreach worker was concerned with outdoor education and had to experiment with where he placed the reflective moments in his work:

> We originally thought that we would take them back to another building where they could have a shower and then talk about things. If they didn't want a shower then the whole thing broke down. So we took it back to basics: 'let's see where it is good' and start building up again. We worked with them coming off the water and as they were changing as well. Some of them in their minds were saying we have changed now, this has finished. Recognizing that, you work then.

The concern is to 'catch the moment', to encourage reflection at critical points, rather than slavishly following some predetermined timetable. This brings with it its own problems, including a certain 'hit or miss' quality and the possibility of undervaluing the use of more formal and disciplined work.

An awareness of this has led many workers to build in projects as part of their work programme.

> You need a reason for being around. It is not just about sitting down and having a fag or bag of chips with a group of young people. If you are bringing groups together or individuals into a group you need

something to do with them. Someone described [one of my groups] as contrived and I am angry about that, because what do we do if we don't contrive situations for people to learn from? Do they honestly believe that they don't contrive situations, they don't manufacture things? We have to contrive, have a project, to build the relationships around. There must be something in it apart from the relationship with me.

Projects typically link into the issues that workers either predict will or do arise in their conversations, for example, around health. Where local educators work to a longer-term plan the use of projects may initially relate to establishing and maintaining working relationships with people. Community workers, for example, may give themselves six months to contact groups in an area. Arising out of this there could be pieces of work – for example, around the establishment of a play scheme or tenants' association – that have to be given time. These may turn out to be ends in themselves or a means of working towards other purposes.

'Owning' space

The desire to 'catch the moment' and to fit in with local routines and practices means that local educators can end up dealing with quite sensitive matters in some very peculiar situations.

> I can't begin to tell you how much time I spend in toilets talking about what this boyfriend has done, or what so-and-so said about the way the person looked, or about the problems they have been having with their periods or their bodies in some way.

Examples such as this immediately raise questions about ownership and production of space. This surfaces most clearly around the use of provision by young women and girls and the experiences of women and different cultural groups within public spaces.

It is no accident that the worker quoted above spends much of her time working with young women in toilets. It is one locale that belongs to young women. It has been labelled 'theirs' by architects and hopefully maintained so by managers. The public space in clubs and centres tends to be controlled by men. In general, it is they who dominate the use of pool tables, sports facilities and the music played. It is their behaviour that is the main reference point for workers (see, for example, Kysel and Coulter 1984). This observation has been a feature of the critique that feminist workers have made of youth provision (see Trimble 1990). However, we must also look at how the young women themselves redefine and produce space. There is a tendency to overlook this aspect of place, as Gregory shows when examining the work of Giddens.

> He constantly talks about locales as settings whose properties are *drawn upon* by actors and emphasizes their *substantially given*

character. This is how actors routinely encounter locales in the
conduct of everyday life, no doubt, but any genuinely critical theory
must go beyond these mundanities to show how particular places
and spaces are *produced*.

(Gregory 1989b: 208)

Like Gregory, I worry about the common assumption that the character
of locales is routinely experienced as 'substantially given'. One theme that
has arisen in recent work on 'youth culture' is how much young people
make creative use of artefacts and in so doing redefine them (Willis *et al.*
1990). This redefinition can then influence design, particularly where
there is a need to attract people in the marketplace. If we return to our
example of young women's use of toilets, for example, we can see how
their use of that space fed back. Centres were built in the 1960s with the
addition of 'en-suite carpeted sitting rooms' (Ministry of Education 1963:
31). Of course, this still left unchallenged the relative power of young men
– and this leads on to the other thing that has to be said.

Questions arise around the theme of 'not invading other people's space'.
There is a tendency, particularly within detached youth work, to see what
are essentially public places as 'their' (meaning the young people's) space
(see, for example, Leissner 1969). Others are aware of this slippage and
define public space communally.

> The shopping area, the streets, these areas are public space, not just
> 'their space'. So if someone is chucking litter on the floor you say
> something. These are things I would do in my own street. You lighten
> it. You might say 'Get a hole in one' rather than 'Don't throw it on
> the floor.' I don't have notions about exclusive space in that sense.
> It is our space.

Questions about 'invading' space also arise in relation to visiting people's
homes.

> You have to knock on people's doors. It is something I have to work
> on. A house really is their space . . . I need to work in some way to
> get myself comfortable with that. I need also to work on some strategy
> whereby it becomes easier to open up conversations with whoever
> else is in the household.

This raises problems for local educators. Simple door-knocking has to be
'psyched-up' for because of the level of rejection that is involved in 'cold-
calling' of any kind. However, this is often more in the anticipation than
the execution. More significant questions occur when their business involves
being invited into the house. Their contact may only be with one person
in the household. Their arrival in the home can arouse questioning or
comment by the other members of the household – parents wanting to
know more about the person who spends time with their children; people
wondering about the nature and impact of the relationship workers have
with their partner. Local educators all have their own set of stories about

such episodes: the husband angry that the worker was turning his wife into a 'feminist'; the mother convinced that the youth worker was 'a bit funny'.

When thinking about local education and the 'ownership' of space, Goffman's (1969) distinction between back and front regions is helpful. Even in settings such as family centres and community centres where people have worked on rules and programmes, workers and users can experience space – the setting for interaction – very differently. The office, for example, may well be seen as 'ours' by workers and they may then talk about 'going out' into the centre (which in some way is seen more as the clients' space). They do this in much the same way that detached youth workers or community workers might talk about 'going out' on their rounds. In this sense the office is, for much of the time, a 'back region'. It is where practitioners can take time off from face-to-face performances with clients and users.

> Here devices such as the telephone are sequestered so that they may be used 'privately' . . . Here the team can run through its perform-ance, checking for offending expressions when no audience is present to be affronted by them; here poor members of the team, who are expressively inept, can be schooled or dropped from the perform-ance. Here the performer can relax; he can drop his front, forgo speaking his lines, and step out of character.
>
> (Goffman 1969: 115)

They perform the function that staffrooms do for teachers (Woods 1983: 38–9). As a result, the lack of an office or suitable 'back region' may be felt strongly.

There are times when the office becomes the setting for a certain type of performance: the space for a 'quiet word'; for 'disciplinary' interviews and discussions; and for 'counselling'. In these circumstances the move into the office signals the shift into a more formal mode where there are clear boundaries.

The cultural experience of time-space

Last, and arising out of questions raised in Chapter 1, local education requires an awareness of the cultural experience of time-space and what this means in 'modern' societies. Again this is not just a matter of workers' thinking and practice. It is also to do with the way in which those with whom they work see the world. This tends to be framed in one of two ways. One strand arises out of comments about timekeeping and how different people see keeping to strict 'clock times' as more or less import-ant. Dealing with extended social systems in 'modern' societies requires people to keep to agreed clock times – for example, for appointments or when going to work (Thompson 1991: 352–404). Enabling people to see and come to terms with this is often a key aspect of the work educators do (Charnley 1993: 48–9). However, there is the question of cultural imperialism: are workers encouraging the adoption of a 'western' view of time? Modernity is a western project (Giddens 1990: 174–6). However, like it or not, it cannot be escaped. It is not possible to sustain communities that are significantly out of time with their neighbours, but it is possible to create points of resistance and some space for other ways of being. Hence the emphasis on providing settings for young people where they can 'hang out' or on working with people to develop and sustain economic, social and political forms which resonate more fully with their view of themselves.

The other strand concerning cultural experiences of time-space arises out of the images or mental maps that people have of where they live and work. The work involves attending closely to where people draw the boundaries of their neighbourhood and how they talk about distance. For example, the high street was seen as a long way off on one estate because it involved crossing a busy dual carriageway. In reality, it was only ten minutes' walk. Local educators' attention can be drawn to this dimension because of the constraints that these images or maps may have upon people's ability to make use of their environment. People build up general pictures of environments, 'that include not only distance and direction but also information about the attributes that exist at various locations together with feelings about those places' (Walmsley 1988: 36). Much of my research was carried out in East London and the lack of use that people made of the opportunities that are 'on their doorstep' was a consistent theme. Enabling people to make use of this resource involved a lot more than pointing them in the direction of the bus stop.

Modes of work

We can now draw out the key ways in which local educators can organize their interactions to create or define time-space (see Massey 1993: 79). Six modes of work emerged in my conversations. These modes might be described as ways of doing or being. They arise out of the way local educators interpret the interaction between purpose, role, issues and strategies (see Chapter 4). The modes were as follows:

- being about;
- being there;
- working with individuals and groups;
- doing projects;
- doing administration and research; and
- reflecting on practice.

We will look briefly at each of these in turn.

Being about

'Being about' involved such activities as walking round the estate, visiting local launderettes, cafés, chip shops, pubs and even wandering into the school at break and lunch times. The aim generally is to be seen, to make and maintain contact with client groups, and to undertake work as it arose.

> Walking about the estate, being able to knock on people's doors; making yourself approachable in that way; just like being there, people will nab you. They might nab you when there is a group. But you can often pick up when they want to talk to you.

This can be a moment of difficulty. Are you to approach the group? Should you signal your awareness? How are you to make yourself available for conversation? This is the terrain of Goffman's (1961; 1963) explorations of encounters. It involves the transition from a moment of 'civil inattention' to the opening of an encounter. To this extent local educators have to be highly skilled in handling encounters, in entering or skirting groups and gatherings. They have to be approachable without being pushy. They have to establish themselves in situations that are open to some ambiguity:

> Walking around the streets, especially as a woman, there are all sorts of connotations – people can be a bit suspicious of what you are . . . It would have been difficult for me to have done that without introductions. I have been making a lot of visits to different groups and individuals.

Or, as another worker put it:

> Initially it was difficult, the suspicion. As time goes on then it is important that people are just used to seeing me. I don't know how it gets them thinking. You are just there, they just take you for granted.

Time is more fluid. Local educators have to be able to stop and talk, but there is also the importance of routine – so that people know where and when they can catch the worker, and, crucially, where the worker can meet people. Again this is a case of workers tuning into local rhythms and habits.

Workers based in buildings have to create and foster environments that allow them to enter into conversations. Within a community education centre, for example, local educators may create spaces where people can just sit and talk, perhaps while other activities are taking place. 'Being about' translates into the time they spend sitting in the bar, coffee lounge or the corner where people can gather after they have dropped their children off in the playgroup. The difficulty with this is that the worker is also identified with the building and with the programme. Administrative and organizational demands – sorting out the bar float, getting a cupboard door mended, arranging cover for an activity – can all too easily take over. However, there are also advantages, as identified by this youth worker:

As a centre-based worker I could be in the company of a young person for nine or ten hours a week, so there was space to be able to develop most things. I can challenge someone in the youth centre on the Monday, knowing that there might be some conflict or rubbing, but also knowing that I have time and space to work with these young people. You haven't got that on the streets. It is residentials and those sorts of experiences that allow us to draw out any long-term work with a group of young people.

'Being about' is seen as a central part of the work – as crucial, in fact – yet, as with all the debates over the use of police time on 'walking the beat', its function and significance is often only recognized when it is skimped on.

Being there

Alongside booking out time or slots for being around, local educators may also set aside time for responding to situations and crises. The range of work involved here is huge. For those involved in the study, it included dealing with people who were homeless; or who were victims or perpetrators of crimes; or who were having to deal with a personal crisis such as pregnancy or the loss of a relative; or who had medical problems associated, for example, with substance abuse. It also involved much less dramatic things like accompanying residents to meetings with officials. Much of this work is 'face to face' with 'clients', but it also often involves spending substantial time speaking to various agencies. By its very nature it is unpredictable and usually requires an immediate response. This mode has an elastic relationship with 'being about'. If there were few 'emergencies' then more time could be spent maintaining contact and so on, and vice versa.

The float time and the being-around time gets quite intermingled. Yesterday if I had got something else booked in I wouldn't have been able to go to the rights project with this woman. So that was the way that floating time was used. You do need a bit of that. One of the things about the work is accepting, unfortunately or fortunately, depending on the way you want to see it, that you are not going to get a normal week to some extent because that is the nature of the job.

This type of responding has two linked components: 'being there' for people and 'working with' the individual or group. 'Being there' is essentially a holding operation. It also involves some element of practical assistance. In the example above, it involved going with someone to a rights project. Other examples include attending court, going with someone to the hospital, to a solicitor, or to the social security office or housing office. A good deal of 'being there' occurs when people have to deal with distant systems and where they lack confidence, or believe they do not have the experience or expertise to handle the situation. The local educator may have to handle or guide some of the encounter, but is often present simply so that the client feels he/she has someone to call upon. The other key aspect of being there is where the worker is a 'shoulder to cry on' or is around in moments of great personal crisis or tragedy such as bereavement or serious illness.

Working with individuals and groups

While being there and being around can be seen as working with people, some of the local educators I talked with reserved the idea of 'working with' to more formal encounters. There was a sense in which it was linked into ideas about depth. It involves moving beyond the making and maintenance of contact, or the holding operation that often takes place when 'being there'. 'Working with' means enabling or helping people to entertain feelings, reflect on their experiences, think about things and make plans.

> You go out on the street, and the rest of your day can be dictated by the first person you come across or whatever problem they have got or whatever you are needed for. I try within that unstructured setting to be structured. So whenever I am working with a group or an individual, I've got structure in my mind, I want a start and a finish.

We can see here that the worker is thinking about this form of encounter in a different way. The purpose of the encounter may become more specific or clearly and openly articulated. It is to sort out a problem, to organize an activity, to work on something that has been bothering an individual or group. Work such as this often cannot be done in the settings where the worker is 'being around'.

> It does inhibit depth. You do need to respond there and then. But the possibility of interruption is there. I am a bit tentative a lot of the time about asking opening questions because it would need 15 or 20 minutes to follow that through. So why open it if I cannot go on? It is frustrating. You are getting into areas which need exploring, which need time, but time is not there in that way. You can't just pop into the office or go into the quiet room for half an hour. It is frustrating.

One ploy is either to find somewhere quiet or out of the way, or to make an arrangement to meet 'in the office' or another formal setting which cannot be interrupted. Where workers are building-based there often are rooms that can be used immediately. Thus, local educators may have clearly advertised 'office hours' where people can come in for 'private' conversations.

Some 'working with' will be concerned with particular problems or issues that have arisen in people's lives, some with more general learning projects they want to pursue. Local educators may devote a significant amount of time to working with people's 'enthusiasms' or assisting with self-directed learning projects. This may involve encouraging an individual to take a particular interest a little further – be it in fuchsias, family history or cats. It can mean working with people to develop a more formal programme of self-study – around, perhaps, religious texts, film or car mechanics (see, for example, Cross 1992: 195). Classically, it can mean working with groups to foster mutual aid in leisure. Such 'organizing around enthusiasm' is important not just for the satisfactions it brings to those involved – friendship, the exchange of information and products, and the opportunity for collective activities and projects (Bishop and Hoggett 1986: 33) – but also for the part it plays in fostering democracy. Sports, hobbyist and arts and crafts groups are mutual aid organizations with an associational structure and as such can act as 'nurseries for the feelings of mutual loyalty and trust which hold the wider community together, and where the skills of self government can be learned and practised' (Marquand 1988: 239; see also Hirst 1993).

The move into a 'working with' mode is often accompanied by clear signals or symbols. The worker may sit differently or adopt a different tone of voice; the setting has usually become more private – the door is closed; the room itself may be more formal; and, crucially, there is usually some overt opening discussion about the task: 'What is it that you want to talk about?' There is a clear beginning. As an earlier worker indicated, there also has to be some clear moment of ending. This may be simply achieved by the person leaving and saying goodbye, or it can be with 'ending-type' lines – 'Is that as far as we can go for the moment?', for example.

Doing projects

The fourth mode or element is 'doing projects or activities'. Such exercises were formal interludes, varying in the amount of time and degree of involvement required. The central things to grasp about 'projects' are that they are:

- planned in advance in terms of when and where they take place, what their aims are and the methods to be used to achieve them, and who will be taking part. However, there will often be a high degree of flexibility concerning actual implementation.
- time-limited. The commitment made is rarely an open-ended one and most often falls into short intensive pieces of work, such as residentials or day events and workshops; or more involved activities, spread over perhaps a three-month period. Examples of the latter include drama workshops; sessions on organizing skills for community groups; young women's groups and so on (Rogers 1994).
- characterized by an explicit commitment to encouraging learning.
- largely driven by the conversations the workers have while 'being about'. They arise out of the work, rather than being imported as 'good ideas'.

There may be some overlap here with 'working with'. A key dividing line is suggested by the naming of the activities: 'working with' and 'doing projects'. The latter is more likely to be seen as the property and responsibility of the worker. It is likely to derive from an initiative on the part of the educator.

Projects give a structure to the work.

> It's about doing ten different things at once all over the place. Now you can see the structure. There are four existing projects set up. They are the main things that happen every week. Then there are the more short-term projects: afternoon at the [centre] on Friday, the trip out, the one-offs. Then the more long-term things, the residentials – although they come before the short term. Then in the middle you have got your street contact, being-around time, whatever.

They are needed by local educators to give focus and depth. They grow out, and connect with the conversations workers have when 'being around'.

> It is a balance. We identified the need with this group of young people, I will use the term anti-social behaviour. If we are to help young people to deal with this, with other people's views, you can't do that sucking a can of Coke, chewing a bag of chips. You have to bring something into that. You need to work that. It is about projects. I was talking with another worker about this time-expiry thing. They can't go on, they must change. Projects are about endings. The ongoing bit is this being about – maintaining relationships.

Doing 'admin' and research

Administration may be seen as a burden. For some workers there can be a feeling that it takes them away from the 'real' business: face-to-face work. Within this category fall things such as line-management meetings and team meetings. For some it symbolizes a lot of the things they sought to escape on entering local education: form-filling, doing returns, writing reports, making applications, and filling in forecast sheets. Undoubtedly, such activities are one means by which organizations can exercise some control over the activities of their employees. For this reason alone they would be viewed with some suspicion. However, there are also other elements here. There are perennial problems concerning communication about process-centred work: how is it to be categorized and described? The rise of 'paperwork' has also been associated with shifts in the funding and organization of welfare and, in particular, the rise of the 'contract culture'. This poses problems for local education as it has tended to be a rather 'oral' culture. However, for most workers it is a necessary and small aspect of their work:

> It is a small proportion, yeh. My co-worker puts it at 80 per cent street work, 20 per cent admin. That is probably a fair balance,

although it wouldn't be fair to say it is like that every week. This week I have a meeting this morning, then a residential. But in the average working week we would endeavour to do about 80 per cent face to face. The majority would be on the street, the remainder would be what happened from the street – going to court, the police station or whatever.

Some workers also quite enjoy this side of the work. As one worker put it: 'there is a streak in me. I like to do my own letters. I do enjoy that side of it.'

There has also been a growing appreciation of the research role of the worker (Everitt *et al.* 1992). Within community work there has been a tradition of workers' undertaking small research projects to inform service development and extension within local authorities and larger non-profit agencies (Thomas 1983: 100–7). It is also seen as simply part of 'getting to know the neighbourhood' (Henderson and Thomas 1987: 54–91). However, it also became legitimated as a 'radical' project. Here the publications coming out of the various Community Development Projects (CDPs) in the 1970s were influential (Loney 1983: 171–88). Research also appears to be growing in youth work with the introduction in some authorities of youth affairs briefs, although there has been a tradition of it within the detached work arena (Goetschius and Tash 1967).

> You need to do your research to work out where you are, the kinds of young people, what their needs are, the kinds of history they have, the way they are viewed by other sectors of the community. You need to look at other agencies and their input. In detached youth-work parlance it is referred to as 'reconnaissance'. I heard that word and it has militaristic overtones for me. So I checked out the dictionary definition and I refused to use it. I refer to that period as research because that is really what it was. I wasn't seeking out the enemy. I was seeking to try and understand the area that I was trying to work.

Perhaps the greatest impetus has arisen from the need to target scarce resources and to make cases for funding. An example of this is in English and Welsh community education with the need to redefine provision following the 1992 Further and Higher Education Act.

Reflecting on practice

The sixth and last mode is sometimes included within administration, particularly where it involves writing up recordings of work. However, reflecting on practice is of a different order. Administration can be seen more as an instrumental activity, something that has to be done so that some external event could happen. Recording, and reflecting on practice, on the other hand, may be seen as something rather more personal and intrinsic. It is a 'backroom' activity, work not seen by clients or the outside world, where 'fronts' can be relaxed or at least changed. Three main arenas are worthy of note. First, there is the medium of recording.

> The work is so instant. It is happening very much in the present. You never know what is going to happen next. If I didn't take that time to write it down I wouldn't reflect on and analyse my work. Also from the writing down I plan my work. I sort out what I am going to try next. In my diary there are things about time management . . . It is very much part and parcel of your working routine . . . That's the problem, because my manager doesn't work like that. I have to do them at home or sneak them in. Sitting down and writing is not seen as work. Writing up case notes is only reluctantly seen as work. He will do these crisis interventions as he calls them. Actually they are crises for him rather than for the other person. He can't recognize when he is being manipulated.

Second, there are conversations with colleagues.

> I have been able to just go back to the office and just relax and have a chat to my co-worker and then go home, or do what I'm going to do. But, what's slowly and surely coming to me is that I'm not dealing with things the way I should be. I shouldn't be taking my anxiety and frustration home with me. That's maybe a lesson for me, which I have got to start learning to deal with.

Lastly, and often driven by realizations such as this, there is the use of supervision, usually by someone who is outside the situation, who does not have managerial responsibility for what is happening.

> It is just nice to talk to somebody who is not involved, who has not got any responsibility to make you do your work and you can talk to about things you are working on. There is an ongoing need for that. There are some things that you cannot say to a line manager – what you might be thinking.

Or, as another worker put it:

> In supervision there needs to be someone who is not connected – independent. The supervision process mirrors how you work with people. You are both trying to get the other person to think about what they are doing.

These activities usually occur away from any arena of face-to-face work. The one exception here is the conversations and writing that occur in the office. However, even here access is restricted and such activity stops when clients appear. Following on from this, such reflection takes place after or before interventions so there is some handling of material across time. Hence the importance of recordings for reflection and the use of supervision. They are a means of concretizing experiences and feelings.

Being, doing, reflecting and working with

A striking feature about the way we have been discussing these aspects is
the nature of the verbs used. These express very different modes of existence and relating to the world. In contrast to 'doing' which tends to
focus attention on an activity, 'being' centres the person. It links me with
some quality: I am tall, I am here. However, being can be taken as something more: as referring to the authentic or essential self (see Jarvis 1992:
101–18). We can see this in the linked notions of being around and being
there. The former tends to be associated with the quality of being visible
and available, the latter with something more – sharing something as a
person with another. The being is a matter not simply of presence, but
also of humanity. We are there, sharing a situation or experience as another person. In fact this distinction is not as clear-cut as this implies,
because the very act of being around a particular neighbourhood can also
be an act of sharing and of making a commitment.

> All the professionals drive through, so actually walking through the
> estate you could be literally anyone. So I think you owe it to the
> community as a whole to let them know what I am doing . . . It's
> about saying I am not part of all that establishment . . . I'm loyal to
> this community, I'm loyal to you lot.

There is also a sense in which 'being' can also appear passive. We are
simply there, not doing anything. In reality, process, activity and movement are elements of being (Fromm 1979: 34). Being is becoming (Kidd
1978: 124–46). When workers talk about 'being there' for someone, they
are not simply passive spectators but active participants. They may or may
not say much, but their very presence enables something to happen. It is
an intervention.

'Doing' is more obviously an active word. Workers 'do' projects and
activities, administration and research. The most evident point is that the
activity initially concerns a thing or object, rather than a person. You act
on this thing. Workers undertake certain processes or procedures. These
involve people, but in the way they talk about them the central point of
reference in description are the processes. These may need planning, or
may have something of a predictable quality. There is a sense in which
workers bring to them a much firmer agenda. Significantly, these things
also provide fixed points.

> I know there are two groups I run; I know that Wednesday morning
> is my admin morning with my clerical worker; that, say if I have got
> some residentials planned, I know I have got to work to see those
> young people. So you set slots of time aside for doing that. There
> might be a couple of meetings to set up. It all depends, my god, I
> look through my diary I see that every week is so incredibly different.
> I think the planning ahead is quite important in being quite clear
> about what you are doing.

Within these activities there may be an opportunity to 'work with' individuals or groups. Here is another contrast. We might work *on* an activity, but we work *with* an individual or a group. 'It is about working alongside, about being there, about not saying go off and do that.' In other words, 'working with' individuals involves a set of understandings about those individuals. For example, that they are not objects to be acted upon, but rather persons who are able to make their own decisions, to think for themselves. This is not a hierarchical relationship in the sense that people can be ordered to do things. 'Working with' is not like an employer–employee relationship.

Lastly, we have the act of reflection. This involves a stepping aside, however momentarily, from the world: a time of withdrawal, and of engagement with 'inner' processes. In many respects it is an inner use of the three previous modes. We might *be* with our feelings and thoughts, *work with* them, *do* certain mental activities or routines. As we have seen in earlier sections, reflection on practice is something that takes place in 'back areas'.

Modes, movement and the whole

The concern with the immediate, and the premium put on 'responding', can mean that there is a lack of commitment to work that requires forward planning. On occasions local educators bear an uncanny resemblance to characters in musicals – that moment where someone says 'Let's do the show here.' People rush round; there is drama and risk; will the thing actually come off? While there can be considerable value in such efforts, all too often the result is simply shoddy. With the move into short-run projects, the continuing need to show the value of work, and the impact of targeted initiatives in the area of health, for example, there has been a renewed emphasis on planned process. As HMI comments:

> the planning needed for a superficially simple task is often elaborate. This leads to the second point: that the youth workers, and in many cases the young people, were fully aware of the complexity of what they were doing. Neither of these points should be taken as arguing against the value of spontaneity and intuition; but these qualities . . . are only effective when the actors are well rehearsed in the basics.
>
> (DES 1987: 20)

The interdependence of these modes comes through strongly in the words here of local educators. For work to have any depth it is necessary to use projects and activities. It is also important to ensure access to appropriate spaces for work with individuals and groups. Time must also be set aside for this, either as 'float time', so that there is space on the diary to respond; or as more formal sessions, where people can come and see you or you can go and see them. Take away one of these elements, for

Figure 5.1: Structuring the work

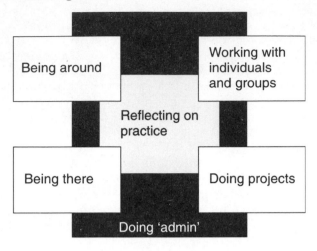

example, to concentrate on 'being around', and the work that is under-taken may remain shallow, barely passing beyond the greeting. In general, there are only limited opportunities for sustained and deeper conversa-tion while in public places. This has been one of the attractions of building-based work where educators can take people into an office or group room. There is a further point here. Writers like Freire (1972) and Fromm (1979) have tended to set 'being' against 'having' (or 'doing'). As Jarvis (1992: 153) has argued, lifelong education can take both forms: 'the being mode often occurs in the creation of relationships between teachers and learners and among the learners, and the having mode when education is regarded merely as a means to an end'.

The interdependence of modes is not linear. It would be easy to fall into the trap of placing each mode or element sequentially in time. You begin by being around, then move on to projects. Having established activities, then people come to you. They can then be worked with. This is a false picture. Each element can only be sustained over time if the others are present: each is a doorway into another. The real problem for many workers is how to maintain a balance between modes. Face-to-face work is underpinned by administration and research. It is also informed by the various reflective activities that educators engage in. Central to all this is not just reflection-*on*-action, but also reflection-*in*-action. Local educators have to think while they are working so that they may move between the various modes or operate within one. This reflection may be quite routine. At other times it can involve consideration of complex ethical and practical questions 'on the hoof'. We can represent this inter-dependence in a simple diagram (Figure 5.1).

The movement between each mode has to be carefully managed. One has to be ended, the other begun. In many respects, it is this process of enabling transitions that makes the work of local educators so sophisticated. They do not operate in one realm. They have to move between situations that are overtly educational, such as those involved with projects, and ones that are simply aspects of daily living. It is a moment where, if workers have misread the situation, or have been clumsy in their signalling, there can be acute embarrassment, physical danger or simply missed opportunity. The consequences of inappropriate action can be substantial. Mostly, however, workers will just be told to go away!

> Sometimes you can be made to feel extremely unwelcome and invading their space and their time. The good thing is that they normally tell you quite directly that they don't want to see you anyway.

This movement between modes can be further complicated because it is also a shift of practice traditions. For example, much of the project work may draw upon educational traditions, while elements of the individual work may be infused by psychoanalytical metaphors and understandings. The difficulties in shifts like this are substantial, as I found in an earlier exploration of informal education (Jeffs and Smith 1990a: 20–1). Workers have to be able to handle what are often very divergent ways of thinking and acting, and to communicate this shift or change in orientation to others. However, for the most part, workers will be influenced by or working within one dominant practice tradition which then threads through the various modes of working.

Having a sense of the whole and the parts allows workers to establish a routine or rhythm. Here I am less concerned with the mechanistic language of time management – of 'having' time to do things – than with what this means for educators' identities or sense of themselves. Workers can approach time as something more than an endless sequence of experiences (Clandinin and Connelly 1991: 261). There is a shape and rhythm. Through experiencing that rhythm, there can be 'that sudden magic that gives us a sense of an inner revelation brought to us about something we have supposed to be known through and through' (Dewey 1934: 170). In this way workers can make sense of what they do – their narratives or 'stories' or practice (see Clandinin and Connelly 1991).

Planning

From what has been said so far, it should be apparent that once the nature of local education is appreciated, the task of planning work programmes is a fairly straightforward enterprise. What we are concerned with here are, essentially, the 'middle elements' we discussed when exploring thinking about direction: issues and strategies. That is to say, work programmes are planned against a background of 'creative participation' and within some overarching agreement concerning purpose and role;

and with attention to the repertoire and disposition of the workers. Following this, the main elements within work plans concern key issues, target groups, basic approaches, and the timing and location of work.

The danger in all this is that the whole exercise becomes too prescriptive and hence anti-conversational. Any approach to planning (and management) which fails to recognize that a high degree of discretion and flexibility is needed in the 'front-line' (Smith 1965) undermines local education. In other words, the very success of the work depends on the ability of educators to respond quickly and in ways that fit in with the situation. At the same time, local educators require a clear organizing framework, and information about the resources they may use, if they are to make sound decisions about practice. Arising out of this a number of rules or guidelines can be seen.

First, as a general principle, any objectives that are set should apply to the nature of the work to be undertaken rather than to outcomes in the individuals and groups worked with. Otherwise we will subvert the character of local education. For example, these were some of the objectives within one local educator's work plan:

> By the end of June I will have:
> ■ established the programme for the play scheme and recruited staff;
> ■ sorted out the office base;
> ■ completed work with the 'Wednesday Group' for Social Services.

The problem that many local educators face is that they have to operate in environments which are satiated with behavioural objectives and, as a result, either become consumed by the numbing 'logic' of such thinking or have to spend considerable amounts of time creating space for their activities (more of this later).

Second, if we accept the desirability of a mix of approaches and are able to reach some agreement about the balance between them, then the basic way of planning is to use 'modes' as building blocks. We set some overall figure for the amount of time to be spent in being around; being there; working with individuals and groups; administration; and reflection on practice. In so doing, we have to bear in mind that the first three elements are particularly elastic in the short run, but it should be possible to make decisions about the overall balance over a longer time period. Here recording is of great importance for both allocating time and thinking about direction.

> I do diary recording on a daily basis, quite short, mostly task but also feelings about things. Then I do the case notes on each session, and they vary according to how I judge the significance of the work. If there is a critical incident I record that separately . . . Then I look back and plan my work.

The discipline of recording also provides workers with a solid base for undertaking periodic evaluations and for writing reports. They are able to go back over particular work periods; to check whether time use has been appropriate; target groups contacted; issues that are coming up; or whether there has been any slippage between the various modes.

Some workers and managers may also want to put some figures on the numbers of clients or groups engaged within each of the modes. For example, a worker on an estate could be expected to be in regular contact with a substantial number of people when 'being around'. Some of the detached youth workers I have talked to, for example, spoke about being in contact with 200 or more young people in this way. We may also make some reasonable judgements about the number and size of projects undertaken, and the number of groups and individuals with whom we can expect to work in some depth in the course of a year.

Third, effective work is linked to the fact that local educators will have a certain number of projects on the go at any one time, and that these are organized around key issues or questions that have arisen in the work. For example, a community worker may be doing all the usual work with local groups plus work around specific campaigns – for example, concerning the siting of a hypermarket; the lack of primary education places; or the state of window frames in rented properties – and running a course, for example, on equal opportunities. Detached youth workers may engage in street work and then run residentials – for example, a motorbike group and a young women's group. Usually, youth workers and community educators are able to have some regular slots in their week for project activities; community workers do not generally have this opportunity as the meeting times for various groups vary, and campaigns tend to consume time in large, energetic blocks. The significance of projects is not simply that they provide room for more formal work; they also have an important symbolic and energizing impact on the rest of the work.

Fourth, the task of managers is less to direct workers, than to interpret policies, look for internal consistency, and facilitate the appropriate use of resources.

> I see my job as a manager as to create the right conditions for workers to work. This means, on the one hand, making sure that the workers are clear about what they are doing; and on the other, working the system to ensure that there are the resources and the appropriate policies to cover what they are doing. [F]

In this respect, the main things looked for in line management concern whether what workers propose are properly thought-out pieces of work: are they clear about aims, rationale, target group and how they are going to go about the work; about whether there is a balance between elements; about what resources will be used; and about how the work is to be evaluated? A further set of concerns links to whether proposals are in line with job descriptions and team and agency priorities (these can be seen as more codified versions of role and purpose; see Chapter 4). Last, decisions have to be made within the usual range of resource constraints: does the work justify the use of scarce resources? Looking back at our discussion concerning direction, there will, broadly speaking, need to be

agreement about purpose, role, key issues and strategy between workers
and managers; questions of tactics and agenda are matters for the local
educator.

Fifth, because many local educators work on their own initiative for
much of the time there is a particular need to develop some collective
appreciation of practice.

> I sometimes feel very envious of those who work from an office full
> of people. It must be so much easier coming in and being able to
> talk about what is happening, there is team planning and everything
> else. There again, I would lose my autonomy.

There have been moves to develop more team-orientated approaches in
local education as these enable larger-scale projects to take place, ensure
some consistency in services, and allow for the development of shared
understandings. For example, one manager put a particular emphasis on
evaluation of work within team meetings 'so we all are clearer what we are
talking about'.

> I saw the value of talking about work issues that were concerning me.
> Very much the sharing of practice. It is such a classic experience –
> you think you are the only one. Issues facing me could be related
> back to this other person's experience, not in a problem-solving way.
> It was just the odd word or two, 'I know what you are feeling', 'We
> have been there ourselves', and taking it off from there.

The move into teams is not without its problems: a team can so easily be
a team in name only because of the front-line nature of practice, and it
is to some of these questions that I will now turn.

Structuring relationships with managers

'Being local' means that workers' interactions with employing organizations are typically distant. For much of their time they are working on
their own or in small teams or pairs. Hours are often 'unsocial'. Their
office base, because it is 'local', is usually some way away from their managers'. Like many other welfare workers, 'front-line' units, with few ex-
ceptions, enjoy considerable freedom. Their work can be carried out largely
independent of other units; and there are major obstacles to direct
supervision (Smith 1965). This is compounded by peculiar administrative
arrangements. Workers have often been seconded to local groups or organizations. Also organizational structures, policies and priorities tend to
be unclear or to conflict. The quality of management within youth work
and community work has not been good (Bradford and Day 1991: 27–39;
Francis and Henderson 1992: 115–18).

Not a little effort is put into keeping things cloudy. Like the social
workers in Pithouse's (1987) study of an area office, local educators manage
the exchange of information between themselves and their central office.

They are 'keen guardians of their hard won local autonomy' (1987: 17). Managers have few chances to see work and to make direct judgements about results. It would be professionally or practically difficult for them to join in much of the work with individuals and groups. There are only some occasions when they can, like a headteacher, sit at the back of the classroom. For these reasons, managers are particularly dependent on the information provided by workers (Arnold *et al.* 1981: 17–19). They are often well aware of this and believe themselves vulnerable. Local educators regularly work in areas and around questions where there is some political sensitivity. Middle managers talk of being a 'buffer' within the organization. Sometimes they are advocates, sometimes 'dampers' for local educators (Linell 1988: 7). As a result, managers want paperwork. Not surprisingly, non-production of reports and forecast sheets, and questions about what is included when they arrive, feature in their conversations. Workers employ a variety of strategies to 'manage their managers', ranging from simple avoidance to swamping them with paper (Rigby 1982; Smith 1984: 23–38, 47–52).

Supplying managers with information and, indeed, keeping colleagues up to date on work can be seen as distractions from 'real' work with local people. 'Administrative work is perceived as an intrusion and higher management the culprits of this diversion' (Pithouse 1987: 15). The professional identity of local educators is wrapped up with the face-to-face interactions discussed above. As a result, 'administration' is typically seen as an outcome of the demands of 'management' or the 'system'. Only some workers see it as a central part of 'good practice' (Francis and Henderson 1992: 116). This is changing with the rise of the 'contract culture' (Chanan 1991; Smith 1991). The need to secure funding both for small-scale pieces of work and for the projects and units has been felt. Some workers are coming to see that survival depends upon making strong cases and writing up activities, and upon using recordings to reflect on their work.

> I found that if I didn't commit myself to paper about what I was experiencing or thinking, a lot of it would have been lost . . . Most of the work has come out of recordings. I look back over them, it helps me to make connections . . . It has not been a flash of light, it has been hard work and some anxious work . . . It is about committing yourself to paper, just to help you, as a tool to your own survival. You need to record who you are with, what you are doing.

Overall, what counts as the 'real' work is altering. There is a growing readiness to write up work and to engage in forms of locally based research. This emphasis has found its way into training (Council for Education and Training in Youth and Community Work 1989: 11; CEVE 1990: 5). In other words, local educators are having to become much better communicators across time and space, as well as maintaining their abilities as face-to-face workers.

Chapter 6

Embedding practice

> There are within this community different communities, and it is about getting these to work together. I sometimes see myself living in a series of different realities, different views of the world which exist at the same time. It's like a medieval town with different communities which meet in the marketplace. There has to be that meeting not just to trade but to share other things.

The notion of 'living in a series of different realities' catches a particular quality of local education: the readiness to engage with diverse views and to embed practice in local ways of living. This wish to 'connect' may arise out of an instrumental wish to be more effective or efficient. It may flow, as is the case with this worker, from deeply held beliefs about community, justice and what makes for well-being. There is, here, a desire to change the character of everyday life so that it holds within it increased possibility. This guides this worker to certain aspects of local life: cultures and idea systems; the groupings and associations that people form; and the networks and relationships that characterize neighbourhoods. Of special importance here also are the ways that people think about, and relate to, one another, and the differences of power involved. These are themes that I keep coming back to in my conversations with local educators, and in this chapter I want to look at each in turn. However, first we need to look at the idea of 'embedding practice'.

The motivation to embed practice

The wish to fix work firmly and deeply in local social systems and events runs through local education. Practitioners work in settings and institutions that are commonly described as 'community-based'. Throughout this book we see community workers involved in meetings of tenants' associations, youth workers talking with groups on the street, and community educators sitting drinking coffee with parents while their children play. This involves becoming part of everyday life.

> Only by the slow and tactful method of inserting yourself unassumingly into the life of the club, not by talking to your club members, but by hanging about and learning from their conversation and occasionally, very occasionally, giving it that twist which leads it to your goal, is it possible to open up a new avenue of thought to them.
>   You must soak yourself in the local atmosphere; you must know the current rates of pay, and slang, and you must be prepared to appreciate standards which are not your own while preserving your own integrity.
>
> (Brew 1943: 16)

Some settings and events are more formal (such as the committee meeting), others may be informal but still have distinctive shapes and patterns – but the concern is similar: establishing work that is part of, and attends to, commonly experienced or familiar forms or ways of life (Smith 1988: 130). Thus, for example, the community worker wanting to encourage women to explore their experience of men and families did not set up a women's study programme or women's group. Rather she started a 'Tuesday Club' where women met, talked and organized things, like outings, for themselves. The afternoon club was a form familiar to the estate.

Effectiveness

The desire to embed practice in this way derives from several sources. First, there can be a straightforward concern for effectiveness. Some may see 'community-based' approaches as being a way of incorporating local groups within state networks. It is a way of quietening opposition (see Cockburn 1977: 97–131), and this has been part of debates within community work for decades (see Bolger *et al.* 1981; Craig *et al.* 1982). For others, the wish to embed practice may flow from a concern for the views of those worked with. For example, local approaches may be used to work with 'disruptive' students. If the institution of the 'school' is seen as a problem by these students then a process which uses forms not too distant from what they see as daily life is one way of enabling them to continue with their education. There is a danger here. We can underestimate people's ability to deal with, and use, systems they find alienating or distant. Our actions, as a result, can end up being paternalistic and misdirected – as has been seen in some adult education initiatives where form has dominated content (Yarnitt 1980). As Brookfield argues: 'teaching and learning are such complex processes, and teachers and learners are such complex beings, that no model of practice or pedagogical approach will apply in all settings' (Brookfield 1990: 197).

Economy and efficiency

Second, there are arguments for embedding practice which flow from concerns with economy and efficiency. Here the aim is to secure the provision of services at the lowest possible cost (economy), and with the best ratio of inputs to outputs (efficiency) (Carter *et al.* 1992: 37). This is not necessarily a worry for many local educators, but it may figure in what managers have to say. Local approaches can be seen as attractive: they appear not to involve heavy demands on plant and capital investment. At the same time, their recurring location in the non-governmental sector seems to allow for more flexibility and for cost savings (Smith 1991: 15–16). Unfortunately, this is an area of assertion and guesswork. There has been no substantial published work comparing the costs and efficiency of different approaches to local education. The suspicion is that many 'savings' are, in fact, simple transfers. Individuals, families and local groups are increasingly bearing the cost of provision (Burridge 1990; Chanan 1991). Furthermore, costs can be underestimated. The result is that some developments in detached youth work, for example, do not have proper budgets for the more formalized aspects of the work such as short-run projects, residentials and activities.

Praxis

Third, and more fundamental, are arguments which derive from a view of education as process and praxis (see, for example, Grundy 1987). Here the desire to embed practice is not born of a wish to 'improve delivery'. Rather, it is seen as the central purpose or 'reason for being' of local educators. It is not just their work which they wish to fix firmly and deeply in local social systems and processes, it is a particular quality: informed and committed action (praxis).

> No one needs to be reminded of how fragile [local] communities are, how easily they are co-opted and perverted . . . It becomes all the more imperative to try and try again to foster and nurture those forms of communal life in which dialogue, conversation, *phronēsis*, practical discourse, and judgment are concretely embodied in our everyday practices.
>
> (Bernstein 1983: 229)

In this way education is a form of praxis that has at its heart the cultivation of praxis. This is the vision of Gadamer and Habermas. It also lies at the centre of what Freire proposes. Local educators work (engage in praxis) to foster communities in which there is praxis. That entails dialogue and a commitment to collective human well-being.

> There is a need for more understanding . . . more co-operation be-
> tween people. For example, there is a lot of infighting and back-
> stabbing in the tenants' association at the moment. People need to
> work together in the community instead of wanting to do their own
> bit and quarrelling.

The desire to encourage people to think of others, to work together is
central to this and other workers' efforts.

Groups

We might expect local educators to place an emphasis on groups. Some,
like this one, organize or describe their work in terms of them.

> Over summer we have the Irish group, the summer scheme and the
> arts project with the club group. Also the local festival. There is a
> hell of a lot being pushed into the summer. Ongoing work includes
> the school group, the EWO girls' group, the health education group,
> street work.

Groups are obvious sites of interaction and within them a sense of con-
nectedness or community with others can be fostered. 'The first and most
immediate social experience of mankind is small group experience . . . The
group is the commonest, as it is the most familiar, of all social units'
(Homans 1951: 1–2). Because they involve recognizable and shared patterns of behaviour, groups allow us to work and organize together (see
Barron *et al.* 1992: 31–45). They also enable us to identify ourselves, to
categorize who and what we are (Turner 1988). Groups can both provide
services to their members and to others, and be a focus for entry into the
political arena (see Chapter 8). Stable and enduring groups allow for
work to happen over time and are the key means of sustaining praxis
within a community. Something of this spirit runs through Knowles's (1950:
9) concern to promote adult informal education, so that every group, of
whatever nature, becomes a '*laboratory of democracy,* a place where people
may have the experience of learning to live co-operatively'.

   Some groups just exist for a moment and become sites for work. Workers may seek to create environments where such groupings can emerge:
this has been a central function of social areas in youth, community and
community education centres. However, many of the groups that workers
engage with exist over substantial periods of time – for example, friendship, activity, formal learning, or community groups. Lindeman, in particular, held that it was the way adult educators work with groups that set
them apart from others. Adult education was for him 'a co-operative venture
in non-authoritarian informal learning the chief purpose of which is to
discover the meaning of experience' (Lindeman 1989: 3; see also Knowles
1970). Similarly, social groupwork became a defining feature of some
traditions of youth work and community work (see, for example, Matthews
1966; Batten 1967).

Frames of reference

The state of mind of the worker in a group is of central significance. It is here that the focus on interactions can be seen.

> There is someone in the group who is rather disruptive. I had been centring on this individual and thinking about what I could do, rather than thinking about the group . . . With the question 'Who are you working with: an individual or a group?' things changed. It is that type of question – making the familiar strange – that is so important. I was taking on an individual in the group. It was almost becoming me and him. When I thought 'What are you doing with this group?' that didn't happen anymore – I had to let the group sort it.

It is easy to fall into the trap of working with an individual in the presence of a group. We have to focus on the interactions rather than what may be happening for a particular person, otherwise the rest of the group tend to become spectators; or all become selfish about their particular space or time. This does not mean that we should not attend to the experiences of individuals, it means simply that we make interactions the focal point. The switch from an individual to a group or interaction frame of reference is not easy (Davies 1975: 60–2).

A specific part of the work may involve encouraging the group to think about the extent to which it is meeting the needs of its members – asking whether people are taking responsibility for what they do and say.

> The way I used to work with groups was very much being in and doing it. And it was suddenly this concept of working in a different way, of not necessarily taking the lead – which is what I had always done. It was hard to stop doing that . . . It suddenly dawned on me what I had heard other people saying. You have got to let the group decide for themselves and take their own decisions. You sit and watch workers and think they are not doing anything, but then you realize they are.

Workers can take some time to come to these sorts of realization. Sometimes, it is simply that workers do not 'see' groups; or that they identify groups with particular formal events such as a class.

> They seem to have the idea that working with groups meant taking them off to another room, deciding on a particular topic, and having quite formal rules. When I started to work with groups in the lounge area there was some difficulty. This was not seen as groupwork. That was something that happened in the 'group room'. [F]

Where the bulk of people's work has been with individuals or the conducting of highly task-centred groups, getting hold of what is required in interactional approach can be an uphill task (Kitto 1986: 185–8).

Groups and individuals

A focus on interactions involves asking questions about relations of power within groups – between members, between workers and members. It means looking for patterns; checking out interpretations; asking whether what is seen is a problem or a symptom (Douglas 1991: 10–14). It involves attending to both task and group maintenance concerns. There are clear differences in dynamics between work with a group and with an individual, yet these can be overplayed. What I have been arguing here is that there should be an interactional focus in both settings. In many respects, this is a view confirmed by developments in psychoanalysis concerning the need for analytical space and mutuality between client and analyst (Casement 1985). A concern with interaction in analysis is necessary because of the impact of transference and counter-transference. There are some similarities between our account of conversation (via Gadamer 1979) and this view of the analytic process.

> The analyst's effectiveness is best demonstrated through learning to follow the analytic process, not in trying to control it. And when the analytic space is most clearly preserved for the patient, providing that unique opportunity for the patient to grow more fully into him/herself, the analytic process can be seen to have a life and direction of its own. Where it might lead cannot be anticipated, and what is experienced by the patient goes far beyond the bounds of expectation.
>
> (Casement 1990: 164–5)

I do not want to push this comparison too far because analysis involves a very particular form of dialogue and set of power relationships (Ricoeur 1981: 84–6). Yet the link is important as it underlines the significance of interaction.

Networks

Attending to interactions orientates us to relationships, and social networks are, at base, a specific type of relation linking a defined set of persons (Mitchell 1969). They are, literally, like nets. The knots represent people (or groups of people) and the strings connections between them. But if the only use of identifying networks was to see who was linked to whom then the effort would only be of limited value. Network analysis, in Knoke and Kuklinski's words, contains a further explicit premise of 'great consequence':

> The structure of relations among actors and the location of individual actors in the network have important behavioural, perceptual and attitudinal consequences both for individual units and for the system as a whole. In Mitchell's (1969) felicitous terms, 'The

patterning of linkages can be used to account for some aspects of the behaviour of those involved.'

(Knoke and Kuklinski 1991: 175–6)

We can look at networks in terms of the *interactions* involved:

- whether the relations between people are multiple or single;
- the 'equalness' of flow (most relations are unequal and reflect differences in power and position);
- the frequency and length of exchanges.

We can also look at the *nature* of what is exchanged and at *structure*: the size of the network; the density; how people are clustered; and how central a particular person or group is. In this way we can start to appreciate how the content of interaction links to the importance of relationships, and how both relate to 'the extent to which individuals experience relationships as entailing obligations to act in certain ways' (Abrams in Bulmer 1986: 89).

Many of these ideas are 'taken for granted'. Early workers with boys, such as Russell and Rigby (1908), recognized the need to harness the energy of 'ring leaders' and 'turbulent spirits' so that they might become an 'active and effective influence for good' (1908: 291). Similarly Baden-Powell (1909: 6) advocated the use of 'leading boys' as patrol leaders. More recently, in the 1970s, the development of training in groupwork has meant that a large number of people were introduced to forms of network analysis. The most usual approach was through the drawing of sociograms – for example, charting friendship patterns, starting with a person who appeared to occupy a central position (see Leighton 1972: 111–16; Button 1974: 51–76). It has also been recommended that workers explore relations of power and support in communities (see, for example, Hadley *et al*. 1987; Dominelli 1990: 63–4).

Networks and communities

It would be surprising if the notion of 'network' had not taken root, given its use within community studies. Bott's (1957) pioneering work has been especially influential. She argued that the immediate social environment of urban families is best considered not 'as the local area in which they live, but rather as the network of actual social relationships they maintain, regardless of whether these are confined to the local area or run beyond its boundaries' (Bott 1957: 99). It has been followed up by studies such as Wallman (1984) and Werbner (1988) and in those concerned with informal care (for example, Willmott 1986; 1987). Workers may routinely use the idea in this sense.

My whole family network is totally different to this. Mine was an incredibly stable family network, I still have both parents, I also had an incredibly happy upbringing. That's very different to a lot of the

young people I work with. There's a lot of instability, and things have
never been as happy, a lot of the kids aren't loved that much anyway.

In the arena of literacy practices, too, some attention has been given to
local relationships and events (Heath 1983; Street 1984) and to networks.
Particular people are known to be able to help with various tasks – writing
to the council, filling in forms, putting the right words in greetings cards
– and these networks of support are fundamental to people's ability to 'get
by' (Barton and Padmore 1991). To this must be added the work done on
the relationships of groups and organizations within localities. Here the
contribution of 'community studies' such as the Banbury research (Stacey
1960; Stacey *et al.* 1975) has been significant. Workers have benefited from
these studies through their assimilation into key practice-skills texts such
as Henderson and Thomas (1987) and their inclusion in training programmes (CEVE 1990).

What this understanding can lead to is a concern to enhance the range
and capacities of networks to respond to the needs of local people. We are
often not aware of their contribution until something goes wrong with
them. As Barton and Padmore (1991: 70) comment with regard to literacy,
people live within such networks and may not identify problems with
reading and writing as help is at hand. When these networks are disrupted
people have to make other arrangements, such as going to basic education classes. At one level this may be viewed as a 'good thing' – change has
provided the impetus for someone to take their learning further. However,
the nature of the moves open to people is significant. If we attend to
networks then change in one local arena can be responded to by alterations
in another. The danger here is that if a local infrastructure does not exist
or is limited then people will have to turn to bureaucratized institutions.
In the case of literacy this entails 'pedagoguization', a growth in 'schooled'
approaches to learning. This has implications wider than the simple gaining
of reading and writing skills (Street and Street 1991: 162–3). Attending to
local events and practices, looking to networks is thus fundamental to
thinking about the nature of power in societies.

Key people

The process of making yourself known as a worker in a locality is greatly
enhanced by approaching the 'central' figures in networks.

One of the key people was someone who has lived and worked
locally for years and who has lots of contacts who you wouldn't get
quickly. For example, we went into one of the local pubs and sat
there talking to a group of men who included one of the biggest
villains in the area. He made a point of introducing me to him so
that now I am OK because he knows what I am. Walking around the
streets, especially as a woman, there are all sorts of connotations –
people can be a bit suspicious of what you are.

In much the same way that ethnographers set out to find 'key informers' and 'gatekeepers' (like 'Doc' in Whyte 1955), local educators have to establish relationships with people who can help them with local knowledge and sponsor them in new situations. It is an area fraught with difficulties. Being sponsored by one particular group or individual may well lead to rejection by other groups. Sponsorship can take ironical forms. One detached youth worker new to an area found ready acceptance by the people with whom he was seeking to work because he was arrested very publicly in the middle of the estate. He had refused to submit to a search by a plain-clothes policeman who would not show his warrant card.

Key individuals are important for another reason. There are networks in which local educators cannot hope to get a working foothold. They have to cultivate intermediaries or leaders (Alinsky 1969: 65) to enable them to take on a more organized educational role.

> There are two different types of work I do: direct work with young people; and this work with groups. There are things I couldn't possibly achieve with those people. One particular woman has managed to get this Gujarati group together. On Saturday evening you have got a lot of Asian young people, starting about 9, going up to 18 plus; boys and girls. You have also got parents coming in. It would be difficult for anyone in the youth service to establish that kind of trust.

They may also use key people to put information into the 'grapevine'. In much the same way as a chain letter spreads, so information can permeate through a network. Workers may see 'word of mouth' as very significant in their activities. Recruitment to youth and community groups is dependent on grapevine information rather than on formal advertising (DES 1983: 36).

However, key people in networks are not important to educators simply because they can act by proxy. They are significant because networks are a fundamental aspect of social life, and their functioning is dependent on people taking on specific roles. Schön (1973: 184–6), for example, talks of brokers, facilitators, managers, manoeuvrers and negotiators. Such roles vary in character, yet make common demands of their practitioners – for example, they require a high degree of personal credibility. If workers want to strengthen networks' capacities to meet the needs of those involved then they have to work with people so that they may fulfil these roles. This can mean a shift in focus and in workers' frames of reference. For example, those used to working directly with 'clients' have to move to the idea of working with (or through) intermediaries (Bayley et al. 1987).

Networking

Workers also have to be aware of the various organizations and groups in an area so that they can do another part of their job.

I think that has to be my role. There are organizations that already exist. I can support them and what I can add is the networking, then bring them together. For me that is the only place I can go.

Linking groups and organizations, and connecting individuals with them is a recurrent theme among the local educators with whom I talk. The making of such connections has been particularly influenced by the number of voluntary groups involved in youth and community work and the need for co-ordination (Jeffs 1979: 1–30).

Community workers must recognize that they are not the be-all and end-all to everybody, that there are other expertises, that at times our work is most effective by being part of a network to enable other learning to go on; and that is where I saw my role. We had a community coffee morning every Wednesday, so I invited the tutor, who offered to pay for the teas and coffees. We leafleted the area. So that was my input – very small, but part of the cog in the wheel.

Others have followed in Lindeman's steps and looked to what might be described as an 'ecological approach' to adult education. For example, Fordham et al. (1979) set out to foster a matrix of independent learning groups and networks. They believed that such a matrix offered 'a positive and dynamic alternative to a number of separate professionally dominated and controlled services which deal with people on a fragmented basis'. Further, to ignore such resources 'is to deny, ultimately, the freedom of people to express themselves, to control their lives, to rejuvenate their own world' (Fordham el al. 1979: 202). Lastly, network can be invoked in relation to building up relations with colleagues in other services and sectors.

At the moment I am working with a number of different workers. The project has grown and there is a lot more opportunity for people. The networks are getting bigger. You need a supportive environment, where you can talk. You need people you can tap into.

From this we can see that while the idea of 'network' is significant, it has not been pushed to quite the extent that has occurred in some research traditions (see Scott 1991). Workers are not likely to spend lots of time exhaustively charting sets of relationships. They may do such an activity from time to time as a way of gaining an insight into a particular problem – for example when working with abuse (Reder et al. 1993: 138–75). The notion of 'network' is useful as a sensitizing idea to encourage further intervention and thought. Workers, like researchers, are advised to use it only for as long as it is useful and interesting (Hannerz 1980: 186).

Culture

The educators with whom I talk use 'culture' in a number of ways: to discuss people's backgrounds or traditions; the norms and routines in

specific small groups ('the culture of the group'); the character of organizational life (after Morgan 1986); and, more broadly, to describe particular communities. While there may be endless debates over definition and
how cultures are formed, there is at least some common ground. Tylor
(1903) is still a good starting point. Culture was, for him, 'that complex
whole which includes knowledge, belief, art, morals, law, custom and
any other capabilities and habits acquired by man as member of society'
(see Lawrence 1987). It is in this sense that we can think of culture as
the whole way of life of a group. It is a pattern of traditions that can be
transmitted over time and space. Three qualities underlie its centrality: it
is learnt; much of it exists at a non- or un-conscious level; and it helps
structure thought, perception and identity.

To address culture, educators need to understand how culture is created; its shape within asymmetrical relations of power; how dominant and
subordinate cultures emerge (Giroux 1983: 163); how one culture relates
to another. Approaching this area of experience, allowing people to step
outside the 'taken-for-granted' and make choices about themselves, places
a number of duties on educators as Giroux (1983: 202–3) has shown. It
involves a number of the qualities already discussed with regard to local
education. First, people must be actively involved in learning. Relationships
have to be structured to facilitate dialogue and exploration. Second, people
must learn to think critically. Third, 'the development of a critical mode
of reasoning must be used to enable students to appropriate their own
histories, i.e. to delve into their own biographies and systems of meaning'
(Giroux 1983: 203). In addressing their culture, people must have the
space to own their experiences and thinking, and hence to speak with
their own voices. Fourth, people must also learn what is good, they must
learn what values are central to human life and well-being and how such
values are transmitted and distorted in the interests of the powerful (Smith
1988: 114). Finally, people must learn about the structural and ideological
forces which influence and restrict their lives. In my conversations with
local educators a number of themes arise with regard to these.

Workers' awareness of their own culture

In the training of local educators there has been an emphasis on participants' enhancing their knowledge of self (Ahmad and Kirby 1988). In part
this is due to the interest in this field in the social and personal development
of people. It would be odd if workers placed great emphasis on development
for others and paid little attention to it for themselves. 'Self-awareness is
the foundation-stone of a social educator's practice. By developing his
knowledge about himself, he can come to understand along what lines
some at least of his practice needs to proceed' (Davies and Gibson 1967:
186). Allied to this is a belief that the personalities of workers are central
to both building relationships with people and handling the relative
freedom and isolation of their jobs (Milson 1970: 78–9). However, the

focus on self-awareness does not necessarily mean that attention is given to culture – workers may well stay in the realm of private troubles rather than public issues (Mills 1959).

Some are aware of cultural questions. Paneth (1944), for example, when evaluating her experience of working around a particular street during the Blitz, posed some familiar questions:

> Have we been intruders, disturbing an otherwise happy community, and is it only the bourgeois in us, coming face to face with his opponents, who minds and wants to change them because he feels threatened? Or *do* they need help from outside?
>
> (Paneth 1944: 121)

Such concerns appear in what some workers have to say about the neighbourhoods in which they worked. As Rosaldo put it, we should not impose our categories on other people's lives: 'they probably do not apply, at least not without serious revision' (Rosaldo 1993: 26). To avoid imposition, we have to know what our categories are. A classic approach is for workers to attempt to stand outside their own, and others', culture and look in. They see themselves both as a part of a culture and as 'outsiders'.

> Sometimes you have to get in there, I am as honest as I possibly can be. For me to have any understanding about where I want to go, I have to stand outside that culture and understand, look at it and evaluate it for myself and make choices. At the end of the day I live within that culture and it's got some good bits about it, but I live within its repressions and I live the images that the men have of women within that culture and I have to deal with it every day.

This was also the disposition that this local educator sought to encourage in those she worked with.

Culture and agency

The belief that people can take hold of their lives, can make changes, that they are not helpless in the face of structural forces, is central to local education. Established patterns of living are not to be taken for granted, they have to be questioned – but this is not the end point. It follows that workers must be orientated also to questions of identity and action. Here we have to avoid approaching culture as a monolithic object, but rather as complex, contradictory phenomenon being made, and kept alive, by people.

> Part of what I am about is looking at that relationship that young people have with that community, peer group. What I have seen are two separate entities. There are those who are very much part of their community and find expression in that community, and there are those who don't.

For some the task is to encourage people to take 'a step outside' the cultures of which they are a part. This is to foster critical engagement; to help people to connect with, and own, those aspects which accord with their sense of themselves, and of what is good and right. At the same time it is to reject certain things, to encourage the desire and ability to change values, behaviours, ideas that are unjust or that inhibit well-being. For others the key aim is to help them to identify the traditions and ideas that express their sense of themselves. Whatever the case, we have to turn to conversation and to a sense of what is good.

> The caste system can be seen in different ways. It can be seen in the religious way or in a historical way – a form of invasion . . . It could be argued that the four original castes were equal. They just referred to people with different capabilities. It is not like that now. Similarly if we look at what the Koran says about women. It is not just about women covering themselves up – it is about men and women dressing modestly. Encouraging that sort of dialogue gets one back to what is important.

This getting beneath the surface, searching for truth, when linked with discussions of what makes for human flourishing, makes action possible.

Promoting cultural diversity and understanding

The final theme I want to discuss is the desire to promote understanding and acceptance of different cultures. If we are to take the politics of difference seriously then the concern is to work not for assimilation but for co-operation on the basis of difference.

> There are lots of different reasons for pursuing this work. I don't see it in isolation as a sort of cultural thing. Making people feel good about the 'melting pot'. It certainly isn't a melting pot. The groups are very distinct. There are lots of suspicions about each other. The question is how you get people working together without making them feel that they are losing something of their culture. Generational questions come into that as well. Young Asian people are rebelling against the strictness of their parents. There is a lot of prejudice to overcome. There is an underlying prejudice between Hindus and Muslims, between Asians and African Caribbeans. How do you overcome it? The slow process of letting people get to know each other and talking about ethics rather than traditions and religion.

The means used by local educators vary enormously. They include promoting explorations of difference and identity, developing situations where people from different cultures can meet, providing information and so on. Some workers make an effort to develop unusual and memorable activities, such as a stay with a bedouin group. There may also be a recognition of the possible knock-on effects as people talk with their friends and neighbours.

> Talking to one lad, his friends can't believe what he has done – eating a meal with a cow looking over his shoulder, going to a wedding in the desert. When he first came back he didn't tell anybody, partly because he hadn't got over the experience himself and partly because he thought they wouldn't believe him. That sort of thing is really worthwhile and does broaden horizons and if one person experiences it, others also do to some extent.

This worker tries to work with other people's points of view. The worker who talked about 'ethics rather than tradition or religion' took an interesting line. He wanted initially to short-circuit arguments about details of religion or the justification for certain practices. Instead, he focused on debates about the underlying values – ideas about what makes for the good. In this way the grounds for dialogue could be set.

> I think it is about accepting and working from where they are and their point of view. Not putting your own priorities or whatever, accepting the ducking and diving, not accepting the racism but hearing what they are saying. Working from there. You would very quickly get shut off if you went in there with your structure of what you are going to do for them.

Here we can see the themes interlocking – being in touch with your cultural identity and prejudgements, having a sense of agency, and looking to an acceptance of diversity and a search for that which is held in common. But this still leaves questions concerning the unequal nature of power relationships in society.

Relations of power

When with groups, workers are encouraged to attend to interpersonal relations of power (see, for example, Whitaker 1985: 372–86; Brown 1988: 90–123; Douglas 1991: 28–84). The concept also appears as an aid to analysing links between individuals:

> I said, what about him, why aren't you talking about him in the same way? Why are you immediately blaming his ex-girlfriend for what is happening? Look at his track record. Let's talk about the power he had over her when they were going out.

It shows up in the way some workers examine their position with 'clients' and the extent to which they recognize the influence they could have because of their position and what their intervention might mean.

> I have had it, parents giving it like I am going to whisk their daughters off. Perhaps not so much parents as boyfriends. They don't like

the girls having that bit of power. It is about me understanding what's going through their mind and managing that. I would be dangerous for the young women if I just went in there and just give them these big ideas and let them get on with it.

Local educators may also recognize they are often in situations where power is an overt issue at an interpersonal level; where they have to work hard to maintain face while not seriously undermining the worth of others. Take, for example, this account of a dispute in a minibus at the start of an outing:

One of the things that he kept saying to me was 'If I don't go, then nobody is going.' I'm saying, I know that. 'If you don't want this van to go then it's going nowhere. But you have got to look at my point of view.' It's about saying I recognize you, your power, but you just look at the shit I might be in. Whether a deal was reached or whether it was just like him saying 'Fuck it', I don't know.

Power may also be a key concept when workers look at the area in which they work. Standard texts on neighbourhood work usually refer to the need to gather information about how power and leadership are exercised in a community. For example, Henderson and Thomas (1987) suggest that workers should look at the nature of:

- business and organized labour;
- elective politics;
- administrative politics;
- civic politics; and
- community politics.

This can feed through into some quite formal analysis by workers, particularly those involved in campaigns. But it is crucial at a more general level.

Aims, rhetoric and 'reality'

Power is not simply a variable to be considered when working, it is integral to local educators' aims.

The aim would be for him to take, to have, to look at – I don't like the word responsibility – but for him to feel a little bit more powerful and clear about his own life.

Formal statements of purpose may contain explicit reference. For example:

Community work is about the active involvement of all people in the issues which affect their lives . . . it is about the ability of all people to act together to create environments where they can reflect on and act on their collective concerns to challenge inequalities and influence and assert control over social, economic and political issues. Community work aims to change the balance of power which will facilitate local democracy. In this sense community work focuses on relations between people and those institutions (both public and private) which shape their everyday lives.

(Federation of Community Work Training Groups/AMA 1991)

Such statements are highly aspirational. The reality of daily practice, as revealed in conversation with workers, is less heady.

> [Workers] associate themselves primarily with reformist styles of community work practice. Community development emerges not only as a preferred model but also as the one which most adequately describes the largest proportion of the work being undertaken.
>
> (Barr 1991: 71)

In some ways this is very welcome. There is in community work, perhaps, less radical posturing and more of an emphasis on securing concrete gains than a decade or more ago (Butcher 1992). In youth work there is still a considerable gap between rhetoric and reality, as various surveys of practice show (see Jeffs and Smith 1990b). Yet there is generally among workers a strong commitment to changing situations where there is exploitation and subordination. However, it is tempered by a reading of what is possible in particular communities and organizations, and here lies the rub.

On the whole workers do not use the room for manoeuvre open to them (Smith 1984). They often lack understanding of the political systems in which they operate; a sufficient repertoire of ideas and actions to draw upon; and do not have what Heller (1976: 202) calls 'civic courage'. It is not difficult to see why this happens. Finding space, resisting dominant and containing ideas and actions, dealing with the self-protectiveness of management, and the sheer scale of oppression and social issues faced can soon tire workers and sap the will to push that little bit further. As Williams (1988) has shown in his detailed study of youth work and race in inner London, apparently progressive-sounding statements are often more to do with closure than possibility. Commenting on difficulties experienced when attempting to implement agreed anti-racist guidelines and policies, he draws attention to workers' complete misunderstanding of the ideological function of the document. 'They saw it as a policy for change, whereas ... its principal role was to legitimize the existing order which originally gave rise to personal and institutional racism' (Williams 1988: 83).

The position is not helped by disputes concerning what is meant by 'power' (see Lukes 1988).

> The problem is that when you are talking about the aims of things you don't want to wrap it up in jargon words. But in fact those are the things, I'm trying not to sound like a jargonistic youth worker, but what is power? You have to get into all those sorts of discussion.

What are the different bases for power, what forms does it take; and to what uses is it put? Some workers may follow Weber. 'In general, we understand by "power" the chance of a man or of a number of men to realize their own will in a communal action even against the resistance of others who are participating in the action' (Weber in Gerth and Mills 1991: 180). However, some go beyond this.

The influence of classic studies of power and decision-making in local communities such as Hunter (1953) and Bachrach and Baratz (1970) has been felt by some local educators. What these studies reveal is that power is not simply the capacity of an individual or group to make and carry out decisions. It is also to do with what actually goes on the decision-making agenda. Power can be used to stop any potentially disruptive opposition from emerging.

> Those in powerful positions may simply fail to respond in any way . . . so that no decision is ever taken (*negative decision making*) . . . Disgruntled groups fail to press their demands because they believe that it would do no good or because they fear for what would happen if they did speak out (*anticipating reactions*) . . . Dominant interests may exert such a degree of control over the way a political system operates, and over the values, beliefs and opinions of less powerful groups within it, that they can effectively determine not only whether certain demands come to be expressed and heeded, but also whether such demands will even cross people's minds (*the mobilization of bias*).
> (Saunders 1980: 29–30; emphasis added)

This account of 'non-decision-making', where things do not cross people's minds; where questions go unasked and demands are not made because people anticipate the reaction, or where people's wishes are simply ignored, has also found its way directly into the literature (see, for example, Craig *et al.* 1982; Smith 1982; Carspecken 1991). We can see how it feeds through into the thinking of this community worker.

> There is an anti-poverty strategy being developed by the council at the moment and I have serious doubts about it. You can look at it from two aspects. One is the effects of poverty and one is the causes. With my point of view I want to look at the causes and not address them, but enable people to address them. I would look at the education of young women so that they knew how to challenge the services here, gain confidence to go for training . . . Others in my team would look at it that they have low income so therefore we must provide a service that they can afford. So we will have low-cost keep fit!

Her concern was to work with people so that they saw that there were questions they could ask, demands they could make. More than that, she sought to work in such a way that people were able to take action on their understandings, to challenge those with power over resources.

Truth and ideology

When all these considerations are placed alongside what we have already discussed about embedding practice or praxis, then three particular questions or directions for the work emerge. The first concerns the impact of asymmetrical relations on what might be regarded as 'truth' or as valid. Our conversations take place in an unequal world, relationships are distorted. People may set out to deceive us or may themselves be unwittingly deceived. We need to turn to the factors that attempt to normalize or legitimate the exercise of power, that render it reasonable (Corlett 1989: 39). Here, after Foucault (1977; 1980), it is especially important that we turn to the categories and dispositions that are carried forward in the discourses of local education. How do key terms like 'client', 'learner' and 'confidentiality' assemble the world rather than reveal it, and so act to subject and discipline (Rojek *et al.* 1988: 114–45)?

Words, signs and actions need to be searched for their:

■ truth. Do they adequately describe the thing we are discussing?
■ rightness. Does what is said accord with recognized norms and values?
■ sincerity. Are speakers truthfully expressing their beliefs, intentions and feelings?

These criteria, Habermas (1984: 307–8) argues, can be used to make judgements and to claim validity for statements. Rejection of what someone says involves taking issue with one of these aspects. It means saying that something is untrue, wrong or insincere. But how do we do this where there is the possibility of 'systematic distortion of communication by the hidden exercise of force' (Ricoeur 1981: 78)? Here we have the problem of ideology, of 'meaning in the service of power' (Thompson 1990: 7).

Luckily, there always is some chink of light, some inconsistency in claims to validity in these circumstances. The dominance of one concept of reality can never be complete: all that can be achieved is a shifting equilibrium. People end up holding contradictory sets of beliefs at the same time (Gramsci 1971: 323–33) and this can be opened up in conversation. Power is never stable and therefore can never be monolithic. In this sense there is possibility – local educators can place an emphasis on people in the community becoming critical. They can encourage people to look for assumptions; the impact of context; and for alternatives (Brookfield 1987b: 15–34).

Second, and linked to what we have just said, an interest in praxis must be infused by a careful interrogation of the forces and interests which affect discourse. In this respect, Mills's oft-quoted dictum concerning the interrelationship of public issues and private problems is important. Education as praxis involves engaging with the experiences of people and the way these are formed in interaction over time. Just as words become indistinguishable without spaces between them, so individuals fade if we ignore their interactions with others and the wider world (see Chapter 2).

Understanding and action

Finally, those local educators concerned with praxis have to address how people may act, as well as understand. This may take them into activities or into arenas that are labelled as 'political'. This is most obvious in the case of community workers (Thomas 1983: 60–106). As Barr's (1991) study showed, the orientation of community workers to the needs of disadvantaged groups often placed them in conflict with dominant interests. At a local level this might be with, for example, the racist management group of the community centre. Councillors, local authority managers, health authorities, representatives of quangos, the management of commercial concerns, developers are all likely to become 'opponents'.

> You can't avoid conflict. These people on this estate get a bad deal. Their housing is crappy, the buses are terrible, they're forgotten by the council. None of this is really fought for by the local councillors. So when I help to organize campaigns things do get a bit difficult sometimes.

At other times opponents can quickly become allies. As one worker put it:

> you need to be on your toes. You have to co-operate with different people at different times to safeguard local interests.

Here we return to basic questions concerning the political role and impact of local educators. There have been various explorations of the extent to which local educators act to quieten opposition to dominant interests (see, for example, Craig *et al.* 1982; Cowburn 1986; Jeffs and Smith 1990b), and there is little need to rehearse the arguments here. However, as Loney (1983: 196) has argued, democratic states are not in a position to direct and regulate every activity of workers, particularly when they are 'involved in innovatory decentralized programmes'. Achievements can be made in terms of getting people to work together and in terms of making improvements in their local situations (Butcher *et al.* 1993). While any steps forward may be stuttering (Taylor and Ratcliffe 1981), local education is part of the democratic struggle. As Lindeman said of adult education:

> The success of democracy depends upon the capacity of the people for generating social movements expressive of their needs . . . Social action is in essence the use of force or coercion. The use of force or coercion is justified only when the force is democratic and this means it must be derived from intelligence and reason. Adult education thus turns out to be the most reliable instrument for social actionists.
>
> (Lindeman 1987b: 116–17)

The experiences of local educators over the last 20 years are hardly likely to lead them to make grand claims about what they can achieve politically, or to have naive beliefs in what is possible. However, the fact that there are small gains to be made, and a belief that attacks on the social and material interests of various subordinated groups have to be resisted, lead some local educators at least to keep trying.

Conclusion

In this chapter we have seen how local educators can embed practice. This process is not a simple technical matter. Some are trying not merely to locate their work deep in local life, but also to foster a particular quality therein: praxis. This involves a focus on interactions and attention to the shared, communal and non-conscious nature of outcomes. It becomes revealed in the way in which local educators may think about and act on certain key phenomena. Groups, networks, power and culture are central organizing ideas here.

What also is revealed in my conversations with local educators is the scale of their commitment to those living in the neighbourhoods in which they work. These workers may be what Gramsci (1971) called 'organic intellectuals'. Some find their social background is similar to those of many local people; they can remain committed and attached to that same fundamental social group (class), and occupy a special place in fostering thinking and organization of the class to which they organically belong. Others do not share the same class or group background but are committed to the emancipation of those with whom they work. Here the idea of 'organic intellectual' is also important.

> Each man . . . carries on some form of intellectual activity, that is, he is a 'philosopher', an artist, a man of taste, he participates in a particular conception of the world, has a conscious line of moral conduct, and therefore contributes to sustain a conception of the world or modify it, that is, to bring into being new modes of thought.
> (Gramsci 1971: 9)

Some workers seek to develop this capacity. However, from what we have seen here, they can also do something more. They can strive to sustain people's critical commitment to the social groups with whom they share fundamental interests. Their purpose is not necessarily individual advancement, but human well-being as a whole.

Chapter 7

Reflecting-in-action

More and more I ask questions while I am working. At first I used to ask after, just go with it. Now I am more aware, I am thinking during the session. Sometimes I make mistakes and the second I have done something I've thought I shouldn't have done that. Before I would have thought it two hours after, sitting at home with a coffee or whatever.

This worker has learnt to reflect-in-action, to think things through in time to act (Schön 1983: 49–69). This process can be contrasted with reflection-on-action, thinking that takes place after the event. In this chapter I want to focus on the former process. The processes and themes I describe find echoes in the literature around reflective practice – for example, in teaching (Clift *et al.* 1990; Day *et al.* 1990; Louden 1991; Russell and Munby 1992; Calderhead and Gates 1993). However, local education, and the pictures and ideas that workers draw upon in practice, bring their own shading and emphasis. Thus, to help make sense of the process we must look at some key practices, such as supervision, and the work of writers whose ideas have been taken up by workers. We have to be mindful of the way in which reflection is not something that simply happens in individual minds, but is a social activity that is situated. What I hope to show is that reflection-in-action does not follow a simple course from point *A* to point *B*: it is a complex mix of moves. I also try to place it firmly within the frame of reference workers bring to a task, and attend to the affective domain.

Reflecting-in-action

When I hear educators talking about their work, or have the chance to observe them in action, I form ideas or judgements about their ability. I suspect most of us do this. I might be impressed by someone's knowledge of an area, but for the most part it is the way people talk about work that catches me. Detailed knowledge is useless if it cannot be used in the best way. We may know a lot and be able to draw on a range of techniques, but what makes workers special is their ability to combine these and improvise. In this they reveal their artistry; they display the fruits of 'educational connoisseurship and educational criticism' (Eisner 1985: 87–102).

Thinking on our feet

When we say that certain people are able to reflect-in-action, what is it that they are able to do? 'Thinking on our feet' is not a bad description of what is going on: as we work we listen to what is said and observe what is happening. At the same time, we try to make sense of the experience, and this helps us to make decisions about how to act (or not to act).

> The practitioner allows himself to experience surprise, puzzlement, or confusion in a situation which he finds uncertain or unique. He reflects on the phenomenon before him, and on the prior understandings which have been implicit in his behaviour. He carries out an experiment which serves to generate both a new understanding of the phenomenon and a change in the situation.
>
> (Schön 1983: 68)

In this we do not closely follow established ideas and techniques – textbook schemes. We are not following a plan like technicians – as many researchers have found with regard to curriculum planning (see Richardson 1990). We may have our own routines or ways of doing things, but these have to be held in tension with each situation. Every case is, in some way, unique, so we have to think things through. But time is limited, we have to act. As a result, this thinking may not feel very complete or 'logical'.

Reflection-on-action comes later: it is distanced in time-space from the original experience. We may write up recordings, talk things through with a supervisor, think about experiences as we drive home from work. We are able to reflect on reflection-in-action. Some writers, like Russell and Munby (1991), argue that distance allows more control; and room for the ordered, deliberate and systematic application of logic. However, to leave it at that would be one-sided – distance also allows us to entertain feelings and emotions that were bottled up or present only dimly in an encounter.

The act of reflecting-on-action enables us to explore why we may have acted and felt as we did, what was happening in a group and so on.

> I don't think I would reflect if I didn't record. The work is so instant. It is happening very much in the present. You never know what is

going to happen next. If I didn't take that time to write it down, I wouldn't reflect on and analyse my work. Also from the writing down I plan my work. I sort out what I am going to try next.

In these processes we develop sets of questions and ideas about practice which are carried into the process of reflection-in-action.

I noticed when I used to go to meet my supervisor I was always chatting things over in my head, and that still happens now. I liken it to when I was learning to drive a car. I could always hear my driving instructor and I can still hear him now when I need it. I still hear my college supervisor, I can hear what he is saying. Whether that is me doing it to myself I don't know. I know how he would think. As I learnt to drive nearly 15 years ago I am assuming that this process will still go on. So you could say I am internalizing it.

This process, which has been described as 'internal supervision' (Casement 1985), and the to-and-fro movement involved, indicates that we need to be cautious about overplaying differences between reflection-in- and -on-action.

Repertoire

You add to that reservoir of knowledge. Yes, I would say you are developing a bank of knowledge, and hopefully . . . you are learning about your attitudes and are developing the skills to be able to utilize the various pieces you are picking up.

We build up a repertoire of images, ideas, examples and actions. Schön, like Dewey (1987: 123), sees this as central to reflective thought (see page 72). By using familiar situations as 'a precedent, or a metaphor, or . . . an exemplar for the unfamiliar one' (Schön 1983: 138), we can engage with a situation. We do not have a full understanding of things before we act, but hopefully we can avoid major problems while 'testing the water'.

I do gauge my reactions. I do think about what I am going to say before I say it . . . I suppose it is because in the past I have put my foot in it a lot. I tended to say what first came into my head and that isn't always the best thing . . . And when your only tool is communication, and you fuck it up or put a spanner in the works or say it wrong, then someone who is feeling pretty vulnerable and not together can be hurt.

In this view, when looking at a situation we are influenced by, and use, what has gone before, what might come, our repertoire, and our frame of reference. We are able to draw upon certain routines. As we work we can bring fragments of memories into play and begin to build theories and responses that fit the new situation. We also create memory traces – of the situation and the processes – and leave physical debris (see Chapter 4).

We interact with others. Educators are not simply deliberating about practice, as Dewey might have put it, but are constructing representations of practice in action (MacKinnon and Erickson 1992: 199). At the same time, we have to handle the fact that there is much that we do not, and cannot, know about the situation or experience. We have to live and work with uncertainties and half-formed ideas. Local educators, like schoolteachers, cannot easily afford the 'luxury of a detached viewpoint: they have to teach, to make choices, whether or not they have a clear view of where they are heading' (Barnes 1992: 15).

These qualities are not just the province of professionals – they need to be generally developed if people are to take their full place in the world (see Chapter 6). However, if the task of educators is to enhance the critical and emancipatory quality of these processes, they themselves have to be in touch with their capacities. They have to develop a particular awareness so that they may both better foster environments for learning and deepen their understanding of the processes that are the subject of their teaching and intervention.

Dimensions of reflection-in-action

Listening to workers talk about their practice, I began to see a linking of elements (see Figure 7.1). Four main foci in the reflective process surfaced:

- engaging with specific contexts, and interacting with others in the situation;
- returning to situations and attending to feelings;
- connecting experiences and feelings with ideas, images and so on, and judging the processes and outcomes;
- framing findings, and rehearsing next moves.

I am not saying that this is the pattern that practitioners do or should follow, merely that this way of looking at reflection-in-action provides some useful metaphors for thinking about practice.

The shape and nature of these elements are, in some ways, close to the process Kolb (1984) talks about as experiential learning (see Chapter 2). This is hardly surprising, given the extent to which this model has become embedded in often unseen ways in training for this arena, and Kolb's debt to Dewey (1929; 1987), Piaget (1932; 1951) and Lewin (1951). However, there are several points of departure – the models describe different things: professional practice (or praxis) in our case, and a form of knowledge production in Kolb's (1984: 41). Further, Kolb's model is individualistic and sequential (Jarvis 1987: 18). The clusters of processes I am exploring are not placed in order, but represent points in a force field which is in constant movement.

At the centre of the picture, and informing all the elements, I have put memory. All the time, as we engage with situations some traces of events,

Figure 7.1: Some aspects of reflection-in-action

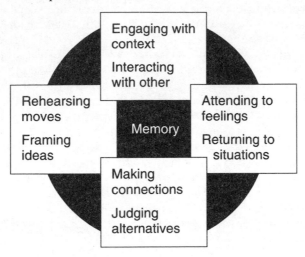

of feelings, and of our processes, are encoded. We also leave various pieces of physical debris. Some traces appear to be lost once we move beyond the immediate moment, others may decay. These traces are representations, clues which can be used later to reconstruct the original in some way or to build something new. What we form can never be a straight reproduction; 'we never recall what actually happened, but only what we think must have happened' (F. Smith 1992: 50). The constructive nature of remembering means that it shares something fundamental with understanding and learning:

> When we look at imagination from a past-tense perspective, we talk of memory. Comprehension is imagination in the present tense, and learning is imagination from the viewpoint of the future. There is no need to postulate separate 'remembering', 'comprehension' and 'learning' processes in the brain. They are simply imagination, perceived and discussed from different vantage points.
>
> (F. Smith 1992: 51–2)

This is not something that can be entirely within an individual, but is an aspect of a dynamic process 'located between person and other (including the context)' (Sampson 1993: 130). In other words, it is situated, local, practical. Further, rather than being contiguous, it is an all-embracing operation that is best seen as a whole – a constellation.

Looking beyond the mirror

To make sense of this we have to look beyond simple mechanical metaphors such as viewing the brain like a computer or the mind as a 'great mirror, containing various representations' (Rorty 1980: 12). We have moved past attempts to reduce thinking and reflection to discrete sets of skills. In this area there is the constant danger of looking at things in an 'ends and means' way. For example, for Kolb, learning is concerned with the production of knowledge: 'Knowledge results from the combination of grasping experience and transforming it' (Kolb 1984: 41). Rather than being knowledge-producing, reflection, as I have tried to approach it, is a process of becoming – a state of being. It is situated. This flows from my view of humans as dialogical beings: 'always in conversation, always in the process of understanding' (Bernstein 1983: 165). We are involved in continuous engagement with others and their work, with situations, with feelings, and with ideas and images. Means and ends are in a reciprocal relationship (Dewey 1948: 74). However, we can easily slip into an individualistic position. Dewey, for example, defined reflective thought as 'active, persistent, and careful consideration of any belief or supposed form of knowledge in the light of the grounds that support it and the further conclusions to which it tends' (Dewey 1987: 118), but this was largely seen as something happening within the person (Cinnamond and Zimpher 1990: 58).

As we engage we create or re-create thoughts, actions and emotions. Thinking does not have a value in and of itself. 'The thinking process is to enable you to reconstruct your environment so that you can act in a different fashion, so that your knowledge lies inside the process and is not a separate affair' (Mead 1936: 350). Reflection, thus, does not occupy a separate place in social processes but is already embedded in them: 'it is inherent in lived experience' (Cinnamond and Zimpher 1990: 63). The real question 'is not in what way being can be understood, but in what way understanding *is* being' (Gadamer 1976: 49).

This way of viewing our 'being in the world' has been a key but not dominant strand in modern western social thought. In that context there has been an undervaluing of other traditions of reflection – of Confucius and Lao Tzu (China), of Gautama (India) or Solomon (Israel). As Houston and Clift (1990: 212) comment:

> When one begins to recognize that reflection can take an Eastern as well as Western approach, to recognize its long and distinguished history, and to recognize that it is not a method nor a technique but a way of life, then one begins to sense the paucity of thought that has too often gone into the conceptualizations of many teacher education programs. One begins, too, to question a conception of teaching that links reflective activity only with problem solving without an equal emphasis on understanding the totality and the unity inherent in the teaching context.

Here we are again brought back to differing notions of selfhood (see Chapter 2). When thinking about thinking we have to be open to the social nature and situatedness of our perspective.

Finally, there are vital questions concerning domination and power. Just as Said has argued about orientalism, the discourses around reflection, while not in a direct link with political power in the raw, are produced in an uneven exchange with various kinds of power. They are

> shaped to a degree by the exchange with the power political (as with a colonial or imperial establishment), power intellectual (as with reigning sciences like comparative linguistics or anatomy, or any of the modern policy sciences), power cultural (as with orthodoxies and canons of taste, texts, values), power moral (as with ideas about what 'we' do and what 'they' cannot do or understand as 'we' do).
>
> (Said 1985: 12)

Here I have tried to bring such concerns to the core. The way I have chosen to do this here, and which makes most sense, is via the frames of reference different people bring to reflection. I have tried to follow Mills's (1959: 225) precept that people should not be seen as isolated fragments.

Triggering reflection

For much of the time we depend on tacit knowledge (Polanyi 1967) – we use ideas, images and examples without being especially aware of them.

> When someone is asked how he would behave under certain circumstances, the answer he usually gives is his espoused theory of action for that situation. This is the theory of action to which he gives allegiance, and which, upon request, he communicates to others. However, the theory that actually governs his actions is his theory-in-use.
>
> (Argyris and Schön 1974: 6–7)

Our theory-in-use may not fit with our espoused theory. Often we are not aware of this. Thus, the role of reflection here is to reveal the theory-in-use and to explore the nature of the 'fit' so that we may further engage with the situation. As Gadamer (1976: 38) put it, 'reflection on a given preunderstanding brings before me something that otherwise happens *behind my back*'.

Thinking begins, according to Dewey (1987: 122), 'in what may fairly enough be called a *forked road* situation that is ambiguous, that presents a dilemma, that proposes alternatives'. More accurately, it is not thinking that begins at such a point, but consciousness of thought. Thinking is not occasional mental activity: 'it goes on all the time, without awareness. Thinking organizes reality for us, and our own place in those realities, and creates alternative realities that we might hope to achieve (or to avoid)' (F. Smith 1992: 30). I have, thus, tended to use 'reflection' instead of 'conscious thought' to contrast with 'commonplace' thinking or what Schön talks about as 'knowing-in-action' – although the usefulness of this distinction in practice is open to question (see Brown and McIntyre 1993: 7).

Workers may talk about moments of disquiet or unease, or of something missing or 'not quite right'. This experience is a spur to exploration.

> Sometimes events trigger things. Sometimes it is a very conscious
> thing. Something begins to happen and I need to think about this.
> Sometimes it is an end product of a sequence of events. The first
> glimmer of light might be 'if I had thought about this three weeks
> ago'. Then you can begin to look back through the process.

One of the things that comes up time and again with workers is the extent
to which they are routinely asking questions of situations.

> I am starting to learn the questions I need to ask myself . . . Trying
> to look at things in a different way . . . So I ask about aims. I ask
> questions about what is happening – did I do the right thing?

This worker was building a framework, a way of viewing the work she did.
She walked into settings already reflecting, ready to ask questions. It is this
quality that many training programmes seek to enhance. In other words,
a 'professional' frame of reference involves a belief in the need to monitor
theory-in-use and to relate it to espoused theory. To this extent, compe-
tent workers arrive at a 'forked road' as they prepare for interaction.
Indeed, experience itself could be described as an oscillating moment 'in
which the human organism alternatively falls out of step with the march
of surrounding things and then recovers unison with it – either through
effort or by some happy chance' (Dewey 1934: 21).

Returning to experience: attending to feelings

Boud *et al.* (1985) reworked Dewey's (1987: 199–209) influential model of
reflective thought (dating from 1933) into three elements:

- *Returning to experience* – that is to say, recalling or detailing salient events.
- *Attending to (or connecting with) feelings* – this has two aspects: using
  helpful feelings and removing or containing obstructive ones.
- *Evaluating experience* – this involves re-examining experience in the
  light of one's intent and existing knowledge and so on. It also involves
  integrating this new knowledge into one's conceptual framework (Boud
  et al. 1985: 26–31).

It is easy to think of these as linear but, as Dewey pointed out, such

> functions of thought . . . do not follow one another in a set order.
> On the contrary, each step in genuine thinking does something to
> perfect the formation of a suggestion and promote its change into
> a leading idea or directive hypothesis.
>
> (Dewey 1987: 206)

In practice phases may telescope, or may be passed over.
The process of 'looking back' is one of re-enactment. We do not look

back to recall what occurred in a particular episode, rather we reconstruct enactments, 'including both the cognitive and affective dimensions' (Richert 1992: 172). In action we may quickly engage with the events and try to pick out key details and feelings. By reconstructing the experience we hope to see further details and patterns. We may also seek to externalize the material, to step outside it and approach it from another angle.

> I can distinctly remember the stirring in me, when for the first time . . . I could actually feel myself drifting away, saying 'something is happening here'. It was significant because at that moment there was revealed my own understanding of a group situation and this particular lad's development.

As well as being situational, this process is state-dependent. When we are happy we tend to reconstruct the good times, when depressed the bad. 'It is often our feelings about past events that we can recall most accurately, in the most detail' (F. Smith 1992: 51). Our disposition – our particular orientation and commitments (motives) and emotions (feelings) – thus has to be a reference point. To understand why we are acting, or acted, in certain ways we have to engage with our commitments and feelings. This may enable us to connect with other ideas and experiences, what some workers describe as using 'gut feeling'.

Intuition and gut feeling

> You get a feeling. Something in the gut tells you something is going down. Do you go in bouncing or do you just pass them . . .? Once you start walking towards that group you can't turn back. You have got to go . . . You are confronted with all these things going on in your head.

Here we can see a worker responding to an apparent 'feeling' – it has entered his consciousness and provoked a response. Perhaps it is something about the others' behaviour or use of words that brings forth images. Unconsciously he may, for example, link the experience with an incident or ordeal in the past. It may simply be that the way the group is standing evokes a sense of something that he has seen before.

To help to see what might be going on it is useful to fall back on Bruner's (1977: 70) distinction between immediate and mediated cognition or apprehension which parallels Dewey's (1929) distinction between 'having' and 'knowing' experience.

> 'Immediate' in this context is contrasted with 'mediated' – apprehension that depends on the intervention of formal methods of analysis and proof. Intuition implies the act of grasping the meaning, significance, or structure of a problem or situation without explicit reliance on the analytical apparatus of one's craft.

In other words, what we usually label as intuition is knowledge or perception not gained through conscious thought or reasoning. It is apparently 'immediate', but that may simply be the surfacing of a thought or image. It may be that a whole chain or process of thinking has taken place without our being alive to it. What we label as intuitive understanding can be better thought of as the outcome of the interaction of our faculties at a largely non-conscious level with the environments, behaviours and feelings that we encounter.

This process can occur with some speed. Without being particularly aware of what is happening we can observe situations, reconstruct something from our repertoire of images and understandings and either 'sense' or make an 'educated guess' as to what is going on. Workers might then label this as 'experiencing an atmosphere'. Here, the worker has to think on the hoof about his approach to the group. Workers may ask themselves what is making them feel a particular way in order to help construct concerns and images. In turn, these can be used to generate a better grasp of the situation and provide for informed action.

Transference and emotions as an integral part of practice

However, there may be more at work in this process. We may be transferring feelings from the past into the present. Freud, in particular, argued that we tend to repeat past patterns of relating in any important relationship. These can be both 'positive' (for example, friendly and affectionate, erotic even) and 'negative' (for example, placing on the other person certain attributes of someone who we believe has done us harm). Both can either assist or get in the way of therapeutic or educative relationships. For example, if neurosis is, as Freud (1914) suggests, a 'compulsion to repeat', then 'by handling the transference responsibly the therapist is able to render the compulsion to repeat harmless, and indeed to turn it into something useful' (Jacobs 1992: 82). Such insights can also be applied to the situations that local educators encounter. The people they work with may also relive in relation to them emotional experiences that they had in their childhood or later (Salzberger-Wittenberg et al. 1983: 32–8). As educators we may be experienced, or seen, as a punishing parent by someone we are working with.

A further problem also creeps in here. There can be a tendency to view emotions and transference negatively, to forget that they are an essential part of practice. Two aspects require comment here. First, there is the question of 'counter-transference'. This is where therapists or, in our case, educators experience a transference response to the other person. Freud only paid limited attention to this area, but it has come to be recognized as valuable (see, for example, Casement 1985: 72–101). By monitoring feelings and thoughts aroused by the other person we can better appreciate what might be going on. Failure to recognize, handle and interpret transference and counter-transference on the part of workers 'can result in blind retaliation – an effort to expel the feelings from consciousness and to punish their source' (Bacon 1988: 187).

Second, we have to appreciate that our emotions are part of our humanity. If we deny our feelings, if we appear like some cold automaton – an educational version of *Star Trek*'s Mr Spock – then we are leaving something of our humanness from our relations with people, and this seriously undermines the character of local education (see Chapter 2). The crucial thing here is that we remain in touch with our capacities. We attend to feelings rather than repress them. The problem is that we cannot generally switch strong feelings on and off to order. It is rather more a case of channelling them or containing them for another place. We need to make our feelings a focus for dialogue.

Our emotions can be a positive aid in another way. They 'drive' us, they can provide us with a positive impetus if harnessed. In the same way, our emotional responses can help us to see events more clearly and can provide the basis for new affective learning. 'Unless we believe in ourselves and our own capabilities we can constrain ourselves to such an extent that we deny ourselves learning opportunities and fail to extract what is available to us in any given situation' (Boud *et al.* 1985: 29). It is in this light that we need to attend to feelings, to utilize the helpful and to contain the obstructive.

Linking the return to experiences and attending to feelings

I have focused on the first two elements of the model of Boud *et al.* (1985) for a number of reasons. First, these two aspects can be linked by workers. For example, one of the striking features of the models of process recording offered to local educators is the way in which talk of feelings is invited (see Little 1994). Description which includes context, interactions, outcomes and the inner processes of the worker, is usually kept apart from analysis, which in turn is separate from further action. Returning to experiences and attending to feelings falls squarely into the first category. Workers are encouraged to link the two and to keep them separate from 'analysis'. This pattern is reinforced by supervision which also attends to emotions (see Gardiner 1989; Hawkins and Shohet 1989). This is partly because it draws so heavily on psychoanalytical and counselling insights.

Second, the way Boud *et al.* (1985: 30–4) approach re-evaluating experience and preparing for action brings out an important danger. Their focus on 'deliberate' learning (1985: 18) does tend to act against an appreciation of reflection as a way of life. As Cinnamond and Zimpher (1990: 67) put it, 'they constrain reflection by turning it into a mental activity that excludes both the behavioural element and dialogue with others involved in the situation'. In part this may flow from their focus on reflection-on-action – and their use of Dewey – but it also highlights again the danger of looking to what happens within people rather than between them.

Connecting and judging

Re-enacting and developing, as imaginative performances, entail making connections and judgements. However, workers may well draw a line between 'description' of an event and analysis. When recording interactions, this line is often physically drawn on the page – with workers recounting the events and their thinking and feeling at the time on one side of the page, and subsequent analysis on the other (see Rogers 1982).

Connecting

> Only connect! That was the whole of her sermon. Only connect the prose and the passion, and both will be exalted, and human love will be seen at its highest. Live in fragments no longer. Only connect, and the beast and the monk, robbed of the isolation that is life to either, will die.
>
> (Forster 1975: 188)

Forster was much concerned with the relationships, and the chance of reconciliation, between pairs of opposites: 'the seen and the unseen, the practical mind and the intellectual, the outer life and the inner' (Stallybrass 1975: 10). Something of the same spirit is abroad here. Workers may build up repertoires of examples, images, understandings and actions and draw upon these. Yet connections are made not only with repertoires, but also with people's frames of reference, and with faint memory traces. Also, immediate physical items like notes and pictures, and interaction with others in the situation can be used. 'Something struck a chord with me. In the back of my mind I was thinking this really relates to so-and-so.' The act of connecting is not like simple data retrieval. It involves imagining, linking and playing with various elements.

In action, we might make a link, might see that there is something about a situation that is similar to, but also different from, some other event, feeling or idea.

> I thought 'I have been here before', this reminds me of someone. As she talked I began to see a picture of her. But it wasn't her now, it was her as a 10- or 11-year-old. It was something about the way she was sitting, the way she sat on her hands. I had this picture of a child – and I knew that there was something here, something I had to get to. [F]

Here the worker has a picture, but not a clear reading of what this relates to. To move on we have to act on a tentative assessment. We can experiment with and test our interpretation in action. In other words, we can frame our actions in such a way as to hold on to the temporary or experimental nature of our thinking. We can engage with the ensuing events and processes, and make further connections.

Workers may draw on material from widely different contexts. Here, two dimensions stand out. First, ideas and images are only useful if we can get at them. The way in which we organize our experiences is crucial – and here the notion of repertoire is helpful. We also need to enhance our ability to remake material. Second, the process involves workers in a conversation with situations. They have to be open to interaction, and able to reframe experiences with regard to what has gone before and what might come. These they then test and remake to fit more closely the particular.

So how do ideas come? 'How is the imagination spurred to put all the images and facts together, to make images relevant and lend meaning to facts?' (Mills 1959: 211). In much the same way as Mills talks about the sociological imagination, we can think about reflection-in-action. The former, he argues, consists in large part of the capacity to shift from one perspective to another, and in the process build up a fuller picture. It can be cultivated.

> [C]ertainly it seldom occurs without a great deal of often routine work. Yet there is an unexpected quality about it, perhaps because its essence is the combination of ideas that no one expected were combinable . . . There is a playfulness of mind . . . as well as a truly fierce drive to make sense of the world which the technician as such usually lacks.
>
> (Mills 1959: 211)

Paradoxically, this process seems, for a number of workers, to involve a kind of 'letting go'.

> One of the things that I have come to realize is that I work too hard sometimes. I want to understand fully, so I look for the details. Over the years I have tried to stand back – not so much to be detached as to allow my mind to wander. I don't mean thinking about shopping lists or the jobs I have got to do. What I mean is that you sort of let what is happening float over you – you pick out odd words, or actions, or shapes. You ask who or what this reminds you of.

In this way images and ideas are released, and we may begin a particular routine or train of action.

Judging

As workers spoke about these matters, the idea that 'connecting' was in a dynamic and special relationship with 'judging' made more sense. We can see something of this in the way this worker talks about supervision:

> Once you start asking questions, invariably you are thinking of answers. I found that through supervision . . . those answers would be tested and tested quite strong. If I was offering my own theory, the question would be why? Very often when you start talking out loud some of my theories weren't necessarily that near the mark.

When we then add in the ability that workers may develop to 'supervise' themselves as they work – what Casement (1985: 29–56) calls the 'internal supervisor' – then we have a powerful form.

> I do it by talking to myself. I do a lot of that anyway. I step outside and talk to myself, I supervise myself from outside. There is a definite standing away from and talking myself out of it. Perhaps it is the outside me knowing that I have been through this before.

This is a very strong image and demonstrates the extent to which under-standings derive from participation in a community of practitioners (Carr and Kemmis 1986). The notion of an 'internal supervisor' is an acknow-ledgement or embodiment of shared notions and intimations of what makes for the good.

We subject our emerging ideas or images to various 'tests'.

> It is also about learning how to question stuff . . . In particular, about how you judge stuff. The judgement I make is based on what people say to me. I need to check that out and by questioning in an ap-propriate manner and not by challenging the [person] . . . in terms of personality but in looking at what happened. It is about what is actually being done, not about the individual who is doing it.

Workers mentioned several questions which they used as means of judg-ing. For example:

- What is it exactly that I am 'saying'?
- What evidence do I have for this and how good is the evidence?
- How does this fit with what I believe happened, what I felt and what I know?
- How does this relate to my values and beliefs?
- What does this mean for further action?

These frameworks emerge through reflection, supervision and discussion with other practitioners (Smith 1994). As one worker put it in relation to a group to which she belonged:

> We are beginning to get a structure for questions – aims, what is your role, how do you think the other people saw you, what do you think they saw their role as, what were you feeling – we seem to go through a set of questions. I don't know how it happened – it just developed.

Here I need to underline four points. First, what we can see here is an emerging frame of reference. By engaging with this, workers can inform judgements with their values and ideas about well-being. In other words, they can engage in a form of practical reasoning. Second, there is an orientation to action. This is, perhaps, an obvious point – after all, we are talking about reflection-in-action. But it does have a profound impact.

> Suddenly you have this coathanger to hang on how we analyse cer-tain situations . . . Then you realize 'Oh I never thought of it like that . . .'.

Understandings are not much use if they do not help educators to think about their actions and what informs them. Third, the conclusions drawn are often very tentative. As one worker put it:

> Suddenly it would be dead clear. And then all of a sudden it would go.

Finally, the images and understandings we use are shared in important ways with others – these local educators participate in a community of practice (Smith 1994).

Framing and rehearsing

Out of the reflective process come ways of thinking and acting that 'make sense' for the situation. 'Making sense' involves fitting the new alongside that which already exists. To do this we have to evoke in various ways particular frames of reference which link to our identity as practitioners. We also have to 'frame' problems:

> The learner has to construct a frame that will encompass the new knowledge but can only do so with the aid of an old frame, which may assimilate the new or conflict with it. If the new ideas or experiences challenge the learner's existing frame, then that frame will need to be revised, thus accommodating the unfamiliar: the world will never appear quite the same again.
>
> (Barnes 1992: 20)

This is not simply an individual act: in interaction the parties have to work to construct a common frame or horizon (see next chapter).

Placing and framing

Seeing possibility in our thoughts and images, we seek to place them in relation to the fabric of our acting and thinking (Brookfield 1987b: 27). We appropriate them or make them our 'own'. That which we cannot take on may be ignored or *placed* on one side. This process of placing is central to the building up of a repertoire. Elements that cannot be taken on can be held on one side. Judgement is suspended until they can be used as an exemplar or metaphor in another situation, or until further relevant data appear. We have to live with the ambiguity (Rosaldo 1993: 92). Appropriation may take the form of a stuttering step forward, a tentative understanding. On other occasions it may involve the transformation of perspectives (Mezirow 1990: 124–8) or the affirmation of existing views. Whether temporary or transformative, the action is one of owning, of taking something for one's own use. In other words, we move beyond knowing about something and understanding it, into acceptance and a readiness to use the learning. We are framing our feelings, actions and understandings. The introduction of a new or strengthened element alters the overall shape and feel of our practice and the way we see things. Here I am following Goffman (1986) and using the notion of frame as a scheme of interpretation in which the particulars of the activities, experiences, understandings and feelings to which we attend are organized and made sensible. The patterns and connections we have made are given a further review and are shaped. This framing process can be seen at work both in respect of particular problems or situations, and in relation to practitioners' overall frame of reference (FOR). In turn, the way in which we frame situations alters our experience of them. This, again, can affirm or otherwise our overall sense of ourselves as workers.

Frames of reference

The overall FOR is crucial to the process of reflection and to practice.

> I have got a few, different, kinds of structures in my head. I always have a structure somewhere because I have got to have something to gel the work, but it is very flexible, because I am the one who is in control, and I can wiggle it about and alter it to the needs of whoever I am working with.

These structures can be given by the sorts of elements we looked at in Chapter 4. Ideas about role, purpose, strategy and issues help to build up a frame of reference. Crucially, we also talked there about disposition – an appeal to a whole set of ideas, feelings, values and images about what makes for the good. Taken together, these things form the setting in which workers can construct and assign meaning to what they do. They are both individual and shared. They take certain typical forms; they are shaped within specific historic and social circumstances.

People's FORs as workers are born of the interplay between their own social and cultural identities and resources, and those running through the various strands of local education. As Brown (1987: 34) has argued in relation to schooling, FORs 'are not only constructed on the basis of past experience, but also include a projection into the future'. This provides people with a sense of continuity. The FOR draws on memories to sustain itself. It is also used to help organize images, ideas, feelings and actions into an associated repertoire. Individuals (and groups) may have a number of FORs which relate to specific contexts. As parents they may take on one frame, as educators another. In each they may draw on the 'same' image or memory of an event, but it is interpreted through a different frame. This is a key point. Repertoires are linked to specific FORs. We do not have one massive repertoire called 'memory'. Rather we have a series of overlapping repertoires which are organized by our FORs.

These frames are shaped within asymmetrical relations of power and use elements from different cultures and traditions. The experiences to be worked on will also be diverse. Just how roles or purposes are cast, for example, will vary as a result. Workers will draw upon assorted traditions of thinking and acting. We can begin to see why debates involving conflicting frames are often not easily resolvable. People 'pay attention to different facts and make different sense of the facts they notice' (Schön 1987: 5).

This touches on one of the weaknesses of Schön's work on reflection-in-action. He tends to focus on a thinking/action process. He creates, arguably, 'a descriptive concept, quite empty of content' (Richardson 1990: 14). While he does look at values and interpretative systems, it is the idea of repertoire that comes to the fore. In other words, what he tends to look at is the process of framing and the impact of frame-making on situations:

> As [inquirers] frame the problem of the situation, they determine the features to which they will attend, the order they will attempt to impose on the situation, the directions in which they will try to change it. In this process, they identify both the ends to be sought and the means to be employed.
>
> (Schön 1983: 165)

The ability to draw upon a repertoire of metaphors and images which allow for different ways of framing a situation is clearly important to creative practice and is a crucial insight. We can easily respond in inappropriate ways in situations through the use of an ill-suited frame. However, what we also must hold in view is the relation of the frame to our FOR.

In the dynamic between our FORs and the images, ideas and feelings that form our repertoires lies the possibility of perspective transformation. And it is in this interplay that many of the constraints to critical thought occur.

> [R]eflection is not a free process ... there are social pressures that constrain the manner by which people think and which, consequently, result in conformity in the outcomes of learning ... Mezirow, almost alone among the theorists of reflection, has recognized that one element in becoming critically aware is being aware of the processes that constrain the thinking process.
>
> (Jarvis 1987: 109)

The task is not so much, as Dewey (1987: 116) said, to rise above traditions but to place ourselves in relation to them (see Chapter 8).

To take account of what has been said, I have redrawn Figure 7.1 so that the process of reflection is grounded in people's FORs and involves their 'repertoires' (see Figure 7.2). This allows us to approach reflective thought as an ethical-political phenomenon, as an expression of practical reasoning (see Chapter 8), rather than as a descriptive concept.

Rehearsing moves

When I first used early versions of this model with workers, one response was that it did not give rehearsal enough emphasis. This is also an aspect that Louden (1991: 168–72) emphasizes in his study of classroom reflection. As a result, I have brought it out into the open. Workers talked of running through the moves they might make before carrying them out. In

Figure 7.2: Reflecting-in-action

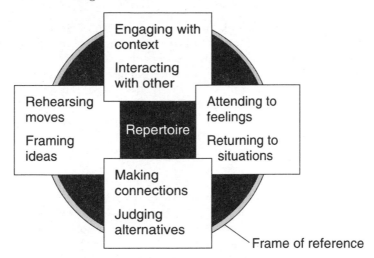

other words, they were imagining possible responses to the tactics they might employ (see Chapter 4).

> I know I often run through what might happen, think of a couple of possible lines. This isn't so much in the middle of things as near the start. Or when something comes up. You think, 'I've got to be careful here.'

These moves depend on how workers frame their next step. Central to this is the nature of their aim. In thinking about this, Schön's, and Dewey's, view of experimentation is helpful. Of course, many actions that workers take are not designed, or thought about, as experiments. However, to reflect-in-action is to play a game with the situation. In this respect, Schön (1987: 70–3) sets out three kinds of experiment: exploratory; move-testing; and hypothesis-testing. When an action is undertaken only to see what follows, this is exploratory. It is 'the probing, playful activity by which we get a feel for things' (1987: 70). With move-testing, workers take action more carefully and have definite aims. They watch to see whether the intended effect comes about. They also determine whether they like this effect in terms of the values, beliefs and commitments they hold (Noordhoff and Kleinfeld 1990: 174). The third form, hypothesis-testing, is where they want to build an explanation. They look for evidence to confirm or refute different explanations. The key point here is that when workers reflect-in-action, and pay attention to the aspects we have looked at in this chapter, then their 'experimenting is at once exploratory, move testing and hypothesis testing. The three functions are fulfilled by the same actions' (Schön 1987: 72).

Engaging and interacting

The last aspect in our constellation involves engaging with the context and interacting with the other(s). I have linked these two together partly because of the way in which some workers talk about their practice: in thinking about their actions they are looking to what other people are saying and doing, and the context in which these arise. However, they also come together in some discussions of the 'other' – where both people and context are treated as dimensions of otherness (see, for example, Sampson 1993: 130). I really do not need to say much about this area as we have spent a lot of time on it already, although I do want to underline several points.

First, when reflecting-in-action we do not leave the situation. However, there may be moments when we disengage to some extent – we 'stand outside the flow'. We might not contribute to a conversation for a few minutes as we listen and try to work out what is going on. We might make interventions that keep the ball rolling, but do not involve us in sustained overt interaction. In this respect our reflection-in-action has to be experienced by others as 'natural' or as valuing them. It should not impede conversation (see Chapter 3). Second, the foci here are on context and interaction. There is a movement back and forth between the two as we use ideas about one to question the other. If we do not hold on to both, we can easily be trapped into a way of viewing the world that disconnects experiences from the contexts in which they arise. In other words, we can lose touch with the situatedness of the experience and the extent to which it is socially constructed. It involves coming to a social understanding.

> [W]hat goes on in interaction is governed by usually unstated rules or principles more or less implicitly set by the character of some larger, though perhaps invisible entity (for example, 'the definition of the situation') 'within' which the interaction occurs.
>
> (Berger 1986: xiii)

As Berger goes on to comment, 'more or less' is a key phrase as the nature of the definition (or framing) of the situation is not always clear. Even when it is, 'participants in interaction may have interests in blurring, changing or confounding it' (1986: xiv). Third, the focus on interaction is crucial. It takes us beyond an 'embodied' notion of reflection and allows us to develop a fully social appreciation.

Zigzagging, the whole and the parts

These aspects are rarely distinct in practice. They overlap and interconnect; the sequencing alters; and some elements will be accorded more attention than others. We can see this movement and flux in this account a worker gives of a demanding situation:

What more could you have done . . . I tell myself off a bit. I go back, I was looking at what had happened to him, thinking, and asking myself what could you have done to change that. And answering, well there is nothing I could have done. What could have been different about tonight? I didn't want to hear all those awful things that were done to that person. Well, how do you think you are going to help the person if you don't listen to what he needed to offload? That sort of thing. The same I would do if a friend had come in. I think I treat myself as a friend then and ask myself questions. I can argue back because I have this feeling of guilt about it.

As Gadamer (1976) asks, in the flux of appearances, in the constant flood of changing impressions, how does anything like permanence come about?

Surely it is first of all the capacity of retention, namely, memory, that allows us to recognize something as the same, and that is the first great achievement of abstraction. Out of the flux of appearances a common factor is spied here and there, and thus, out of accumulating recognitions that we call experience, the unity of experience slowly emerges.

(Gadamer 1976: 63)

In this way we form and develop our FORs and their linked repertoires. There is movement between the various elements and the whole.

Hopping back and forth between the whole conceived through the parts that actualize it and the parts conceived through the whole that motivates them, we seek to turn them, by a sort of intellectual perpetual motion, into explications of one another.

(Geertz 1983: 69)

This movement is a classic expression of hermeneutics – of understanding as dialogue. As Yinger (1990: 82) put it, the conversation metaphor 'expresses the multifaceted give-and-take nature of human thought. Thinking is responsive interchange between thought and action, between the organism and the environment.'

Within each of the elements, too, a zigzagging occurs. There is movement between situations and interactions; the return to experience and feelings; connecting and judging; and between framing and rehearsing. The zigzagging parallels what Erikson has described as free-floating attention in psychoanalysis. It 'turns inward to the observer's ruminations while remaining turned outward to the field of observations and which, far from focusing on any one item too intentionally, rather waits to be impressed by recurring themes' (Erikson 1959, quoted in Schön 1987: 224). We need to listen for talkback from the situation, ready to be impressed by recurring themes. We have to hold on to several dimensions of experience at any one time.

Erikson's comments highlight a danger. Reflecting-in-action does not mean putting our brains into overdrive. Rather, it is to allow a space for ideas and feelings to surface, be entertained and worked on. In conversations, rather than trying to follow the minute twists and turns of content, we might listen first to the form of the communication (for instance, its sheer weight or volume) (Casement 1985: 43). As Bion (1974: 37) has commented, instead of trying to bring 'a brilliant, intelligent, knowledgeable light to bear on obscure problems', perhaps we should turn down our illumination. Where there is a faint or flickering light, it is best revealed by creating darkness.

'Non-reflective' practice

As we begin to look at this model we can also see some of the jumps that we make. Here I want to comment on three examples of non-reflective, but not necessarily limited, practice.

Mechanical practice or routines

Non-reflective practice tends to occur when there is a straight up-and-down movement between interacting with others and connection with repertoire. 'Goals, values and strategies are simply taken for granted and the emphasis is on techniques and making techniques more efficient; it operates within a closed and self-confirming world of understandings' (Usher and Bryant 1989: 87). What occurs is only a limited, almost non-conscious, judgement and connection. The experience is not returned to in any detail, feelings are left unattended and a mark is hardly left on the memory (and certainly not on the overall frame). It is akin to what Argyris and Schön (1974) have labelled theories-in-use. What they describe as a 'single loop' occurs. This can be contrasted with a 'double loop' where sustained reflection is triggered and changes are made to framing (Argyris and Schön 1974: 18–19).

If workers *only* operated at a mechanical level then there would be a problem; but there would be a problem if they *never* operated mechanically. As Louden (1991) has argued, teaching is a struggle to establish a settled practice, a set of routines and patterns of actions to handle different situations. 'Non-reflective' practice in this sense is a necessary aspect of interaction. When considering practice we have to take care not to expend all our energies on the problematic and non-routine.

Leaving unfinished business

Another possibility occurs when the movement is between direct experience and framing. Here practitioners may simply 'deposit' raw strips of experience in memory and alter their framing only so far as to note the presence of the new data. In other words, material is not immediately explored. There may be times when practitioners attend to feelings and revisit experiences and 'jump' to framing (the horizontal movement), leaving out any consistent attempt to connect with their repertoire and frame of reference. At other times they may be struggling with a problem, attempting to make connections, which they place 'on hold', unable to name relationships and hold shapes. Later, with extra data, things may fall into place. Alternatively, in the interim period, the process put on hold in the conscious domain continues to operate within the unconscious.

> You are in a session and you recognize that this is my stuff and you have got to deal with it later. In supervision you can go and get it when you want it. The other stuff is when your little light lights up. When your supervisor has been questioning you and you haven't quite caught on. And he'll say 'Let's leave it.' And because it is in my mind, when something happens, 'Oh now I understand that.'

Here the worker deliberately leaves unfinished business, because it is her own, and dealing with it at that moment would get in the way of work with the other person. We can see, too, the impact of leaving a question or idea in the mind – what we often call 'sleeping on it'. Dewey describes this well.

> Then after the mind has ceased to be intent on the problem, and consciousness has relaxed its strain, a period of incubation sets in. Material rearranges itself; facts and principles fall into place; what was confused becomes bright and clear; the mixed-up becomes or- derly, often to such an extent that the problem is essentially solved.
> (Dewey 1987: 345)

Focusing on parts
There are also situations when there is inadequate movement or zigzagging between the paired elements. We have already commented upon two instances of this. The first is where there is a failure to link the cognitive and affective domains – for example, where we return to experiences, but leave feelings unattended. A second occurs where in interaction we place an excessive emphasis upon individualized exchanges with people at the cost of developing a fully social engagement with the situation. In other words, where we focus on some aspect of a person's experience and fail to appreciate the way in which that experience is constructed and has meaning as part of a greater social whole.

There are a number of other patterns that we could etch out. These include memorization and simply skimming across the surface of all the elements (see Jarvis 1987). However, for now, these examples should suffice.

In conclusion

Reflecting-in-action involves more than decision-making. It includes processes such as imagining, remembering, interpreting, judging, caring and feeling (Buchman 1990: 43). The process is rarely mechanical or

confined to one plane. We conjure up images and metaphors, and fragments of conversations; we recall stories and emotions; and we bring to
bear what theories we possess. We place these alongside the situations we
encounter and the experiences they generate. At the same time, we throw
these into a dialogue with our individual, and shared, values, purpose and
role.

Such processes cannot be repeated in full for everything we do. We
have to take certain things as read. We have to fall back on routines in
which previous thought and sentiment have been sedimented (see Chapter 3). It is here that the full importance of reflection-on-action becomes
clear. As we think and act, questions arise that cannot be answered in the
present. The space afforded by recording, supervision and conversation
with our peers allows us to approach these. Reflection requires space in
the present and the promise of space in the future.

Chapter 8

Fostering community, conversation and praxis

As I hinted in the Introduction, my interest in community, conversation and praxis springs from a particular ethical-political position. In this concluding chapter I want, in the light of my conversations with local educators, to return to three key ideas.

Community

Groups and social networks, as we saw in Chapter 6, allow people to grow, to work together and to amuse themselves, but they also have the capacity to constrain and exclude. They can be the arena for petty jealousies, the means of organizing against different groups in the community, and can be used to control the activities of their members. Sometimes this is desirable, as when seeking to ensure that children are able to play in safety around an estate; often it is odious, for example, when people group together to make life difficult for neighbours of another race or with a different lifestyle. There is a need to cultivate everyday practices which embody thought for others and social justice, and a key starting point is people's experience of local groups.

Local groups can benefit their members in a number of ways. First, they provide a means by which people with common interests or concerns can exchange information and specialist products. This can range from enthusiast groups such as those around model-building to self-help groups, for example, linked with anorexia nervosa. They also provide the space for collective rather than individual projects (such as art exhibitions, campaigning or team sports). Finally, they

provide opportunities for making friends and meeting people, suggesting that the substantive activity itself may be of secondary
importance . . . For many organizations this purely social dimension
to their existence may not be quite legitimate to discuss openly but
may shape their final identity far more than the nature and rules of
their ostensible leisure activity.

(Bishop and Hoggett 1986: 33)

Such groups also have a number of features which make them a vital
part of any democracy (see Smith, M. K. 1992). They have an associational
structure: officers, committees and a way of working which allows members a say. Further, they are a window on to larger political processes.
Often they have been formed to campaign – for example, to protect the
interests of residents on an estate. They also have to relate to their own
regional, national or international bodies. In these ways, local organizations provide the means through which most people engage with the
traditional political arena (Entwistle 1981). These associations are not just
the cement of civil society, they hold the possibility of being the primary
means of organizing social life (Hirst 1993: 117). Community groups and
organizations usually carry within them some valuing of co-operation, a
commitment to those in membership, and some understanding of the
need for engaging in educational activity. Of crucial importance here is
the extent to which they help sustain friendships. As Aristotle (1976: 258)
argued, friendship seems to be the bond that holds communities together.

Many community groups may be thought of as mutual aid organizations
in themselves. They involve people joining together to produce goods and
services for their own enjoyment. The basis is reciprocity, and relationships are informed by ideas of 'give and take' (Bishop and Hoggett 1986).
In short, local groups and associations provide both a means of taking
part in political life and a way of learning about it. As Freire has said of
Brazil:

People could learn social and political responsibility only by *experiencing* that responsibility, through intervention in the destiny of their
children's schools, in the destinies of their trade unions and places
of employment, through associations, clubs and councils, and in the
life of their neighbourhoods, churches and rural communities by
actively participating in associations, clubs and charitable societies.

(Freire 1974: 36)

The rationale for local educators working to build up relationships and
networks is clear. In so doing they help to develop groups and organizations which allow people to be and work together so that they may meet
their needs and flourish. In this there is a care for democracy. Because
such institutions exist over time they can carry forward relationships and
projects; they can engage with wider systems. Just as schools need to be defined as public spaces 'that seek to recapture the idea of critical democracy

and community' (Giroux 1989: 201), so local groups have to be similarly developed.

Fostering a sense of community

Education is not simply about skills and knowledge. It is also about commitment and hence the concern of some to foster a 'sense of community'. This is, in part, to cultivate a sense of belonging to a place, a plank for construction of self-identity. It is also to encourage a commitment to other human beings, to their needs and wishes. This we may describe as solidarity with others.

> Part of the role I have defined for myself is to harmonize what is going on in the neighbourhood. To get a good neighbourhood feel, to make people proud of living where they are. The feeling I have I would like to share with other people.

The traditional way of spelling this out, as Rorty (1989: 189) puts it, is to say that there is something in each of us – our essential humanity – 'which resonates to the presence of this same thing in other human beings'. Rorty doubts this 'essential' quality and argues that solidarity is a goal to be achieved by imagination. It has to be learnt and is necessary if people are to develop. Thus, educators should be working so that people's own needs are not automatically given preferential treatment, but weighed in relation to the needs and wishes of others (White 1982: 98).

> A lot of it is having contact with a group and it is just a matter of challenging – their attitudes, maybe their lifestyles, making them aware of where they are in the community. That sort of work can go on with any group, anywhere.

At one level it does not matter whether solidarity and co-operativeness are learnt or innate qualities. What is innate still has to be cultivated and added to. At another level it is important. If the feeling of human solidarity is 'deeply lodged in men's understanding and heart, because it has been nurtured by all our preceding evolution' (Kropotkin 1939: 229), then there is a deep disposition to co-operation. In this respect, the co-ordination found in social interaction provides strong evidence, against Rorty, for unlearnt processes.

> In many ways human nature is co-operative. We are more like ants and wolves than like cats. We readily join groups and form attachments, and receive powerful biological and emotional rewards for doing so. Our co-operative tendencies are culturally universal, partly innate, the result of evolution.
>
> (Argyle 1991: 247)

If this is the case, then there is something in us all that can be appealed to to form the basis for conversation and the formation of community. This quality may be suppressed or distorted, but it does provide hope.

'That which is held in common': culture and tradition

> Men live in a community in virtue of the things which they have in
> common; and communication is the way in which they come to pos-
> sess things in common. What they must have in common to form a
> community or society are aims, beliefs, aspirations, knowledge – a com-
> mon understanding – like-mindedness as the sociologists would say.
>
> (Dewey 1966: 4)

While working for common understanding is a necessary part of sustaining community, as we saw in Chapter 2, we have to be mindful of the
extent to which it can act to marginalize and exclude the voices of subordinate groups. As Giroux (1992: 32) has argued, 'the central values of a
democratic revolution – freedom, equality, liberty and justice – must provide the principles by which differences are affirmed within rather than
outside of a politics of solidarity forged through public spheres'. To affirm
difference and work for solidarity involves us in a careful exploration of
the cultures and traditions that touch our lives.

We may think of traditions as clusters of customs, thoughts, beliefs,
artefacts and practices which are handed down from one generation to
the next. They give people a place in the world and provide concrete ways
of dealing with things. For example, one worker talked of groups 'still
immersed in their tradition', another of having to deal with 'layers of
tradition'. At times this is seen as a problem, something in the way of
needed change; at other times as a positive quality. The various elements
of a tradition, and the way they relate to each other, are distinctive. Traditions can, thus, be seen as 'establishing or symbolizing social cohesion
or the membership of groups, real or artificial communities' (Hobsbawm
1983: 9). In other words, they are those elements of cultures which are
seen as part of the common inheritance of social groups.

It is easy to fall into the trap of thinking that culture is a living, changing
phenomenon and that tradition is fixed. In reality, traditions also change
and, indeed, are invented. Traditions in this sense involve a conscious
attempt to pass on a coherent set of practices to others. They 'inculcate
certain values and norms of behaviour by repetition, which automatically
implies continuity with the past' (Hobsbawm 1983: 1). Examples of invented
traditions are the rituals surrounding the royal family in Britain (Cannadine
1983) or scouting (Ranger 1983: 226).

We can never fully distance or free ourselves from what has been transmitted from the 'past'. Nor should we want to.

> Rather, we stand always within tradition, and this is no objectifying
> process, i.e. we do not conceive of what tradition says as something
> other, something alien. It is always part of us, a model or exemplar,
> a recognition of ourselves which our later historical judgment would
> hardly see as a kind of knowledge, but as the simplest preservation
> of tradition.
>
> (Gadamer 1979: 250)

It is in and through the encounter with that which is handed 'down' to us through tradition that we discover which of our prejudices (prejudgements) are oppressive and which are enabling.

The significance of tradition for educators was well recognized by Gramsci (1971) – as, indeed, it was by Dewey. Cultural creativity 'requires that the would-be innovator take a tradition into himself' (Entwistle 1979: 46). Approaching tradition, 'making the familiar strange', and enabling people to make judgements about themselves and the cultures of which they are a part are concerns among local educators (see Chapter 6). Traditions do not have any special authority – they have no special claims to truth – but because they are so much a part of our lives their influence can go unquestioned. Reflection brings things to awareness so that they may be confronted, and then accepted or thrown out (Gadamer 1976: 34). While educators may focus on fostering environments for learning, they also need to think carefully about what might be learnt. Otherwise 'education gets reduced to words without sense' (Entwistle 1979: 49).

Yet it is not only one's own culture or traditions that are important. Many 'progressive' educators shy away from examining the extent to which it is necessary for people to engage with supposedly elitist or dominating traditions of thought (Donald 1992: 141). This is the challenge that Gramsci, in particular, sets us. He dismissed work which failed to enable people to approach established systems of thought. People have to analyse and think on a par with the intellectual traditions they must overcome. To do this we need to gain certain habits: diligence, precision, poise. We also have to learn to concentrate on specific subjects. This, Gramsci argues, 'cannot be achieved without the mechanical repetition of disciplined and mechanical acts' (Gramsci 1971: 37). All this has a conservative feel – it is a view of learning that can be linked with what Freire described as 'banking'. 'Education becomes an act of depositing, in which the students are the depositories and the teacher is the depositor. Instead of communicating, the teacher issues communiqués and "makes deposits"' (Freire 1972: 43–4). Yet there is the danger here of thinking in simplistic dichotomies between 'traditional' and 'progressive', 'banking' and 'problem-posing', 'subjects' and 'topics'. This has been the problem of primary education in the UK. It has also bedevilled local education, particularly through the unthinking adoption of Freirian approaches. Indeed, it is a problem that goes to the heart of the Freirian project. As Alexander et al. (1992: 5) put it (after Dewey 1963) with regard to primary education, 'the move to a more mature and balanced discussion of the issues is long overdue'.

Problems with community

The idea of 'community' has a range of meanings for workers. Lindeman's (1921: 14–15) classic statement of what an ideal community should furnish to its human constituents – order, economic well-being, physical well-being, constructive use of leisure time, ethical standards, intellectual diffusion, free avenues of expression, democratic forms of association and spiritual motivation – indicates how widely debates can range. It is also worth noting some of the abuses to which the concept is put. 'Community' can be used very selectively – for example, one study of adult education (Newman 1979: 197–209) found it commonly used in six ways. Community equals:

- the working class;
- quiescent poor;
- the disadvantaged;
- the 'whole community';
- acceptable community; and
- society.

It is easy to make sweeping statements about 'the community' based on contact with just a few people. This is especially so when it concerns the experiences of very disparate groups. Also, being such a 'warm' word, community can be used to good effect. Many policy developments in the 1980s had the word placed in front of them to smooth their path: community care, community charge, community policing, and so on (Willmott 1989: 21–31).

One response is to avoid using the word. For example, Stacey (1960; Stacey et al. 1975) gave up on it as a 'non-concept' and instead studied local social systems. Others have explored community as a symbolic construction. As Cohen (1985: 12) says, 'community' involves two related suggestions: that the members of a group have something in common with each other; and that this sets them apart in significant ways from others. We can, thus, look at how people define themselves: the boundaries they draw around 'their' community and the symbols they use to mark that boundary. I have not avoided the word – it has such a central place in the vocabulary of local educators. However, I have tried to be more specific: I have looked to the sense in which the word is used. Thus, I have referred to localities or neighbourhoods (community as place); networks (community as social system); solidarity and co-operativeness (sense of community); and tradition and culture (community as that which is held in common). As we have seen, concepts like 'local' (see Chapter 1) and 'network' (see Chapter 6) allow for greater rigour. They also allow us to focus on the interaction of individuals and institutions in specific areas (Bell and Newby 1971: 49). At the same time, the word clearly has meaning for practitioners and for those with whom they work. It is not simply a place where they work, it is something that they seek to approach and foster.

Conversation

Conversation is also not just the means which local educators use, it is also a quality they want to cultivate in local life. A 'humane collective life depends on vulnerable forms of innovation-bearing, reciprocal and unforcedly egalitarian everyday communication' (Habermas 1985: 82). Since Socrates' debates with the Sophist philosophers, the differences between dialogue as a practice which can be described, and as an ideal, have not always been appreciated (Maranhão 1990: 5). Part of the confusion arises because when we discuss dialogue as an ideal we tend to use the language of description (1990: 9).

Horizons of understanding

'Dialogue', Freire says, 'is the encounter between men, mediated by the world, in order to name the world' (Freire 1972: 61). Gadamer describes conversation thus:

> [It] is a process of two people understanding each other. Thus it is a characteristic of every true conversation that each opens himself to the other person, truly accepts his point of view as worthy of consideration and gets inside the other to such an extent that he understands not a particular individual, but what he says. The thing that has to be grasped is the objective rightness or otherwise of his opinion, so that they can agree with each other on a subject.
>
> (Gadamer 1979: 347)

In conversation, knowledge is not a fixed thing or commodity to be grasped. It is, rather, an aspect of a process. We bring prejudices (or prejudgements) to these encounters. We each have our own 'horizon of understanding'. This is 'the range of vision that includes everything that can be seen from a particular vantage point' (Gadamer 1979: 143). With these prejudgements and understandings we involve ourselves in what is being said. In conversation we try to understand a horizon that is not our own in relation to our own. We have to put our own prejudices (prejudgements) and understandings to the test.

> Only by seeking to learn from the 'other', only by fully grasping its claims upon one can it be critically encountered. Critical engaged dialogue requires opening of oneself to the full power of what the 'other' is saying. Such an opening does not entail agreement but rather the to-and-fro play of dialogue.
>
> (Bernstein 1991: 4)

We seek to discover other people's standpoint and horizon. As we do so their ideas become intelligible, without our necessarily having to agree with them (Gadamer 1979: 270), and we can come to terms with the other (Crowell 1990: 358). The concern is not to 'win the argument' but to advance understanding and human well-being. This can be found in the way this worker talked about conversation:

> I am not trying to get him to see things my way . . . It would be great if he did change his view and he did understand what I was saying.

What do I want to do? I would just like him to see the other side of
the story.

Agreement cannot be imposed, but rests on common conviction (Habermas
1984: 285–7). In this, the understanding we bring from the past is tested
in encounters with the present and forms what we take into the future
(Louden 1991: 106). We experience a 'fusion of horizons'.

> The horizon of the present is being continually formed, in that we
> have continually to test all our prejudices. An important part of that
> testing is the encounter with the past and the understanding of the
> tradition from which we come . . . In a tradition this process of
> fusion is continually going on, for there old and new continually
> grow together to make something of living value, without either
> being explicitly distinguished from the other.
>
> (Gadamer 1979: 273)

Whether 'fusion' is quite the right word is a matter of debate. It does not
quite fit the 'ruptures that disturb our attempts to reconcile different
ethical-political horizons' (Bernstein 1991: 10). However, what we do know
is that in that 'moment' our own horizon is enriched and we gain knowledge of ourselves.

Conversation, power and distortion

As soon as we reflect on what is required for a conversation based on
mutual trust, respect, a willingness to listen and risk one's opinions, we
can see that we have 'defined a powerful regulative ideal that can orien-
tate our practical and political lives' (Bernstein 1983: 163). Bernstein
continues:

> If the quintessence of what we are is to be dialogical – and if this is
> not just the privilege of the *few* – then whatever the limitations of the
> practical realization of this ideal, it nevertheless can and should give
> practical orientation to our lives. We must ask what it is that blocks
> and prevents such dialogue, and what is to be done, 'what is feasible,
> what is possible, what is correct here and now' to make such genuine
> dialogue a concrete reality.
>
> (Bernstein 1983: 163)

We may have a powerful regulative ideal – but what sense does it make in
a world riven by inequality and distorted communication? Is it the case, as
Freire (1972: 61) suggests, that dialogue cannot occur between those who
want to name the world, and those who do not want this naming; or
between those who have been denied the right to speak, and those who
deny the right?

Writers such as Gadamer can be criticized for not fully addressing how
great inequalities in power condition dialogue; or how the meanings of

the words we use can be systematically distorted. Yet, as we saw in Chapter 6, problems of ideology and distortion can be addressed – hegemony can never be complete. In the movement of social relations, actions and ideas still have to be justified, people have to talk and be convinced. For as long as people require others to do their bidding, or to join with them in some enterprise, there has to be conversation, otherwise they cannot hope fully to achieve their aims. For subordinated groups the room for manoeuvre here may be small for much of the time, but in any system there are moments of crisis and dysfunction where voice takes on new meaning and levers can be placed under oppressors' positions.

Once there is conversation there is hope. As Habermas argues, in dialogue there is a 'gentle but obstinate, a never silent although seldom redeemed claim to reason' (Habermas 1979: 3): what Goffman calls the requirement to demonstrate sanity (see Manning 1992: 156–7). However distorted our ways of communicating are, there is within their structures a 'stubbornly transcending power' (Habermas 1979: 3).

> When we assert a belief that we hold, we also offer an implied promise to provide at least some of the evidence and reasons behind that belief, if asked. We may not be asked; we may not be able to provide those reasons fully; and we may not convince others if we do – but by making the assertion we commit ourselves to that broader obligation.
>
> (Burbules 1993: 75)

The claims each and every statement has to make as to its own validity hold some possibility of dialogue and hence of furthering understanding.

Freire, dialogue and local education

A number of the educators with whom I talked have been influenced by Freire's thinking, as indeed have I. We may share with him a similar political intent. Our experience of working in situations where there are major imbalances in wealth and power may well lead us to work for fundamental change. Some are attracted by Freire's mix of Christian personalism and his use of the Marxist notion of the human being as unfinished and always in the process of becoming (Elias and Merriam 1980: 148). Others find his casting of social reality in black and white terms 'is more the characteristic of the simplistic religious preacher than the critical philosopher (1980: 153). As might be expected from the broadly pragmatist position adopted here, I am not happy with his appeal to transcendentalism – the idea that there is some 'real' or 'authentic' view of reality. However, this is not my focus here – I want to look at some of the differences in the contexts in which Freire's thinking was formed and those in which it might be applied by local educators in northern societies.

The most obvious contrast lies in the societies in which these educators are working. Inequality and poverty help to structure the daily experience of people in northern countries like Britain. Yet health care, education, housing, food, material goods and means of communication (telephone, television, newspapers, books) are available to the bulk of the population on a scale that is literally 'worlds apart' from the vast majority of southern societies (George 1976; 1989). While not wanting to use a simple model of difference between North and South (see Hoogvelt 1982), we do need to recognize the appalling material conditions endured by those at whom Freire aimed his work. The social and economic context inevitably informs the way in which educators see their work. Thus, we should be suspicious of work in northern countries which simply reproduces his 'approach' (Aronowitz 1993). There is a tendency to treat his method as 'a recipe ready made and directly applicable' (Mackie 1980: 9). His suggestions need to be reworked, as he himself insists. There is a danger in simply transplanting ideas: it is a practice that can be 'ideologically alienating and benefits the dominating group' (Freire 1985: 172).

In some respects this is the problem that has occurred around 'banking' notions of education. Many northern local educators have rejected didactic roles, they have equated teaching with banking. Instead, they have seen their role more as 'problem-posers', as 'facilitators' of dialogue. Part of this is to do with their reaction against the institution of the school:

> I . . . have a problem associating myself with a school, being seen to be a teacher. I know that is coming from within me.

However, the polar opposites that Freire (1972: 45–59) uses to make his arguments may have added to this. Problem-posing and inquiry do not preclude teaching and 'depositing information'. To believe so is to make a fundamental mistake, as Freire later acknowledged (Kirkwood 1991). Indeed, as Taylor (1993) has convincingly shown, Freirian approaches smuggle in a range of assumptions and orientations under the guise of problem-posing. An analysis of Freire's literacy programme shows that

> the rhetoric which announced the importance of dialogue, engagement, and equality, and denounced silence, massification and oppression, did not match in practice the subliminal messages and modes of a Banking System of education. Albeit benign, Freire's approach differs only in degree, but not in kind, from the system which he so eloquently criticizes.
>
> (Taylor 1993: 148)

Educators have to teach. They have to transform transfers of information into a 'real act of knowing' (1993: 43). Linked to this are problems regarding Freire's model of literacy. While it may be taken as a challenge to the political projects of northern states, his analysis carried within it certain assumptions about cognitive development and about the relation of literacy to rationality that are suspect (Street 1984: 14). His work has not 'entirely shrugged off the assumptions of the "autonomous model" ' (1984: 14). As soon as we overlook questions of content, or seek to avoid mechanical forms of learning, then we do a grave disservice to those with whom we work. The question we should be asking is 'what is the place and meaning of subject-matter and of organization *within* experience' (Dewey 1963: 20).

A further, crucial, point of departure is that Freire's pedagogy was constructed around formal educational situations. While Freire may originally have been concerned not with schooling, but with the less structured world of 'non-formal' education, the educational encounters he explores remain formal (Torres 1993: 127). They remain curriculum-based and entail transforming settings into a particular type of pedagogical space. There is a special danger here of unthinking application – that of the pedagoguization or 'schooling' of the everyday (Street and Street 1991). In contrast, the workers I focus on here are, by and large, informal educators (Jeffs and Smith 1990a).

> We are educators in our local area. It is right . . . The mix of informal and formal education is an interesting one because I know that I do both. You have planned programmes and sessions for some bits of work. You sometimes need a particular task or an activity to achieve the learning. I found this working with informal groups, you get a task and it becomes more formal, and then it sort of lapses back again. The shift is really noticeable.

This means that local educators do not make use of a formal curriculum for much of their work. They work in settings not usually associated with education. Much of their conversation, as a result, is not immediately distinguishable from what might be said between friends or neighbours. This is the way it has to be – if they attempt to problematize things that are said in the way they might in a classroom or in some formal session, they may well be shunned. They have to work within the boundaries set by the 'daily round' to make openings for conversation.

The context of the work, and the way this affects workers' frames of reference, led me to move away from a focus on 'dialogue'. While, as a process, conversation and dialogue share meaning, the latter does have a more formal side. Working in public places, engaging in commonplace social encounters, and going with the 'flow' leads local educators to focus on some rather different aspects of process. As a result, writers such as Goffman (1961; 1963; 1981) who look at everyday (and not so everyday) social encounters, have a special appeal. Their focus on process, on what particular individuals are thinking, and the situations they analyse – the meeting on the street, the gathering of friends – echoes the concerns of practitioners.

Cultivating conversation lies at the centre of what local educators do. It is not simply the form that their work takes, but also part of their purpose. Through conversation, testing out prejudices (prejudgements), searching out meaning, we become more critical. Language, discourse 'exists not for the sake of expression alone but for the sake of the community it makes possible among those who become parties to it' (Gunn 1992: 90). We become better able to name our feelings and thoughts, and place ourselves in the world. We can develop a language of critique and possibility which allows us to act (Giroux 1989: 208).

Praxis

As Lindeman said of adult education, local education is 'education for use' (Lindeman 1987a: 103).

> Man must prove the truth, i.e. the reality and power, the this-sideness of his thinking in practice . . . All social life is essentially practical. All mysteries which lead theory to mystics, find their rational solution in human practice and in the comprehension of this practice . . . The philosophers have only interpreted the world, in various ways; the point is to change it.
>
> (Marx 1977: 156–8)

In other words, educators are involved with praxis: acts which shape and change the world. But what does this consist of?

Reflection and action

Only a few of the workers I am focusing on spoke of praxis. Those that did tended to link it to Freire where interpretation can mean change.

> The word is more than an instrument which makes dialogue possible; accordingly, we must seek its constituent elements. Within the word we find two dimensions, reflection and action, in such radical interaction that if one is sacrificed – even in part – the other immediately suffers. There is no true word that is not at the same time a praxis. Thus to speak a true word is to transform the world.
>
> (Freire 1972: 60)

Yet while praxis may not form part of many workers' overt vocabulary, practice, a pale derivative, does.

Practice is often depicted as the act of doing something. It is usually contrasted to 'theory': abstract ideas about some thing or phenomenon. Thus, for many workers, theory is what you learn in college and then apply to the situations you find in your work. The result is practice. In a similar way, local educators may talk of, for example, the failure of a group they have worked with to practise what they have learnt. In this 'theory' tends to be put on a pedestal. From theory can be derived general principles (or rules). These in turn can be applied to the problems of practice. Theory is 'real' knowledge, while practice is the application of that knowledge to solve problems. In many ways, this is a legacy of Aristotle and his threefold classification of disciplines as theoretical, productive or practical. The basis of the distinction lies in the *telos*, or purpose, each serves. In brief:

> The purpose of a theoretical discipline is the pursuit of truth through contemplation; its *telos* is the attainment of knowledge for its own sake. The purpose of the productive sciences is to make something; their *telos* is the production of some artefact. The practical disciplines are those sciences which deal with ethical and political life; their *telos* is practical wisdom and knowledge.
>
> (Carr and Kemmis 1986: 32)

This way of separating areas of knowledge can be seen, for example, in the way that we might view 'pure maths' (theoretical), tool-making (productive), and social work training (practical).

The form of thinking Aristotle saw as appropriate to theoretical activities was contemplative. It involves mulling over facts and ideas that the person already possesses.

> The Aristotelian contemplator is a man who has already acquired knowledge; and what he is contemplating is precisely this knowledge already present in his mind . . . the contemplator is engaged in the orderly inspection of truths which he already possesses; his task consists in bringing them forward from the recesses of his mind, and arranging them fittingly in the full light of consciousness.
>
> (Barnes 1976: 38)

This for Aristotle was the highest form of human activity. It was the ultimate intellectual virtue: a life of unbroken contemplation being something divine (Aristotle 1976: 333). Educators, if they were to follow this line, would have to place the gaining of knowledge for its own sake above, for example, the cultivation of affection and sympathy for other people. As Barnes comments, human excellence runs in a broader and more amiable stream. The fulfilled person will be a lover of others and an admirer of beauty as well as a contemplator of truth: 'a friend and an aesthete as well as a thinker' (Barnes 1976: 42).

If the form of thinking associated with theoretical activities was contemplative, the enquiry involved in productive disciplines was a 'making' action or *poietike*. Aristotle associated this form of thinking and doing with the work of craftspeople or artisans. Hence, the making action is not simply mechanical. It also involves some creativity. This making action is dependent upon the exercising of skill (*techne*). It always results from the idea, image or pattern of what the artisan wants to make. In other words, the person has a guiding plan or idea. For example, potters will have an idea of the article they want to make. While working, they may make some alterations, develop an idea and so on. But they are restricted in this by their original plan.

The ends–means relationship that exists within this approach to knowledge, where theory is set above practice, has dominated our understanding

Figure 8.1: The practical: making judgements

People begin with a situation or question
which they consider in relation to what they
think makes for human flourishing.

(the good)

They are guided by a moral disposition to
act truly and rightly.

(phronēsis)

This enables them to engage with the
situation as committed thinkers and actors.

(praxis)

The outcome is a process.

(interaction)

Source: based on Grundy (1987: 64)

of science. Yet in contemporary conversations about the nature of rationality, social theorists are having to unhook themselves from such technical-
rational views of scientific knowledge. They are having to question the
obsession with science and scientific knowledge (*episteme*).

> The more closely we examine the nature of this scientific knowledge
> that has become the paradigm of theoretical knowledge, the more
> we realize that the character of rationality in the sciences, especially
> in matters of theory choice, is closer to those features of rationality
> that have been characteristic of the tradition of practical philosophy
> than to many of the modern images of what is supposed to be the
> character of genuine *episteme*.
>
> (Bernstein 1983: 47)

It is to this we must now turn.

Practical reasoning

Where the productive begins with a plan or design, the practical cannot
have such a concrete starting point. Instead, we begin with a question or
situation. We then start to think about this situation in the light of our
understanding of what is good or what makes for human flourishing.
Thus, for Aristotle, praxis is guided by a moral disposition to act truly and
rightly, a concern to further human well-being and the good life. This is
what the Greeks called *phronēsis*, and requires an understanding of other
people. I have set this process out in Figure 8.1.

In praxis there can be no prior knowledge of the right means by which
we realize the end in a particular situation. For the end itself is only
specified in deliberating about the means appropriate to a particular

situation (Bernstein 1983: 147). Practical wisdom is 'grounded in experience and, in the light of a conception of the good, enables individuals to choose an appropriate course of action' (Blenkin *et al.* 1992: 121). Here we can see how fluid the process is. As we think about what we want to achieve, we alter the way we might achieve it. As we think about the way we might go about something, we change what we might aim at. There is a continual interplay between ends and means. In just the same way, there is a continual interplay between thought and action. This process involves interpretation, understanding and application in 'one unified process' (Gadamer 1979: 275). It is something we engage in as human beings and it is directed at other human beings.

When comparing the practical with the productive there is the danger of making an either/or judgement. Just as the debates about traditional/ progressive or banking/problem-posing forms of education are, in the end, sterile, so can this be. These are different ways of thinking, but both are necessary and valuable to different situations. The practical can engage with the productive. Ruskin demonstrates this in his discussion of the nature of the Gothic (see Thompson 1955: 32–8). Craftspeople working on Venice's churches did not apply established ideas and techniques in some standardized way. Rather, they had to develop an understanding of each situation. Furthermore, the builders 'never suffered ideas of outside symmetries and consistencies to interfere with the real use and value of what they did' (Ruskin 1920: 196).

Well-being

Practical wisdom (*phronēsis*) involves moving between the particular and the general.

> The mark of a prudent man [is] to be able to deliberate rightly about what is good and what is advantageous for himself; not in particular respects, e.g. what is good for health or physical strength, but what is conducive to the good life generally.
>
> (Aristotle 1976: 209)

Running through what some local educators say about their work is a deep sense of what makes for human flourishing – the good life. Not having syllabuses, nor inhabiting a particular subject, they have to go back to first principles and look to the processes they view as desirable. They need to ask how any action they might take contributes to, or inhibits, well-being. This requires that workers are in touch with their values and their ideas about what makes for the good.

> As a worker you have to hold on to values . . . it is your anchor. It keeps you going. It gives me a direction. If I am talking to a particular person, it is not a question of trying to lead them to my values, but often to try and express some different values. I find that is quite

important because each peer group has its norms and they drift along.

Allied to this are a vision of the sort of society they would like to see, and a critique of the one in which they live and work. As Dewey (1966: 97) put it, 'education as a social process and function has no meaning until we define the kind of society we have in mind'. So what sort of society do local educators have in mind? Given their variety, and an emphasis on interaction and process, it would be surprising if some clear design emerged. Indeed, having too fixed an idea would limit what could emerge. Yet certain things do come through – in particular, a concern with the quality of daily life. Listening to local educators talking about direction and purpose in their work, certain qualities come to mind, such as the desire to cultivate wisdom and critical thought, and to develop a sense of community (see Chapter 4). Underpinning these is a belief that people can create possibilities for themselves and for others. This is not to say that the range of actions open to them is limitless. Imbalances in power and deep-seated structural forces curb opportunity. Yet there is here a sense of agency; a conviction that people are able to act to change aspects of their lives and the world of which they are a part. Linked to this is also a belief that educators can make a difference.

To act in this way entails, according to Doyal and Gough (1991: 54) two preconditions: physical survival and personal autonomy. 'They constitute the most basic human needs – those which must be satisfied to some degree before actors can effectively participate in their form of life to achieve any other valued goal.' To be autonomous, people need to have a developed self – the capacity to work out options, to own them and to act. They also require some understanding of themselves, of their culture and what is expected of them (1991: 60). A third aspect is freedom from external constraints. Autonomous people are not manipulated by others, they are able to act in pursuit of self-chosen goals (Lindley 1986: 6). However, these statements take on a different meaning according to whether we approach them with an individualistic or social understanding of the self. If, as has been argued here, the significant thing about people is not what is contained within them but what transpires between them (Sampson 1993: 20), then autonomy is understood better as a state of interdependence than as one of independence.

Praxis: informed, committed action

We can now see the full quality of praxis. It is not simply action based on reflection. It is action which embodies certain qualities. These include a commitment to human well-being and the search for truth, and respect for others. It is the action of people who are free, who are able to act for themselves. Moreover, praxis is always risky. It requires that a person 'makes a wise and prudent practical judgment about how to act in *this* situation'

(Carr and Kemmis 1986: 190). These qualities were caught beautifully by one worker.

> Praxis is important to me. I went through an 'academic' stage where I thought I could sort out the problems of the world in my mind. To understand what the truth of the world was, to create nice systems. I have come round to thinking that you don't sort things out that way. You sort them out through struggle, through commitment, through practice. It is not that you don't think about things, but it is an ongoing process that you never finish. That is a value for me – questioning – the crucial role of the question mark.

Our 'chief business' as educators is to enable people to 'share in a common life' (Dewey 1966: 7). Local education involves grounding practice – or praxis, to be more accurate – in local life. It stresses solidarity, co-operation and social responsibility. It requires workers to seek and value conversation; to engage with the views of others and the traditions we all inhabit. Its practitioners want to see people take their place in, and change, the world as free but committed and connected agents. Their task, in short, is to foster those forms of local life which nurture community, conversation and praxis.

References

Ahmad, Y. and Kirby, R. (1988) 'Training the professional worker' in T. Jeffs and M. Smith (eds) *Welfare and Youth Work Practice*. London: Macmillan.

Alexander, R. (1992) *Policy and Practice in Primary Education*. London: Routledge.

Alexander, R., Rose, J. and Woodhead, C. (1992) *Curriculum Organisation and Classroom Practice in Primary Schools. A Discussion Paper*. London: Department of Education and Science.

Alinsky, S. D. (1969) *Reveille for Radicals*. New York: Random House. First published in 1946.

Allen, G. and Martin, I. (eds) (1992) *Education and Community. The Politics of Practice*. London: Cassell.

Allen, G., Bastiani, J., Martin, I. and Richards, K. (eds) (1987) *Community Education. An Agenda for Educational Reform*. Milton Keynes: Open University Press.

Anzaldua, G. (1987) *Borderlands/La Frontera. The New Mestiza*. San Francisco: Spinsters/Aunt Lute.

Argyle, M. (1991) *Cooperation. The Basis of Sociability*. London: Routledge.

Argyle, M. (1992) *The Social Psychology of Everyday Life*. London: Routledge.

Argyris, C. and Schön, D. (1974) *Theory into Practice. Increasing Professional Effectiveness*. San Francisco: Jossey-Bass.

Aristotle (1976) *The Nicomachean Ethics* (trans. J. A. K. Thomson; revised H. Tredennick). London: Penguin.

Arnold, J., Askins, D., Davies, R., Evans, S., Rogers, A. and Taylor, T. (1981) *The Management of Detached Work. How and Why*. Leicester: National Association of Youth Clubs.

Aronowitz, S. (1993) 'Paulo Freire's radical democratic humanism' in P. McLaren and P. Leonard (eds) *Freire. A Critical Encounter*. London: Routledge.

Bachrach, P. and Baratz, M. S. (1970) *Power and Poverty. Theory and Practice*. New York: Oxford University Press.

Bacon, R. (1988) 'Counter transference in a case conference' in G. Pearson, J. Treseder and M. Yelloly (eds) *Social Work and the Legacy of Freud. Psychoanalysis and Its Uses.* London: Macmillan.

Baden-Powell, R. (1909) *Scouting for Boys. A Handbook for Instruction in Good Citizenship* (rev. edn). London: Pearson.

Banks, M., Bates, I., Breakwell, G., Bynner, J., Emler, N., Jamieson, L. and Roberts, K. (1992) *Careers and Identities.* Milton Keynes: Open University Press.

Banton, M. (1968) *Roles. An Introduction to the Study of Social Relations.* London: Tavistock.

Barnes, D. (1992) 'The significance of teachers' frames for teaching' in T. Russell and H. Munby (eds) *Teachers and Teaching. From Classroom to Reflection.* London: Falmer Press.

Barnes, J. (1976) 'Introduction' in Aristotle, *The Nicomachean Ethics.* London: Penguin.

Barr, A. (1991) *Practising Community Development. Experience in Strathclyde.* London: Community Development Foundation.

Barron, R. S., Kerr, N. and Miller, N. (1992) *Group Process, Group Decision, Group Action.* Buckingham: Open University Press.

Barrow, R. (1984) *Giving Teaching Back to the Teachers. A Critical Introduction to Curriculum Theory.* Brighton: Wheatsheaf Books.

Barton, D. and Padmore, S. (1991) 'Roles, networks and values in everyday writing' in D. Barton and R. Ivanic (eds) *Writing in the Community.* Newbury Park, CA: Sage.

Batten, T. R. (1967) *The Non-Directive Approach in Group and Community Work.* London: Oxford University Press.

Bayley, M., Parker, P., Seyd, R. and Tennant, A. (1987) *Practising Community Care. Developing Locally-Based Practice.* Sheffield: Sheffield University Joint Unit for Social Services Research.

Bell, C. and Newby, H. (1971) *Community Studies.* London: Unwin.

Berger, B. (1986) 'Foreword' in E. Goffman, *Frame Analysis. An Essay on the Organization of Experience.* Boston: Northeastern University Press.

Bernstein, R. J. (1983) *Beyond Objectivism and Relativism. Science, Hermeneutics and Praxis.* Oxford: Blackwell.

Bernstein, R. J. (1991) *The New Constellation. The Ethical-Political Horizons of Modernity/Postmodernity.* Cambridge: Polity Press.

Bion, W. R. (1974) *Brazilian Lectures.* Rio de Janeiro: Imago Editora.

Bishop, J. and Hoggett, P. (1986) *Organising around Enthusiasm. Mutual Aid in Leisure.* London: Comedia.

Blackburn, M. and Blackburn, D. (1990) 'Informal education in residential settings' in T. Jeffs and M. Smith (eds) *Using Informal Education.* Buckingham: Open University Press.

Blenkin, G. M., Edwards, G. and Kelly, A. V. (1992) *Change and the Curriculum.* London: Paul Chapman.

Bolger, S., Corrigan, P., Docking, J. and Frost, N. (1981) *Towards Socialist Welfare Work. Working in the State.* London: Macmillan.

Bott, E. (1957) *Family and Social Network. Roles, Norms, and External Relationships in Ordinary Urban Families.* London: Tavistock.

Boud, D., Keogh, R. and Walker, D. (eds) (1985) *Reflection. Turning Experience into Learning.* London: Kogan Page.

Bracey, H. E. (1964) *Neighbours. On Estates and Subdivisions in England and USA.* London: Routledge & Kegan Paul.

Bradford, S. and Day, M. (1991) *Youth Service Management. Aspects of Structure, Organisation and Development.* Leicester: National Youth Agency.

Brew, J. Macalister (1943) *In the Service of Youth.* London: Faber.

Brew, J. Macalister (1946) *Informal Education: Adventures and Reflections.* London: Faber.

Brookfield, S. D. (1983) *Adult Learning, Adult Education and the Community.* Milton Keynes: Open University Press.

Brookfield, S. D. (1986) *Understanding and Facilitating Adult Learning. A Comprehensive Analysis of Principles and Effective Practices.* Milton Keynes: Open University Press.

Brookfield, S. D. (1987a) 'Introduction' to S. D. Brookfield (ed.) *Learning Democracy. Eduard Lindeman on Adult Education and Social Change.* Beckenham: Croom Helm.

Brookfield, S. D. (1987b) *Developing Critical Thinkers. Challenging Adults to Explore Alternative Ways of Thinking and Acting.* Milton Keynes: Open University Press.

Brookfield, S. D. (1990) *The Skillful Teacher. On Technique, Trust and Responsiveness in the Classroom.* San Francisco: Jossey-Bass.

Brown, P. (1987) *Schooling Ordinary Kids. Inequality, Unemployment and the New Vocationalism.* London: Tavistock.

Brown, R. (1988) *Group Processes. Dynamics within and between Groups.* Oxford: Blackwell.

Brown, S. and McIntyre, D. (1993) *Making Sense of Teaching.* Buckingham: Open University Press.

Bruner, J. (1977) *The Process of Education.* Cambridge, MA: University of Harvard Press.

Buchman, M. (1990) 'How practical is contemplation in teaching?' in C. W. Day, M. Pope and P. Denicolo (eds) *Insight into Teachers' Thinking and Practice.* Basingstoke: Falmer Press.

Bulmer, M. (1986) *Neighbours. The Work of Philip Abrams.* Cambridge: Cambridge University Press.

Burbules, N. C. (1993) *Dialogue in Teaching. Theory and Practice.* New York: Teachers College Press.

Burns, T. (1992) *Erving Goffman.* London: Routledge.

Burridge, D. (1990) *What Local Groups Need. Their Efficiency and Effectiveness and the Role of Local Authorities.* London: National Council for Voluntary Organisations.

Butcher, H. (1992) 'Community work: current realities, contemporary trends' in P. Carter, T. Jeffs and M. K. Smith (eds) *Changing Social Work and Welfare.* Buckingham: Open University Press.

Butcher, H., Glen, A., Henderson, P. and Smith, J. (eds) (1993) *Community and Public Policy.* London: Pluto Press.

Button, L. (1974) *Developmental Group Work with Adolescents.* London: Hodder & Stoughton.

Cahill, M. (1992) 'Personal mobility and social inequality' in P. Carter, T. Jeffs and M. K. Smith (eds) *Changing Social Work and Welfare.* Buckingham: Open University Press.

Calderhead, J. (1989) 'Reflective teaching and teacher education', *Teaching and Teacher Education,* 5(1): 43–51.

Calderhead, J. (1990) 'Representations of teacher knowledge' in P. Goodyear (ed.) *Teaching Knowledge and Intelligent Tutoring.* New York: Ablex Publishing.

Calderhead, J. and Gates, P. (eds) (1993) *Conceptualizing Reflection in Teacher Development.* London: Falmer Press.

Callaghan, G. (1992) 'Locality and localism. The spatial orientation of young adults in Sunderland', *Youth and Policy*, 39: 23–33.

Cannadine, D. (1983) 'The context, performance and meaning of ritual: the British monarchy and the "invention of tradition", *c*.1820–1977' in E. Hobsbawm and T. Ranger (eds) *The Invention of Tradition*. Cambridge: Cambridge University Press.

Cannan, C., Berry, L. and Lyons, K. (1992) *Social Work and Europe*. London: Macmillan.

Carr, W. and Kemmis, S. (1986) *Becoming Critical. Education, Knowledge and Action Research*. Lewes: Falmer.

Carspecken, P. F. (1991) *Community Schooling and the Nature of Power*. London: Routledge.

Carter, N., Klein, R. and Day, P. (1992) *How Organisations Measure Success. The Use of Performance Indicators in Government*. London: Routledge.

Casement, P. (1985) *On Learning from the Patient*. London: Routledge.

Casement, P. (1990) *Further Learning from the Patient. The Analytic Space and Process*. London: Routledge.

Central Statistical Office (1993) *Social Trends 23*. London: HMSO.

Chanan, G. (1991) *Taken for Granted. Community Activity and the Crisis of the Voluntary Sector*. London: Community Development Foundation.

Charnley, C. (1993) 'Arts work in informal education' in M. K. Smith (ed.) *Youth or Adult? The First Five Years*. London: YMCA National College/Rank Foundation.

Cinnamond, J. H. and Zimpher, N. L. (1990) 'Reflectivity as a function of community' in R. T. Clift, W. R. Houston and M. C. Pugach (eds) *Encouraging Reflective Practice in Education. An Analysis of Issues and Programs*. New York: Teachers College Press.

Clandinin, D. J. and Connelly, F. M. (1991) 'Narrative and story in practice and research' in D. A. Schön (ed.) *The Reflective Turn. Case Studies in and on Educational Practice*. New York: Teachers Press, Columbia University.

Clift, R. T., Houston, W. R. and Pugach, M. C. (eds) (1990) *Encouraging Reflective Practice in Education. An Analysis of Issues and Programs*. New York: Teachers College Press.

Coats, M. (1994) *Women's Education*. Buckingham: Open University Press.

Cockburn, C. (1977) *The Local State. Management of Cities and People*. London: Pluto Press.

Cohen, A. P. (1982) 'Belonging: the experience of culture' in A. P. Cohen (ed.) *Belonging. Identity and Social Organisation in British Rural Cultures*. Manchester: Manchester University Press.

Cohen, A. P. (1985) *The Symbolic Construction of Community*. London: Tavistock.

Cohen, L. and Manion, L. (1989) *A Guide to Teaching Practice* (3rd edn). Cookstown: Routledge.

Coleman, J. S. (1976) 'Differences between experiential and classroom learning' in M. T. Keeton (ed.) *Experiential Learning*. San Francisco: Jossey-Bass.

Collins, M. (1991) *Adult Education as Vocation. A Critical Role for the Adult Educator*. London: Routledge.

Collins, N. and Hoggarth, L. (1977) *No Man's Landmarks*. Leicester: National Youth Bureau.

Collins, P. Hill (1990) *Black Feminist Thought. Knowledge, Consciousness and the Politics of Empowerment*. London: HarperCollins.

Community Education Validation and Endorsement (Scotland) (1990) *Pre-Service Training for Community Education Work*. Edinburgh: Scottish Community Education Council.

Coombs, P. H. (1968) *The World Educational Crisis. A Systems Analysis.* Oxford: Oxford University Press.

Corlett, W. (1989) *Community without Unity. A Politics of Derridan Extravagance.* Durham, NC: Duke University Press.

Cornbleth, C. (1990) *Curriculum in Context.* Basingstoke: Falmer Press.

Cosgrove, D. (1989) 'Geography is everywhere: culture and symbolism in human landscapes' in D. Gregory and R. Walford (eds) *Horizons in Human Geography.* London: Macmillan.

Council for Education and Training in Youth and Community Work (1989) *Guidelines to Endorsement. Initial Training in Youth and Community Work.* Leicester: Council for Education and Training in Youth and Community Work.

Coutinho, J. D.-V. (1972) 'Preface' to P. Freire, *Cultural Action for Freedom.* Harmondsworth: Penguin.

Cowburn, W. (1986) *Class, Ideology and Community Education.* Beckenham: Croom Helm.

Coyle, G. L. (1930) *Social Process in Organized Groups.* New York: Richard R. Smith.

Craig, G., Derricourt, N. and Loney, M. (eds) (1982) *Community Work and the State.* London: Routledge & Kegan Paul.

Cross, K. P. (1992) *Adults as Learners. Increasing Participation and Facilitating Learning.* San Francisco: Jossey-Bass. First published in 1981.

Crow, G. (1989) 'The use of the concept of "strategy" in recent sociological literature', *Sociology*, 23(1): 1–24.

Crowell, S. G. (1990) 'Dialogue and text: re-marking the difference' in T. Maranhão (ed.) *The Interpretation of Dialogue.* Chicago: University of Chicago Press.

Davenport, J. (1993) 'Is there any way out of the andragogy morass?' in M. Thorpe, R. Edwards and A. Hanson (eds) *Culture and Processes of Adult Learning.* London: Routledge.

Davies, B. (1975) *The Use of Groups in Social Work Practice.* London: Routledge & Kegan Paul.

Davies, B. and Gibson, A. (1967) *The Social Education of the Adolescent.* London: University of London Press.

Day, C., Pope, M. and Denicolo, P. (eds) (1990) *Insight into Teachers' Thinking and Practice.* Basingstoke: Falmer Press.

Dennis, F., Henriques, F. and Slaughter, C. (1969) *Coal Is Our Life. An Analysis of a Yorkshire Mining Community.* London: Tavistock. First published in 1956.

Department of Education and Science (1982) *Experience and Participation. Review Group on the Youth Service in England* (Thompson Report). London: HMSO.

Department of Education and Science (1983) *Young People in the 80's. A Survey.* London: HMSO.

Department of Education and Science (1987) *Effective Youth Work. A Report by HM Inspectors. Education Observed No. 6.* London: DES.

Department of Education and Science (1990) *Responsive Youth Work. The Youth Service and Urgent Social Needs.* London: HMSO.

Derrida, J. (1978) *Writing and Difference* (trans. A. Bass). Chicago: University of Chicago Press.

Dewey, J. (1929) *Experience and Nature.* New York: Dover. First published in 1925.

Dewey, J. (1934) *Art as Experience.* New York: Capricorn.

Dewey, J. (1948) *Reconstruction in Philosophy.* New York: Mentor. First published in 1920.

Dewey, J. (1963) *Experience and Education.* New York: Macmillan. First published in 1938.

Dewey, J. (1966) *Democracy and Education. An Introduction to the Philosophy of Education.* New York: Free Press. First published in 1916.

Dewey, J. (1987) 'How we think. A restatement of the relation of reflective thinking to the educative process' [1933] in J. Dewey, *The Later Works 1925–1953, Vol. 8: 1933 essays and How We Think (Revised Edition).* Edited by J. A. Boydston. Carbondale: Southern Illinois University Press.

Dominelli, L. (1990) *Woman and Community Action.* Birmingham: Venture Press.

Donald, J. (1992) 'Dewey-eyed optimism: the possibility of democratic education', *New Left Review,* 192: 133–44.

Douglas, T. (1976) *Groupwork Practice.* London: Tavistock.

Douglas, T. (1991) *A Handbook of Common Groupwork Problems.* London: Routledge.

Doyal, L. and Gough, I. (1991) *A Theory of Human Need.* London: Macmillan.

Eisner, E. W. (1985) *The Art of Educational Evaluation. A Personal View.* Lewes: Falmer.

Elias, J. L. and Merriam, S. (1980) *Philosophical Foundations of Adult Education.* Malabar, FL: Krieger Publishing Co.

Ellis, J. W. (1990) 'Informal education: a Christian perspective' in T. Jeffs and M. Smith (eds) *Using Informal Education.* Buckingham: Open University Press.

El-Solh, C. F. (1991) 'Somalis in London's East End. A community striving for recognition', *New Community,* 17(4): 539–52.

Entwistle, H. (1979) *Antonio Gramsci. Conservative Schooling for Radical Politics.* London: Routledge & Kegan Paul.

Entwistle, H. (1981) 'The political education of adults' in D. Heater and J. A. Gillespie (eds) *Political Education in Flux.* London: Sage.

Erikson, E. H. (1959) 'The nature of clinical evidence in psychoanalysis' in D. Lerner (ed.) *Evidence and Inference.* New York: Free Press.

Everitt, A., Hardiker, P., Littlewood, J. and Mullender, A. (1992) *Applied Research for Better Practice.* London: Macmillan.

Eyles, J. (1989) 'The geography of everyday life' in D. Gregory and R. Walford (eds) *Horizons in Human Geography.* London: Macmillan.

Federation of Community Work Training Groups/Association of Metropolitan Authorities (1991) *Learning for Action. Community Work and Participative Training.* Sheffield: Federation of Community Work Training Groups.

Fisher, E. (1993) 'A health education project' in M. K. Smith (ed.) *Youth or Adult? The First Five Years.* London: YMCA National College/Rank Foundation.

Flynn, P., Johnson, C., Lieberman, S. and Armstrong, H. (eds) (1986) *You're Learning All the Time. Women, Education and Community work.* Nottingham: Spokesman.

Fordham, P., Poulton, G. and Randle, L. (1979) *Learning Networks in Adult Education. Non-formal Education on a Housing Estate.* London: Routledge & Kegan Paul.

Foreman, A. (1990) 'Personality and curriculum' in T. Jeffs and M. Smith (eds) *Using Informal Education.* Buckingham: Open University Press.

Forster, E. M. (1975) *Howards End.* Harmondsworth: Penguin. First published in 1910.

Foucault, M. (1977) *Discipline and Punish. The Birth of the Prison.* Harmondsworth: Penguin.

Foucault, M. (1980) *Power/Knowledge. Selected Interviews and Other Writings 1972–1977.* Brighton: Harvester Wheatsheaf.

Francis, D. and Henderson, P. (1992) *Working with Rural Communities.* London: Macmillan.

Freire, P. (1972) *Pedagogy of the Oppressed.* Harmondsworth: Penguin.

Freire, P. (1974) *Education: The Practice of Freedom.* London: Writers and Readers Publishing Cooperative.

Freire, P. (1985) *The Politics of Education. Culture, Power and Liberation.* London: Macmillan.

Freud, S. (1914) *Remembering, Repeating, Working Through. Standard Edition Vol. XII.* London: Hogarth Press.

Fromm, E. (1979) *To Have or To Be?* London: Abacus.

Fryer, P. (1988) *Black People in the British Empire. An Introduction.* London: Pluto Press.

Gadamer, H.-G. (1976) *Philosophical Hermeneutics* (trans. and ed. D. E. Linge). Berkeley: University of California Press.

Gadamer, H.-G. (1979) *Truth and Method* (2nd edn). London: Sheed and Ward.

Galbraith, J. K. (1992) *The Culture of Contentment.* London: Sinclair-Stevenson.

Gallagher, A. (1977) 'Women and community work' in M. Mayo (ed.) *Women in the Community.* London: Routledge & Kegan Paul.

Galton, M. and Williamson, J. (1992) *Group Work in the Primary Classroom.* London: Routledge.

Galton, M., Simon, B. and Croll, P., with Jasman, A. and Willcocks, J. (1980) *Inside the Primary Classroom.* London: Routledge & Kegan Paul.

Gardiner, D. (1989) *The Anatomy of Supervision. Developing Learning and Professional Competence for Social Work Students.* Milton Keynes: Open University Press.

Geertz, C. (1973) *The Interpretation of Cultures.* London: Hutchinson.

Geertz, C. (1983) *Local Knowledge. Further Essays in Interpretive Anthropology.* New York: Basic Books.

George, S. (1976) *How the Other Half Dies. The Real Reasons for World Hunger.* Harmondsworth: Penguin.

George, S. (1989) *A Fate Worse than Debt.* London: Penguin.

Gerth, H. H. and Mills, C. W. (eds) (1991) *From Max Weber. Essays in Sociology.* London: Routledge. First published in 1948.

Gibbs, C. (1989) 'Confidentiality and consent', *Young People Now,* 1(6): 54–5.

Giddens, A. (1984) *The Constitution of Society. Outline of the Theory of Structuration.* Cambridge: Polity Press.

Giddens, A. (1987) *Social Theory and Modern Sociology.* Cambridge: Polity Press.

Giddens, A. (1990) *The Consequences of Modernity.* Cambridge: Polity Press.

Giddens, A. (1991) *Modernity and Self-Identity. Self and Society in the Late Modern Age.* Cambridge: Polity Press.

Gilroy, P. (1987) *There Ain't No Black in the Union Jack. The Cultural Politics of Race and Nation.* London: Hutchinson.

Giroux, H. A. (1983) *Theory and Resistance in Education. A Pedagogy for the Opposition.* London: Heinemann.

Giroux, H. A. (1989) *Schooling for Democracy. Critical Pedagogy in the Modern Age.* London: Routledge.

Giroux, H. A. (1992) *Border Crossings. Cultural Workers and the Politics of Education.* London: Routledge.

Gitlin, A. and Smyth, J. (1989) *Teacher Evaluation. Critical Educative and Transformative Alternatives.* Lewes: Falmer.

Goetschius, G. W. and Tash, J. (1967) *Working with Unattached Youth. Problem, Approach, Method.* London: Routledge & Kegan Paul.

Goffman, E. (1961) *Encounters. Two Studies in the Sociology of Interaction.* Indianapolis: Bobbs-Merrill.

Goffman, E. (1963) *Behavior in Public Places. Notes on the Social Organization of Gatherings.* New York: Free Press.

Goffman, E. (1969) *The Presentation of Self in Everyday Life.* Harmondsworth: Penguin. First published in 1959.

Goffman, E. (1971) *Relations in Public. Microstudies of the Public Order.* Harmondsworth: Penguin.

Goffman, E. (1972) *Interaction Ritual. Essays on Face-to-Face Behaviour.* Harmondsworth: Penguin. First published in 1967.

Goffman, E. (1981) *Forms of Talk.* Oxford: Blackwell.

Goffman, E. (1986) *Frame Analysis. An Essay on the Organisation of experience.* Boston: Northeastern University Press. First published in 1974.

Goulet, D. (1974) 'Introduction' to P. Freire, *Education: The Practice of Freedom.* London: Writers and Readers Publishing Cooperative.

Gramsci, A. (1971) *Selections from Prison Notebooks* (trans. and ed. Q. Hoare and G. Nowell Smith). London: Lawrence and Wishart.

Gregory, D. (1989a) 'Area differentiation and post-modern human geography' in D. Gregory and R. Walford (eds) *Horizons in Human Geography.* London: Macmillan.

Gregory, D. (1989b) 'Presences and absences: time-space relations and structuration theory' in D. Held and J. B. Thompson (eds) *Social Theory of Modern Societies. Anthony Giddens and His Critics.* Cambridge: Cambridge University Press.

Grice, H. P. (1975) 'Logic and conversation' in P. Cole and J. L. Morgan (eds) *Syntax and Semantics. Vol. 3: Speech Acts.* New York: Academic Press.

Grundy, S. (1987) *Curriculum: Product or Praxis.* Lewes: Falmer.

Gumperz, J. J. (1982) *Discourse Strategies.* Cambridge: Cambridge University Press.

Gunn, G. (1992) *Thinking across the American Grain. Ideology, Intellect and the New Pragmatism.* Chicago: University of Chicago Press.

Habermas, J. (1979) *Communication and the Evolution of Society* (trans. T. McCarthy). London: Heinemann.

Habermas, J. (1984) *The Theory of Communicative Action. Vol. 1: Reason and the Rationalization of Society* (trans. T. McCarthy). Cambridge: Polity Press.

Habermas, J. (1985) 'A philosophico-political profile – an interview with Habermas', *New Left Review*, 151: 75–105.

Hadley, R., Cooper, M., Dale, P. and Stacy, G. (1987) *A Community Social Worker's Handbook.* London: Tavistock.

Halsey, A. H. (ed.) (1972) *Educational Priority. Volume 1: EPA Probems and Policies.* London: HMSO.

Hamilton, E. and Cunningham, P. M. (1989) 'Community-based adult education' in S. B. Merriam and P. M. Cunningham (eds) *Handbook of Adult and Continuing Education.* San Francisco: Jossey-Bass.

Hammersley, M. (1990) *Classroom Ethnography. Empirical and Methodological Essays.* Buckingham: Open University Press.

Hannerz, U. (1980) *Exploring the City. Inquiries towards an Urban Anthropology.* New York: Columbia University Press.

Harvey, D. (1982) *The Limits to Capital.* Oxford: Blackwell.

Hawkins, P. and Shohet, R. (1989) *Supervision in the Helping Professions. An Individual, Group and Organizational Approach.* Milton Keynes: Open University Press.

Heath, S. Brice (1983) *Ways with Words. Language, Life and Work in Communities and Classrooms.* Cambridge: Cambridge University Press.

Heller, A. (1976) 'Marx's theory of revolution and the revolution in everyday life' in A. Heller (ed.) *The Humanization of Socialism. Writings of the Budapest School.* London: Alison and Busby.

Henderson, P. and Thomas, D. N. (1987) *Skills in Neighbourhood Work* (2nd edn). London: George Allen & Unwin.

Hirst, P. (1993) 'Associational democracy' in D. Held (ed.) *Prospects for Democracy. North, South, East, West.* Cambridge: Polity.

Hobsbawm, E. J. (1983) 'Introduction. Inventing Traditions' in E. Hobsbawm and T. Ranger (eds) *The Invention of Tradition.* Cambridge: Cambridge University Press.

Hobsbawm, E. J. and Ranger, T. (eds) (1983) *The Invention of Tradition.* Cambridge: Cambridge University Press.

Homans, G. C. (1951) *The Human Group.* London: Routledge & Kegan Paul.

Hoogvelt, A. M. H. (1982) *The Third World in Global Development.* London: Macmillan.

Houle, C. O. (1972) *The Design of Education.* San Francisco: Jossey-Bass.

Houle, C. O. (1980) *Continuing Learning in the Professions.* San Francisco: Jossey-Bass.

Houston, R. J. and Clift, R. T. (1990) 'The potential for research contributions to reflective practice' in R. T. Clift, W. R. Houston and M. C. Pugach (eds) *Encouraging Reflective Practice in Education. An Analysis of Issues and Programs.* New York: Teachers College Press.

Howe, D. (1993) *On Being a Client. Understanding the Process of Counselling and Psychotherapy.* London: Sage.

Hugman, R. (1991) *Power in Caring Professions.* London: Macmillan.

Hunter, F. (1953) *Community Power Structure. A Study of Decision Makers.* Chapel Hill: University of North Carolina Press.

Jacobs, M. (1992) *Sigmund Freud.* London: Sage.

Jarvis, P. (1985) *The Sociology of Adult and Continuing Education.* Beckenham: Croom Helm.

Jarvis, P. (1987) *Adult Learning in the Social Context.* Beckenham: Croom Helm.

Jarvis, P. (1992) *Paradoxes of Learning. On Becoming an Individual in Society.* San Francisco: Jossey-Bass.

Jeffs, T. (1979) *Young People and the Youth Service.* London: Routledge & Kegan Paul.

Jeffs, T. (1992) 'The state, ideology and the community school movement' in G. Allen and I. Martin (eds) *Education and Community. The Politics of Practice.* London: Cassell.

Jeffs, T. and Smith, M. (eds) (1987) *Youth Work.* London: Macmillan.

Jeffs, T. and Smith, M. (eds) (1988) *Welfare and Youth Work Practice.* London: Macmillan.

Jeffs, T. and Smith, M. (eds) (1990a) *Using Informal Education. An Alternative to Casework, Teaching and Control?* Buckingham: Open University Press.

Jeffs, T. and Smith, M. (eds) (1990b) *Young People, Inequality and Youth Work.* London: Macmillan.

Jeffs, T. and Smith, M. (1990c) 'Taking issue with issues', *Youth and Policy*, 28: 16–19.

Jones, R. (1987) *Like Distant Relatives. Adolescents' Perceptions of Social Work and Social Workers.* Aldershot: Gower.

Joshi, H. (ed.) (1989) *The Changing Population of Britain.* Oxford: Blackwell.

Kelly, T. (1970) *A History of Adult Education in Great Britain. From the Middle Ages to the Twentieth Century.* Liverpool: Liverpool University Press.

Kidd, J. R. (1978) *How Adults Learn* (3rd edn). Englewood Cliffs, NJ: Prentice Hall Regents.

Kirkwood, G. (1991) 'Education in the community. Fallacy: the community educator should be a non-directive facilitator' in B. O'Hagan (ed.) *The Charnwood Papers. Fallacies in Community Education.* Ticknall, Derbyshire: Education Now.

Kitto, J. (1986) *Holding the Boundaries. Professional Training of Face to Face Workers at a Distance.* London: YMCA National College.

Kliebard, H. M. (1987) *The Struggle for the American Curriculum 1893–1958.* New York: Routledge & Kegan Paul.

Knight, D. and Morgan, G. (1990) 'The concept of strategy in sociology: A note of dissent', *Sociology,* 24(3) 475–83.

Knoke, D. and Kuklinski, J. H. (1991) 'Network analysis: Basic concepts' in G. Thompson, J. Frances, R. Levacic and J. Mitchell (eds) *Markets, Hierarchies and Networks. The Coordination of Social Life.* London: Sage.

Knowles, M. S. (1950) *Informal Adult Education.* New York: Association Press.

Knowles, M. S. (1970) *The Modern Practice of Adult Education. Andragogy versus Pedagogy.* New York: Association Press.

Kolb, D. (1976) *Learning Style Inventory. Technical Manual.* Boston: McBer and Co.

Kolb, D. (1984) *Experiential Learning. Experience as the Source of Learning and Development.* Englewood Cliffs, NJ: Prentice Hall.

König, R. (1968) *The Community* (trans. E. Fitzgerald). London: Routledge & Kegan Paul.

Kropotkin, P. (1939) *Mutual Aid. A Factor of Evolution.* Harmondsworth: Penguin. First published in 1902.

Kuenstler, P. H. K. (1955) 'Spontaneous youth groups' in P. H. K. Kuenstler (ed.) *Spontaneous Youth Groups.* London: University of London Press.

Kutnick, P. J. (1988) *Relationships in the Primary School Classroom.* London: Paul Chapman Publishing.

Kyriacou, C. (1986) *Effective Teaching in Schools.* Oxford: Blackwell.

Kysel, F. and Coulter, A. (1984) *The Youth Service. A Fair Deal for Girls?* London: Inner London Education Authority.

Larkins, R. (1991) 'Youth service evaluation. A study and analysis of its current failure and potential introduction'. Unpublished MSc thesis, Polytechnic of East London.

Lave, J. and Wenger, E. (1991) *Situated Learning. Legitimate Peripheral Participation.* Cambridge: Cambridge University Press.

Lawrence, P. (1987) 'Tylor and Frazer: The intellectualist tradition' in D. J. Austin-Broos (ed.) *Creating Culture.* Sydney: Allen & Unwin.

Leighton, J. P. (1972) *The Principles and Practice of Youth and Community Work.* London: Chester House.

Leissner, A. (1969) *Street Club Work in Tel Aviv and New York.* London: Longmans with National Bureau for Cooperation in Child Care.

Levine, K. (1986) *The Social Context of Literacy.* London: Routledge & Kegan Paul.

Lewin, K. (1947) 'Frontiers in group dynamics. Concept, method and reality in social science', *Human Relations,* 1: 5–41.

Lewin, K. (1948) *Resolving Social Conflicts. Selected Papers on Group Dynamics.* New York: Harper and Row.

Lewin, K. (1951) *Field Theory in Social Science.* New York: Harper and Row.

Lieberman, J. (ed.) (1939) *New Trends in Group Work.* New York: Association Press.

Lightfoot, J. (1990) *Involving Young People in their Communities.* London: Community Development Foundation.

Lindeman, E. (1921) *The Community. An Introduction to the Study of Community Leadership and Organization.* New York: Association Press.

Lindeman, E. (1987a) 'New needs for adult education' [1944] in S. Brookfield (ed.) *Learning Democracy. Eduard Lindeman on Adult Education and Social Change.* Beckenham: Croom Helm.

Lindeman, E. (1987b) 'World peace through adult education' [1945] in S. Brookfield (ed.) *Learning Democracy. Eduard Lindeman on Adult Education and Social Change.* Beckenham: Croom Helm.

Lindeman, E. (1987c) 'Building a social philosophy of adult education' [1951] in S. Brookfield (ed.) *Learning Democracy. Eduard Lindeman on Adult Education and Social Change.* Beckenham: Croom Helm.

Lindeman, E. (1989) *The Meaning of Adult Education.* Norman: Oklahoma Research Centre for Continuing Professional and Higher Education. First published in 1926.

Lindley, R. (1986) *Autonomy.* London: Macmillan.

Linell, J. (1988) *Power and Delivery. The Role of the Area Officer in Local Authorities.* Leicester: National Youth Bureau.

Linge, D. E. (1976) 'Editor's introduction' to H.-G. Gadamer (1976) *Philosophical Hermeneutics* (trans. and ed. D. E. Linge). Berkeley: University of California Press.

Little, P. (1994) 'Recording and record keeping' in P. Carter, T. Jeffs and M. K. Smith (eds) *Social Working.* London: Macmillan.

Loney, M. (1983) *Community against Government.* London: Heinemann.

Louden, W. (1991) *Understanding Teaching. Continuity and Change in Teachers' Knowledge.* London: Cassell.

Lovett, T. (1975) *Adult Education, Community Development and the Working Class.* London: Ward Lock.

Lovett, T. (ed.) (1988) *Radical Approaches to Adult Education: A Reader.* Beckenham: Croom Helm.

Lovett, T., Clarke, C. and Kilmurray, A. (1983) *Adult Education and Community Action. Adult Education and Popular Social Movements.* Beckenham: Croom Helm.

Lukes, S. (ed.) (1988) *Power.* Oxford: Blackwell.

Lynd, R. S. and Lynd, H. M. (1929) *Middletown. A Study in American Culture.* New York: Harcourt Brace.

Lynd, R. S. and Lynd, H. M. (1937) *Middletown in Transition. A Study in Cultural Conflicts.* New York: Harcourt Brace.

Mackie, R. (1980) 'Introduction' in R. Mackie (ed.) *Literacy and Revolution. The Pedagogy of Paulo Freire.* London: Pluto Press.

MacKinnon, A. and Erickson, G. (1992) 'The roles of reflective practice and foundational disciplines in teacher education' in T. Russell and H. Munby (ed.) *Teachers and Teaching. From Classroom to Reflection.* London: Falmer Press.

Macpherson, C. B. (1962) *The Political Theory of Possessive Individualism.* Oxford: Oxford University Press.

Manning, P. (1992) *Erving Goffman and Modern Sociology.* Cambridge: Polity.

Maranhão, T. (1990) 'Introduction' to T. Maranhão (ed.) *The Interpretation of Dialogue.* Chicago: University of Chicago Press.

Marquand, D. (1988) *The Unprincipled Society. New Demands and Old Politics.* London: Fontana.

Marsella, A. J., Devos, G. and Hsu, F. L. K. (eds) (1985) *Culture and Self. Asian and Western Perspectives.* London: Tavistock.

Marsick, V. J. and Watkins, K. E. (1990) *Informal and Incidental Learning in the Workplace.* London: Routledge.

Marx, K. (1977) 'Thesis on Feuerbach' [1845] in D. McLellan (ed.) *Karl Marx: Selected Writings.* Oxford: Oxford University Press.

Massey, D. (1984) *Spatial Divisions of Labour. Social Structures and the Geography of Production*. London: Macmillan.

Massey, D. (1993) 'Politics and time/space', *New Left Review*, 196: 65–84.

Matthews, J. E. (1966) *Working with Youth Groups*. London: University of London Press.

McPeck, J. (1981) *Critical Thinking and Education*. Oxford: Martin Robertson.

Mead, G. H. (1934) *Mind, Self and Society. From the Standpoint of a Social Behaviorist* (ed. C. W. Morris). Chicago: University of Chicago Press.

Mead, G. H. (1936) *Movements of Thought in the Nineteenth Century* (ed. M. A. Moore). Chicago: University of Chicago Press.

Mewett, P. G. (1982) 'Associational categories and the social location of relation-ships in a Lewis crofting community' in A. P. Cohen (ed.) *Belonging. Identity and Social Organisation in British Rural Communities*. Manchester: Manchester University Press.

Mezirow, J. D. (ed.) (1990) *Developing Critical Self-Reflection. Tools for Transformative Learning*. San Francisco: Jossey-Bass.

Midwinter, E. (1972) *Priority Education. An account of the Liverpool Project*. Harmonds-worth: Penguin.

Miller, D. L. (1973) *George Herbert Mead. Self, Language and the World*. Chicago: University of Chicago Press.

Mills, C. W. (1959) *The Sociological Imagination*. New York: Oxford University Press.

Milson, F. (1970) *Youth Work in the 1970's*. London: Routledge & Kegan Paul.

Ministry of Education (1963) *Youth Club: Witheywood, Bristol. Building Bulletin 22*. London: HMSO.

Mitchell, J. Clyde (ed.) (1969) *Social Networks in Urban Situations*. Manchester: Manchester University Press.

Moller, J. C. and Watson, K. (1944) *Education in Democracy. The Folk High Schools of Denmark*. London: Faber and Faber.

Morgan, D. H. J. (1989) 'Strategies and sociologists: a comment on Crow', *Sociology*, 23(1): 25–30.

Morgan, G. (1986) *Images of Organization*. Beverley Hills, CA: Sage.

Newman, M. (1979) *The Poor Cousin. A Study of Adult Education*. London: George Allen & Unwin.

Noordhoff, K. and Kleinfeld, J. (1990) 'Shaping the rhetoric of reflection for multicultural settings' in R. T. Clift, W. R. Houston and M. C. Pugach (eds) *Encouraging Reflective Practice in Education. An Analysis of Issues and Programs*. New York: Teachers College Press.

Oakley, A. (1982) *Subject Women*. London: Fontana.

Oppenheim, C. (1990) *Poverty. The Facts*. London: Child Poverty Action Group.

Pahl, R. (1984) *Divisions of Labour*. Oxford: Blackwell.

Palmer, A. (1989) *The East End. Four Centuries of London Life*. London: John Murray.

Paneth, M. (1944) *Branch Street*. London: George Allen & Unwin.

Parkin, F. (1979) *Marxism and Class Theory. A Bourgeois Critique*. London: Tavistock.

Pearson, G. (1975) *The Deviant Imagination: Psychiatry, Social Work and Social Change*. London: Macmillan.

Peräkylä, A. and Silverman, D. (1991) 'Reinterpreting speech-exchange systems: Communication formats in AIDS counselling', *Sociology*, 25(4): 627–51.

Perkin, H. (1989) *The Rise of Professional Society. England since 1880*. London: Routledge.

Piaget, J. (1932) *The Moral Judgement of the Child*. New York: Free Press.

Piaget, J. (1951) *Play, Dreams and Imitation in Childhood*. New York: W. W. Norton.

Pithouse, A. (1987) *Social Work. The Social Organisation of an Invisible Trade.* Aldershot: Avebury.

Polanyi, M. (1967) *The Tacit Dimension.* New York: Doubleday and Co.

Poster, C. (1990) 'The role of the community educator' in C. Poster and A. Kruger (eds) *Community Education in the Western World.* London: Routledge.

Poster, C. and Krüger, A. (eds) (1990) *Community Education in the Western World.* London: Routledge.

Postman, N. and Weingartner, C. (1971) *Teaching as a Subversive Activity.* Harmondsworth: Penguin.

Preston-Shoot, M. (1987) *Effective Groupwork.* London: Macmillan.

Priestley, P., McGuire, J., Flegg, D., Helmsley, V. and Welham, D. (1978) *Social Skills and Personal Problem Solving. A Handbook of Methods.* London: Tavistock.

Principal Community Education Officers, Scotland (1989) *Youth Work in the Community Education Service.* Edinburgh: Scottish Community Education Council.

Principal Community Education Officers, Scotland (1990) *Adult Education in the Community Education Service.* Edinburgh: Scottish Community Education Council.

Principal Community Education Officers, Scotland (1992) *Community Development in the Community Education Service.* Edinburgh: Scottish Community Education Council.

Pusey, M. (1987) *Jürgen Habermas.* London: Tavistock.

Putnam, R. (1990) *In Search of Adventure. A Study of Opportunities for Adventure and Challenge for Young People* (ed. J. Hunt). Guildford: Talbot Adair Press.

Ranger, T. (1983) 'The invention of tradition in colonial Africa' in E. Hobsbawm and T. Ranger (eds) *The Invention of Tradition.* Cambridge: Cambridge University Press.

Reder, P., Duncan, S. and Gray, M. (1993) *Beyond Blame. Child Abuse Tragedies Revisited.* London: Routledge.

Reid, K. E. (1981) *From Character Building to Social Treatment. The History of the Use of Groups in Social Work.* Westport, CT: Greenwood Press.

Richardson, V. (1990) 'The evolution of reflective teaching and teacher education' in R. T. Clift, W. R. Houston and M. C. Pugach (eds) *Encouraging Reflective Practice in Education. An Analysis of Issues and Programs.* New York: Teachers College Press.

Richert, A. E. (1992) 'The content of student teachers' reflection within different structures for facilitating the reflective process' in T. Russell and H. Munby (ed.) *Teachers and Teaching. From Classroom to Reflection.* London: Falmer Press.

Ricoeur, P. (1981) *Hermeneutics and the Human Sciences* (trans. and ed. J. B. Thompson). Cambridge: Cambridge University Press.

Rigby, A. (1982) 'Managing management – the nooks and crannies of community work', *Community Development Journal* 17(1): 47–53.

Rogers, A. (1981) *Starting Out in Detached Work.* Leicester: National Association of Youth Clubs.

Rogers, A. (1982) *Recording and Reporting.* Leicester: National Association of Youth Clubs.

Rogers, A. (1992) *Adult Learning for Development.* London: Cassell.

Rogers, A. (1994) 'Setting up and managing projects' in M. K. Smith (ed.) *Setting Up and Managing Projects.* London: YMCA National College/Rank Foundation.

Rogers, C. (1942) *Counselling and Psychotherapy. Newer Concepts in Practice.* Boston: Houghton Mifflin.

Rogers, C. (1965) *Client Centred Therapy. Its Current Practice, Implications and Theory.* London: Constable. First published in 1951.

Rogers, C. (1974) *On Becoming a Person. A Therapist's View of Psychotherapy.* London: Constable. First published in 1961.

Rogers, C. (1980) *A Way of Being.* Boston: Houghton Mifflin.

Rogers, C. (1983) *Freedom to Learn in the '80s.* Columbus, OH: Charles Merrill.

Rogers, J. (1977) *Adults Learning* (2nd edn). Milton Keynes: Open University Press.

Rojek, C. (1985) *Capitalism and Leisure Theory.* London: Tavistock.

Rojek, C., Peacock, G. and Collins, S. (1988) *Social Work and Received Ideas.* London: Routledge.

Rorty, R. (1980) *Philosophy and the Mirror of Nature.* Oxford: Blackwell.

Rorty, R. (1989) *Contingency, Irony and Solidarity.* Cambridge: Cambridge University Press.

Rosaldo, R. (1993) *Culture and Truth. The Remaking of Social Analysis.* London: Routledge. First published in 1989.

Rosseter, B. (1987) 'Youth workers as educators' in T. Jeffs and M. Smith (eds) *Youth Work.* London: Macmillan.

Ruskin, J. (1920) *The Stones of Venice Vol II. The Sea Stories* (New Universal Library edn). London: George Routledge. First published in 1853.

Russell, C. E. B. and Rigby, L. M. (1908) *Working Lads' Clubs.* London: Macmillan.

Russell, T. and Munby, H. (1991) 'Reframing. The role of experience in developing teachers' professional knowledge' in D. A. Schön (ed.) *The Reflective Turn. Case studies in and on educational practice.* New York: Teachers Press, Columbia University.

Russell, T. and Munby, H. (ed.) (1992) *Teachers and Teaching. From Classroom to Reflection.* London: Falmer Press.

Sadler, J. E. (1974) *Concepts in Primary Education.* London: George Allen & Unwin.

Said, E. W. (1985) *Orientalism.* Harmondsworth: Penguin. First published in 1978.

Salzberger-Wittenberg, I., Henry, G. and Osborne, E. (1983) *The Emotional Experience of Learning and Teaching.* London: Routledge & Kegan Paul.

Sampson, E. E. (1993) *Celebrating the Other. A Dialogic Account of Human Nature.* Hemel Hempstead: Harvester Wheatsheaf.

Sargant, N. (1991) *Learning and 'Leisure'. A Study of Adult Participation in Learning and Its Policy Implications.* Leicester: National Institute of Adult Continuing Education.

Saunders, P. (1980) *Urban Politics.* Harmondsworth: Penguin.

Schön, D. A. (1973) *Beyond the Stable State. Public and Private Learning in a Changing Society.* Harmondsworth: Penguin. First published in 1971.

Schön, D. A. (1983) *The Reflective Practitioner. How Professionals Think in Action.* London: Temple Smith.

Schön, D. A. (1987) *Educating the Reflective Practitioner. Towards a New Design for Teaching and Learning in the Professions.* San Francisco: Jossey-Bass.

Schweder, R. A. and Bourne, E. J. (1984) 'Does the concept of the person vary cross-culturally?' in R. A. Schweder and R. A. LeVine (eds) *Culture Theory. Essays on Mind, Self and Emotion.* Cambridge: Cambridge University Press.

Scott, C. (1908) *Social Education.* Boston: Ginn & Co.

Scott, J. (1991) *Social Network Analysis. A Handbook.* London: Sage.

Scottish Education Department (1975) *Adult Education. The Challenge of Change. Report by a Committee of Inquiry Appointed by the Secretary of State for Scotland under the Chairmanship of Professor K. J. W. Alexander.* Edinburgh: HMSO.

182   Local education

Seay, M. F. and Associates (1974) *Community Education: A Developing Concept*. Midland, MI: Pendell Publishing.

Sennett, R. (1973) *The Uses of Disorder. Personal Identity and City Life*. Harmondsworth: Penguin.

Sennett, R. (1991) *The Conscience of the Eye. The Design and Social Life of Cities*. London: Faber & Faber.

Shaw, M. (1990) 'Strategy and social process: military context and sociological analysis', *Sociology*, 24(3): 465–73.

Smith, D. (1965) 'Front-line organization of the state mental hospital', *Administrative Science Quarterly*, 10: 381–99.

Smith, F. (1992) *To Think. In Language, Learning and Education*. London: Routledge.

Smith, M. (1980) *Creators not Consumers. Rediscovering Social Education*. Nuneaton: National Association of Youth Clubs.

Smith, M. (1982) *Creators not Consumers. Rediscovering Social Education* (2nd edn). Leicester: National Association of Youth Clubs.

Smith, M. (1984) *Questions for Survival. Some Problems of Political Education and How to Combat Them*. Leicester: National Association of Youth Clubs.

Smith, M. (1988) *Developing Youth Work. Informal Education, Mutual Aid and Popular Practice*. Milton Keynes: Open University Press.

Smith, M. K. (ed.) (1991) *The Challenge for Voluntary Youth Work Organizations*. London: YMCA National College/Rank Foundation.

Smith, M. K. (1992) 'The possibilities of public life. Educating in the community' in I. Martin and G. Allan (eds) *Education and Community. The Politics of Practice*. London: Cassell.

Smith, M. K. (1993) Local Education – Methodology. Mimeo paper available from the writer.

Smith, M. K. (1994) *Developing Critical Conversations about Practice*. London: YMCA National College.

Spender, D. (1980) *Man Made Language*. London: Routledge & Kegan Paul.

Spurling, L. (1988) 'Casework as dialogue: A story of incest' in G. Pearson, J. Treseder and M. Yelloly (eds) *Social Work and the Legacy of Freud. Psychoanalysis and Its Uses*. London: Macmillan.

Stacey, M. (1960) *Tradition and Change. A Study of Banbury*. Oxford: Oxford University Press.

Stacey, M. (1969) 'The myth of community studies', *British Journal of Sociology*, 20(2): 134–47.

Stacey, M., Batstone, E., Bell, C. and Murcott, A. (1975) *Power, Persistence and Change. A Second Study of Banbury*. London: Routledge & Kegan Paul.

Stallybrass, O. (1975) 'Editor's introduction' to E. M. Forster, *Howards End*. Harmondsworth: Penguin.

Standing Conference on Community Development (1990) *A Working Statement on Community Development*. Sheffield: Standing Conference on Community Development.

Stanley, M. (1890) *Clubs for Working Girls*. London: Macmillan.

Stenhouse, L. (1975) *An Introduction to Curriculum Research and Development*. London: Heinemann.

Stewart, D. S. (1987) *Adult Learning in America. Eduard Lindeman and His Agenda for Lifelong Education*. Malabar, FL: Robert E. Krieger.

Stewart, J. (1986) *The Making of the Primary School*. Milton Keynes: Open University Press.

Stone, M. (1981) *The Education of the Black Child. The Myth of Multicultural Education*. London: Fontana.

Strathern, M. (1981) *Kinship at the Core. An Anthropology of Elmdon, Essex*. Cambridge: Cambridge University Press.

Strauss, A. and Corbin, J. (1990) *Basics of Qualitative Research. Grounded Theory Procedures and Techniques*. Newbury Park, CA: Sage.

Street, B. V. (1984) *Literacy in Theory and Practice*. Cambridge: Cambridge University Press.

Street, J. C. and Street, B. V. (1991) 'The schooling of literacy' in D. Barton and R. Ivanic (eds) *Writing in the Community*. Newbury Park, CA: Sage.

Taylor, P. V. (1993) *The Texts of Paulo Freire*. Buckingham: Open University Press.

Taylor, T. and Ratcliffe, R. (1981) 'Stuttering steps in political education'. *Schooling and Culture*, 9: 26–9.

Tennant, M. (1988) *Psychology and Adult Learning*. London: Routledge.

Thomas, D. N. (1983) *The Making of Community Work*. London: George Allen & Unwin.

Thompson, E. P. (1955) *William Morris. Romantic to Revolutionary*. London: Merlin Press.

Thompson, E. P. (1991) *Customs in Common*. London: Merlin Press.

Thompson, J. (1990) *Ideology and Modern Culture*. Cambridge: Polity.

Thompson, J. L. (ed.) (1980) *Adult Education for a Change*. London: Hutchinson.

Thorne, B. (1992) *Carl Rogers*. London: Sage.

Thorpe, M., Edwards, R. and Hanson, A. (eds) (1993) *Culture and Processes of Adult Learning*. London: Routledge.

Tiffany, G. A. (1993) 'Environment and dialogue' in M. K. Smith (ed.) *Youth or Adult? The First Five Years*. London: YMCA National College/Rank Foundation.

Tiles, J. E. (1988) *Dewey*. London: Routledge.

Torres, C. A. (1993) 'From the "Pedagogy of the Oppressed" to "A Luta Continua": The Political Pedagogy of Paulo Freire' in P. McLaren and P. Leonard (eds) *Freire. A critical encounter*. London: Routledge.

Tough, A. (1993) 'Self-planned learning and major personal change' [1976] in R. Edwards, S. Sieminski and D. Zeldin (eds) *Adult Learners, Education and Training*. London: Routledge.

Townsend, S. (1984) *The Growing Pains of Adrian Mole*. London: Methuen.

Toynbee, W. S. (1985) *Adult Education and the Voluntary Associations in France*. Nottingham: University of Nottingham, Department of Adult Education.

Trimble, J. (1990) *Equality of Opportunity. Provision for Girls and Young Women in the Full Time Sector of the Northern Ireland Youth Service*. Belfast: Youth Action Northern Ireland.

Turner, J. C. (1988) *Rediscovering the Social Group. A Self-Categorization Theory*. Oxford: Blackwell.

Turner, R. H. (1962) 'Role taking: process versus conformity' in A. H. Rose (ed.) *Human Behavior and Social Processes*. Boston: Houghton Mifflin.

Twelvetrees, A. (1982) *Community Work*. London: Macmillan.

Tyler, R. W. (1949) *Basic Principles of Curriculum and Instruction*. Chicago: University of Chicago Press.

Tylor, E. B. (1903) *Primitive Culture: Researches into the Development of Mythology, Philosophy, Religion, Language, Art and Custom*. Vols 1 and 2. London: John Murray. First published in 1871.

Usher, R. and Bryant, I. (1989) *Adult Education as Theory, Practice and Research. The Captive Triangle.* London: Routledge.

Vertovec, S. (1992) 'Community and congregation in London Hindu temples: divergent trends', *New Community*, 18(2): 251–64.

Vygotsky, L. S. (1962) *Thought and Language.* (trans. and ed. by E. Hanfmann and G. Vakar). Cambridge, MA: MIT Press.

Wallman, S. (1984) *Eight London Households.* London: Tavistock.

Walmsley, D. J. (1988) *Urban Living. The Individual in the City.* Harlow: Longman.

Wardhaugh, R. (1985) *How Conversation Works.* Oxford: Blackwell.

Werbner, P. (1988) 'Taking and giving: Working women and female bonds in a Pakistani immigrant neighbourhood' in S. Westwood and P. Bhachu (eds) *Enterprising Women. Ethnicity, Economy and Gender Relations.* London: Routledge & Kegan Paul.

Westwood, S. (1992) 'When class became community: radicalism in adult education' in A. Rattansi and D. Reeder (eds) *Rethinking Radical Education. Essays in Honour of Brian Simon.* London: Lawrence and Wishart.

Whitaker, D. Stock (1985) *Using Groups to Help People.* London: Tavistock/Routledge.

White, J. (1982) *The Aims of Education Restated.* London: Routledge & Kegan Paul.

Whyte, W. F. (1955) *Street Corner Society. The Social Structure of an Italian Slum* (2nd edn). Chicago: University of Chicago Press.

Wild, J. (1982) *Street Mates.* Liverpool: Merseyside Youth Association.

Williams, L. O. (1988) *Partial Surrender. Race and Resistance in the Youth Service.* Lewes: Falmer Press.

Willis, P. with Jones, S., Canaan, J. and Hurd, G. (1990) *Common Culture. Symbolic Work at Play in the Everyday Cultures of the Young.* Buckingham: Open University Press.

Willmott, P. (1986) *Social Networks, Informal Care and Public Policy.* London: Policy Studies Institute.

Willmott, P. (1987) *Friendship Networks and Social Support.* London: Policy Studies Institute.

Willmott, P. (1989) *Community Initiatives. Patterns and Prospects.* London: Policy Studies Institute.

Wilson, E. (1991) *The Sphinx in the City. Urban Life, the Control of Disorder, and Women.* London: Virago.

Wong, A. (1986) 'Creole as a language of power and solidarity' in D. Sutcliffe and A. Wong (eds) *The Language of the Black Experience. Cultural Experience through Word and Sound in the Caribbean and Black Britain.* Oxford: Blackwell.

Woods, P. (1983) *Sociology and the School. An Interactionist Viewpoint.* London: Routledge & Kegan Paul.

Woodward, D. and Green, E. (1988) ' "Not tonight, dear!" The social control of women's leisure' in E. Wimbush and M. Talbot (eds) *Relative Freedoms. Women and Leisure.* Milton Keynes: Open University Press.

Worpole, K. (1992) *Towns for People. Transforming Urban Life.* Buckingham: Open University Press.

Wright, S. (1992) 'Image and analysis: new directions in community studies' in B. Short (ed.) *The English Rural Community. Image and Analysis.* Cambridge: Cambridge University Press.

Yarnitt, M. (1980) 'Second Chance to Learn, Liverpool; class and adult education' in J. L. Thompson (ed.) *Adult Education for a Change.* London: Hutchinson.

Yeaxlee, B. A. (1929) *Lifelong Education. A Sketch of the Range and Significance of the Adult Education Movement.* London: Cassell and Co.

Yinger, R. J. (1990) 'The conversation of practice' in R. T. Clift, W. R. Houston and M. C. Pugach (eds) *Encouraging Reflective Practice in Education. An Analysis of Issues and Programs.* New York: Teachers College Press.

Young, R. (1992) *Critical Theory and Classroom Talk.* Clevedon: Multilingual Matters.

Index

WOMEN'S EDUCATION

Maggie Coats

This book is about women's education; it is not about education for women. 'Women's education' is education which is possessed or owned by women; education which is provided by women for women, which focuses on the needs of women, and which is designed for and about women.

Maggie Coats celebrates the achievements of women's education over the past twenty years, paying tribute to the women who have been involved in it. She describes and analyses the meaning, development and distinctive characteristics of women's education, arguing that we should build upon the lessons learnt during the last two decades; that we should expand rather than contract provision; and that we should make a long-term commitment to women's education.

Contents

What is women's education? – The background to women's education today – Feminist ideologies and women's education – The case for women-only provision – The curriculum of women-only provision: six case studies – The curriculum of women-only provision: the main themes – The curriculum of women-only provision: recommendations and guidelines – Education or training? The significance of women-only provision – Women's education: challenging the backlash – Appendix – Bibliography – Index.

192pp   0 335 15734 3 (Paperback)   0 335 15735 1 (Hardback)

USING EXPERIENCE FOR LEARNING

David Boud, Ruth Cohen and David Walker (eds)

This book is about the struggle to make sense of learning from experience. What are the key ideas that underpin learning from experience? How do we learn from experience? How does context and purpose influence learning? How does experience impact on individual and group learning? How can we help others to learn from their experience?

Using Experience for Learning reflects current interest in the importance of experience in informal and formal learning, whether it be applied for course credit, new forms of learning in the workplace, or acknowledging autonomous learning outside educational institutions. It also emphasizes the role of personal experience in learning: ideas are not separate from experience; relationships and personal interests impact on learning; and emotions have a vital part to play in intellectual learning. All the contributors write themselves into their chapters, giving an autobiographical account of how their experiences have influenced their learning and what has led them to their current views and practice.

Using Experience for Learning brings together a wide range of perspectives and conceptual frameworks with contributors from four continents, and is a valuable addition to the field of experiential learning.

Contents

Introduction: understanding learning from experience – Part 1: Introduction – Through the lens of learning: how the visceral experience of learning reframes teaching – Putting the heart back into learning – Activating internal processes in experiential learning – On becoming a maker of teachers: Journey down a long hall of mirrors – Part 2: Introduction – Barriers to reflection on experience – Unlearning through experience – Experiential learning at a distance – Learning from experience in mathematics – Part 3: Introduction – How the T-Group changed my life: a sociological perspective on experiential group work – Living the learning: internalizing our model of group learning – Experiential learning and social transformation for a post-apartheid learning future – Experiential learning or learning from experience: does it make a difference? – Index.

Contributors

Lee Andresen, David Boud, Angela Brew, Stephen Brookfield, Ruth Cohen, Costas Criticos, Kathleen Dechant, Elizabeth Kasl, Victoria Marsick, John Mason, Nod Miller, John Mulligan, Denis Postle, Mary Thorpe, Robin Usher, David Walker.

208pp   0 335 19095 2 (Paperback)   0 335 19096 0 (Hardback)

THE TEXTS OF PAULO FREIRE

Paul V. Taylor

Paulo Freire can be numbered among the few, great educators this century. His classroom is the world of the oppressed: his subject is the literacy of liberation.

This volume provides a (re)introduction to Freire. The first part is a fresh, biographical sketch of his life, the context within which he worked and the texts which he has produced. The second part uncovers the genius of his eclecticism and discovers that, contrary to the myth, his revolutionary method is more a radical reinvention of classical pedagogy.

This sets the scene for a review and questioning of Freire's method and of his philosophy of contradiction. There is then a critical examination of his view of literacy through a close reading of the teaching material on which his successful method is based.

The concluding section attempts to reconstruct a practice of literacy, illustrating the importance of Freire's pedagogy of questioning for all those who are working in the field of literacy today.

Contents
Introduction: The textualizing and contextualizing of Freire – A biographical sketch – Backgrounds and borrowings: a review of selected sources and influences – Education and liberation: the means and ends of Dialogue and Conscientization – The 'Método Paulo Freire': generative words and generating literacy – Generating literacy: decoding Freire's ten learning situations – A reconstruction of literacy – Conclusion – Notes – Bibliographies – Index.

176pp   0 335 19019 7 (Paperback)   0 335 19020 0 (Hardback)

Learning Resources
Centre